THE
RENAISSANCE
REDISCOVERY
OF *intimacy*

Kathy Eden

THE RENAISSANCE REDISCOVERY OF *intimacy*

THE UNIVERSITY OF CHICAGO PRESS

Chicago and London

The University of Chicago Press, Chicago 60637
The University of Chicago Press, Ltd., London
© 2012 by The University of Chicago
All rights reserved. Published 2012.
Paperback edition 2017
Printed in the United States of America

23 22 21 20 19 18 17   2 3 4 5 6

ISBN-13: 978-0-226-18462-3 (cloth)
ISBN-10: 0-226-18462-5 (cloth)
ISBN-13: 978-0-226-52664-5 (paper)
ISBN-13: 978-0-226-18464-7 (e-book)

Library of Congress Cataloging-in-Publication Data

Eden, Kathy, 1952 –
    The Renaissance rediscovery of intimacy / Kathy Eden.
        p.cm.
    Includes bibliographical references and index.
    ISBN-13: 978-0-226-18462-3 (hardcover : alkaline paper)
    ISBN-10: 0-226-18462-5 (hardcover : alkaline paper)
1. European letters—Renaissance, 1450–1600—History and criticism. 2. Intimacy (Psychology) in literature. 3. European letters—Classical influences. 4. Classical letters—Influence. 5. Rhetoric, Ancient. 6. Rhetoric, Renaissance. 7. Petrarca, Francesco, 1304–1374. Familiarum rerum libri. 8. Erasmus, Desiderius, d.1536—Criticism and interpretation. 9. Montaigne, Michel de, 1533–1592. Essais. I. Title.
    PN4400.E34 2012
    908.6—dc23
                    2011038169

∞ This paper meets the requirements of ANSI/NISO Z39.48-1992 (Permanence of Paper).

FOR RICHARD

Columen familiae, Anchora domus
—*Adagia* I.iii.42, 43

Contents

Acknowledgments / ix

INTRODUCTION
Rediscovering Style / 1

CHAPTER ONE
A Rhetoric of Intimacy in Antiquity / 11

CHAPTER TWO
A Rhetoric and Hermeneutics of Intimacy in Petrarch's *Familiares* / 49

CHAPTER THREE
Familiaritas in Erasmian Rhetoric and Hermeneutics / 73

CHAPTER FOUR
Reading and Writing Intimately in Montaigne's *Essais* / 96

CONCLUSION
Rediscovering Individuality / 119

Bibliography of Secondary Sources / 125

Index / 145

Acknowledgments

During the past decade, a number of friends, colleagues, and students have supported my efforts to write this book. For the generosity of their support, I wish to thank Steve Baker, Teodolinda Barolini, Hall Bjørnstad, Mary Carruthers, Terence Cave, Bradin Cormack, Pierre Force, Lorna Hutson, Victoria Kahn, William Kennedy, Ian Maclean, Charles McNamara, Margaret Mitchell, Hattie Myers, Richard Scholar, Kirsti Sellevold, Richard Strier, and Leah Whittington. I have also learned a great deal about my topic from audiences at Barnard, the University of California, Berkeley, the University of North Carolina at Chapel Hill, the University of Chicago, Corpus Christi and Merton Colleges at the University of Oxford, Fitzwilliam College at the University of Cambridge, the Heyman Center for the Humanities and the Italian Academy at Columbia University, the Centre d'Etudes Supérieures de la Renaissance at Tours, the University of Oslo, Rutgers University at New Brunswick, St. Andrews University, and Yale University, as well as from the participants in two seminars, one at Columbia in spring 2009, the other at the Folger Shakespeare Library in spring 2010. Two visiting fellowships during the winter and spring of 2010, one from All Souls College, Oxford, and the other from the Rockefeller Institute at Bellagio, afforded me the leisure and resources to complete a full draft. Finally, for reasons he knows best, I have dedicated this book to Richard Bernstein.

An earlier version of chapter 2, with the title "Petrarchan Hermeneutics and the Rediscovery of Intimacy," appeared in the volume *Petrarch and the Textual Origins of Interpretation*, ed. Teodolinda Barolini and H. Wayne Storey (Leiden, 2007), 231–44.

INTRODUCTION **Rediscovering Style**

In one of the many sections in *Timber, or Discoveries* (1641) devoted to literary matters, Ben Jonson first asserts that "[i]n writing there is to be regarded the Invention, and the Fashion" and then goes on to explain that "fashion" pertains to "the Qualities of your style."[1] What Jonson does not disclose is that both assertion and explanation are taken word for word without attribution from John Hoskyns's *Directions for Speech and Style* (c. 1599). Well, not quite word for word. Inadvertently or otherwise, Jonson has dropped from his source the explicit focus on letter writing. "In the writing *of letters*," reads Hoskyns's original (my italics), "there is to be regarded the invention and the fashion."[2] Well, not quite original. For Hoskyns himself is leaning heavily on *his* unacknowledged Latin source, the *Institutio epistolica* (1590) of Justus Lipsius, who in turn has adapted a recently rediscovered ancient Greek manual on style, complete with the oldest instructions on letter writing, routinely attributed to Demetrius.[3]

Flourishing first in antiquity and then again in full flower by the beginning of the seventeenth century, this family tree of literary theorists featuring Demetrius, Lipsius, Hoskyns, and Jonson may strike the reader as an odd way

---

1. *The Poems, The Prose Works*, ed. C. H. Herford Percy and Evelyn Simpson, 11 vols. (Oxford, 1925–52), 8: 629, ll. 2161–62, and 630, l. 2192. On these literary discussions, including not only their borrowings but changing attitudes to these borrowings, see Lorna Hutson's introduction in *The Cambridge Complete Works of Ben Jonson*, ed. David Bevington, Ian Donaldson, Martin Butler, and David Gants (Cambridge, Eng., forthcoming 2012), 7: 3–14.

2. *Directions for Speech and Style*, ed. Hoyt H. Hudson (Princeton, 1935), 4.

3. On Hoskyns's reliance on Lipsius and Jonson's on Hoskyns, see Wesley Trimpi, *Ben Jonson's Poems: A Study of the Plain Style* (Stanford, 1962), 60–75, where Trimpi makes the case that there was "a tendency among those interested in reviving the Attic, or plain, style to consider the familiar letter as the ideal stylistic model" and concludes that "[i]t is not strange, therefore, that Jonson should apply to style in general a passage on letter writing from John Hoskyns's *Direccōns for Speech and Style*. This passage, which Hoskyns took from Lipsius' *Institutio Epistolica* and which Lipsius derived originally from Demetrius, defines Jonson's basic rhetorical position" (74). Demetrius's *On Style* is discussed below in chap. 1, pp. 34–36.

to introduce a book about rediscovering intimacy. Let me offer a number of reasons why it is fitting. In the first place, it introduces the central role in this rediscovery of a number of recovered ancient texts, including Demetrius. (As we will see in chapter 2, the textual recoveries behind the rediscovery of intimacy begin with Petrarch's spectacular encounter with Cicero's lost letters to Atticus in 1345.)[4] In the second place, this little bit of lineage sets in high relief how utterly foundational the genre of the so-called familiar letter (Lat. *epistola familiaris*) is to the long heritage of Western literature considered here. Although the letter, as we will see in chapter 1, only gradually and with difficulty invades the ancient *ars rhetorica,* grounded as it was in the adversarial nature of the oration, by the seventeenth century, epistolary writing has very nearly captured the larger literary field. As evidence of this capture, as noted earlier, Jonson extends Hoskyns's epistolary considerations—the writing of letters—to *all* writing. Over time, the intimacy characteristic of the written communication between close friends will thoroughly captivate readers of not only letters but essays and novels, including epistolary novels. As we will see in chapter 3, it will even change the way early modern Christians read Scripture. If writing intimately for the ancients, including Cicero and Demetrius, meant letter writing exclusively, Renaissance writers, while relying on ancient theory and practice, apply no such exclusion.

Finally, the line of descent from Demetrius to Jonson places front and center the question of style.[5] In its preoccupation with style, in other words, Renaissance theory adheres to its ancient sources. As featured in my title, then, the intimacy rediscovered refers to a particular style of written communication, which, as we will see in the chapters that follow, has its own complex history. In its complexity, this history of intimacy is like others that have been written during the last few decades. It is also like them in that it

---

4. In 1587, according to J. H. Waszink ("Classical Philology," in *Leiden University in the Seventeenth Century: An Exchange of Learning,* ed. Th. H. Lunsingh Scheurleer and G. H. M. Posthumus Meyjes [Leiden, 1975], 161), Lipsius lectured on both epistolography and Cicero's *Letters to Atticus.*

5. The question of style is also front and center in Ronald Witt, *'In the Footsteps of the Ancients': The Origins of Humanism from Lovato to Bruni* (Leiden, 2000), who argues persuasively that "a litmus test for identifying a humanist was his intention to imitate ancient Latin style" (22). In contrast to the humanist preoccupation with style, Witt notes the current "scorn for stylistic matters" (25 n. 53). See also his "Medieval Italian Culture and the Origins of Humanism as a Stylistic Ideal," in *Renaissance Humanism: Foundations, Forms, and Legacy,* ed. Albert Rabil Jr., 3 vols. (Philadelphia, 1988), 1: 29–70.

is responding more or less directly to a challenge implicit in one scholarly lament of the 1980s which reads: "In the history of the self and of intimacy, almost everything remains to be written."[6]

Unlike these other histories, however, mine does not turn to social history or the philosophy of psychology to understand early modern intimacy as a condition of physical (including geographical), sexual, or mental life. Instead, it aims to deepen our understanding of intimacy as a style that determines the reading and writing practices of the period.[7] To this end, I analyze these practices as theorized by three of the most influential practitioners of the Renaissance, Petrarch, Erasmus, and Montaigne,[8] taking as my point of departure *their* point of departure, namely, the reading and writing practices treated by such ancient theorists—newly recovered in part or in whole— as Aristotle, Cicero, Seneca, Quintilian, and Demetrius.[9] Beginning with

---

6. Orest Ranum, "The Refuge of Intimacy," in *A History of Private Life*, ed. Roger Chartier, vol. 3: *Passions of the Renaissance*, trans. Arthur Goldhammer (Cambridge, Mass., 1989), 207.

7. For the contribution of social historians to our understanding of early modern intimacy, see, for instance, the multivolume collection entitled *Histoire de la vie privée*, ed. Philippe Ariès and Georges Duby, esp. vol. 2, *De l'Europe féodale à la Renaissance* (Paris, 1985), and Dora Thornton, *The Scholar in His Study: Ownership and Experience in Renaissance Italy* (New Haven, 1997); and for that of philosophers of psychology, see Charles Taylor, *Sources of the Self: The Making of the Modern Identity* (Cambridge, Mass., 1989). For early modern reading practices with aims other than intimacy, see, for instance, Anthony Grafton and Lisa Jardine, "'Studied for Action': How Gabriel Harvey Read His Livy," *Past and Present* 29 (1990): 30–78; Anthony Grafton, "The Humanist as Reader," in *A History of Reading in the West*, ed. Guglielmo Cavallo and Roger Chartier, trans. Lydia G. Cochrane (Amherst, 1999), 179–212; Peter Mack, "Rhetoric, Ethics and Reading in the Renaissance," *Renaissance Studies* 19 (2005): 1–21; William H. Sherman, *John Dee: The Politics of Reading and Writing in the English Renaissance* (Amherst, 1995).

8. Although subsequent chapters will refer to other scholarly treatments of this triad of influential writers, including their influence on one another, two articles by Nancy Struever must be mentioned here because they connect these humanists on the basis of their attention not only to intimacy but to an intimacy that looks back to Cicero: "The Rhetoric of Familiarity: A Pedagogy of Ethics," *Philosophy and Rhetoric* 31 (1998): 91–106, and "Montaigne's Ciceronian Pessimism: Rhetoric, Politics, Ethics," *Montaigne Studies* 14 (2002): 49–64.

9. On the humanists' recovery of ancient texts, see Remigio Sabbadini, *Le scoperte dei codici latini e greci ne' secoli XIV e XV*, 2 vols. (Florence, 1905, 1914); L. D. Reyn-

Petrarch's rediscovery of the epistolary Cicero, the gradual recovery of these authors directs the equally gradual shift away from the dictaminal theory and practice of earlier centuries to those of early modernity.[10] For these rediscoveries, including their assumptions about stylistic intimacy, change fundamentally the way Europeans between the fourteenth and sixteenth centuries expect to read and write. With his slight but significant misappropriation of Hoskyns, Jonson bears witness to these changes.

A study of early modern assumptions about reading and writing intimately, this book relies in turn on some assumptions of its own. Chief among these is the Gadamerian insight regarding the inseparability of rhetoric and hermeneutics—literary composition and literary interpretation. Here, as in my previous work, I take as axiomatic Gadamer's dictum that the "rhetorical and hermeneutical aspects of human linguisticality completely interpenetrate each other"—that how a culture writes is inextricably linked to how it reads.[11]

---

olds and N. G. Wilson, *Scribes and Scholars: A Guide to the Transmission of Greek and Latin Literature* (Oxford, 1968); and John Monfasani, "Humanism and Rhetoric," in Rabil, *Renaissance Humanism*, 3: 171–235, esp. 177–95.

10. According to Ronald Witt, "Medieval 'Ars Dictaminis' and the Beginnings of Humanism: A New Construction of the Problem," *Renaissance Quarterly* 35 (1982): 1–35, esp. 26, reform of personal correspondence is a hallmark of Petrarchan humanism, differentiating Petrarch from Dante, whose lack of intimacy in his personal letters "surely does not stem from shortcomings in his personality or talents but from the means of expression available to him" (19). On the Petrarchan rejection of the style of the *ars dictaminis* as key to his humanism, see Witt, "Medieval Italian Culture and the Origins of Humanism as a Stylistic Ideal," 43–55. More recently, in *El arte epistolar en el Renascimiento Europeo 1400–1600* (Bilbao, 2005), Pedro Martín Baños makes a similar point: "Ni los epistolarios medievales ni el ars dictaminis ignoran, en rigor, las cartas amistosas, pero lo que Petrarca reivindica es la familiaritas de las epístolas clásicas" (270). See also Jerrold E. Seigel, *Rhetoric and Philosophy in Renaissance Humanism: The Union of Eloquence and Wisdom, Petrarch to Valla* (Princeton, 1968), 200–225. On the *ars dictaminis* and its gradual replacement by humanist letter writing, see John O. Ward, "Rhetorical Theory and the Rise and Decline of Dictamen in the Middle Ages and Early Renaissance," *Rhetorica* 19 (2001): 175–223; Gideon Burton, "Renaissance Letter-Writing Manuals in the Context of Humanism" in *Letter-Writing Manuals and Instruction from Antiquity to the Present*, ed. Carol Poster and Linda C. Mitchell (Columbia, S.C., 2007), 88–101. And in the same volume, see Lawrence D. Green, "Dictamen in England, 1500–1700," 102–126; and see below, chap. 2, n. 19.

11. Hans-Georg Gadamer, "On the Scope and Function of Hermeneutical Reflection," trans. G. B. Hess and R. E. Palmer, in *Philosophical Hermeneutics*, ed. David E.

Fully in keeping with this linkage (Gadamer's "interpenetration") of literary production and reception, an early modern rhetoric of intimacy, as I hope to show in the course of this study, presumes a corresponding hermeneutics.

Without treating intimacy in detail, Gadamer himself alerts us to this presumption. Singling out *epistolary* reading and writing for special attention in a way strikingly resonant with the tradition examined in these pages, Gadamer acknowledges, albeit in passing, that how we understand a letter serves as a paradigm for how we understand literature more broadly.[12] "Just as the recipient of a letter understands the news that it contains," Gadamer explains,

> and first sees things with the eyes of the person who wrote the letter— i.e., considers what he writes as true, and is not trying to understand the writer's peculiar opinion as such—so also do we understand traditional texts on the basis of expectations of meaning drawn from our own prior relation to the subject matter. (294)[13]

The precondition for understanding, and especially for textual understanding, Gadamer insists, is a prior relation between the reader and the writer that motivates the reader not only to take the writer at his word—"to consider what he writes as true"—but also to approach the matter, as the letter reader would, from the writer's point of view, as if with *his* eyes.

In a seemingly unrelated passage much earlier in *Truth and Method*,

---

Linge (Berkeley, 1976), 25. For some key examples of this rhetorical and hermeneutical "interpenetration," see my *Hermeneutics and the Rhetorical Tradition: Chapters in the Ancient Legacy and Its Humanist Reception* (New Haven, 1997). For a reminder that these deep links between reading and writing were humanist and therefore elite in orientation and that "reading and writing were distinct in the practices of many, perhaps most, early modern people," see Heidi Brayman Hackel, *Reading Material in Early Modern England: Print, Gender, Literacy* (Cambridge, Eng., 2005), 68.

12. On the paradigmatic nature of the letter, see also Jacques Derrida, *The Post Card*, trans. A. Bass (Chicago, 1987), who writes: "Mixture is the letter, the epistle, which is not a genre but all genres, literature itself" (48). On this status of the letter before the Renaissance, see Carol Dana Lanham, "Freshman Composition in the Early Middle Ages: Epistolography and Rhetoric before the *Ars Dictaminis*," *Viator* 23 (1992): 115–34.

13. *Truth and Method*, trans. Joel Weinsheimer and Donald G. Marshall, 2nd ed. (New York, 1989); *Wahrheit und Methode*, 3rd ed. (Tübingen, 1972). All quotations from the English translation (*TM*) and the German original (*WM*) are to these editions and cited by page number in the text.

Gadamer describes this hermeneutic relation between reader and writer as intimacy:

> The written word and what partakes of it—literature—is the intelligibility of mind transferred to the most alien medium. Nothing is so purely the trace of the mind as writing, but nothing is so dependent on the understanding mind either. In deciphering and interpreting it, a miracle takes place: the transformation of something alien and dead into total contemporaneity (*Zugleichsein*) and familiarity [i.e., intimacy] (*Vertrautsein*). This is like nothing else that comes down to us from the past. (*TM* 163, *WM* 156)

Understanding any written text, Gadamer affirms (in a generalizing move that recalls Jonson's adaptation of Hoskyns), necessarily involves the reader as interpreter in the "miracle" of understanding what the writer had in mind, and this understanding inevitably creates some kind of intimacy (*Vertrautsein*) between them. With this affirmation, Gadamer positions himself in a long line of theorists of interpretation from Seneca to Jonson (and beyond) that identifies written language as the most revealing image—in Gadamer's terms, the "trace"—of the mind.[14] For most if not for all of these theorists, this "transfer" of the image (or trace) to the alien medium of language is identified with style.

In a brief appendix at the end of *Truth and Method* (493–97), Gadamer addresses the crucial concept of style as it pertains to his larger argument for "historical consciousness."[15] Although this appendix counts for little more than an afterthought, two of its preliminary remarks figure prominently in this book. The first refers to what Gadamer characterizes as the "fairly unexplored history of the word [style]" (493), which he associates with early modern French jurisprudence: *style* was a "manière de procéder—i.e., the way of conducting a trial that satisfied particular legal requirements." "Af-

---

14. On Socrates as the source of this tradition, see Cicero, *Tusc. Disp.* 5.47, and Erasmus, *Apotheg. Liber* 3.70 (*Desiderii Erasmi Roterodami opera omnia*, ed. Jean LeClerc, 10 vols. [Leiden, 1703–6], IV, 162D [hereafter LB]; cf. 698C) and *Adagia* II.vi.54. For the Senecan version, see epp. 75.4–5 and 114.2. In *Timber, or Discoveries* (8: 625, ll. 2031–33), Jonson rehearses the Socratic apothegm with the injunction "*Language* most shewes a man: speake that I may see thee. It springs out of the most retired, and inmost parts of us, and is the Image of the Parent of it, the mind." For the central role of this apothegm in the history of the plain style, see Trimpi, *Ben Jonson's Poems*, 53–59.

15. On the argument for "historical consciousness," see especially *TM* 265–307.

ter the sixteenth century," Gadamer maintains, "the word [style] is used in a general way to describe the manner in which something is presented in language" (493–94).

While Gadamer neither substantiates this claim nor mentions the author of the *Essais* anywhere in *Truth and Method*, Montaigne, whose rhetoric and hermeneutics of intimacy are the focus of chapter 4, provides a telling example of the very shift in meaning of the term *style* that Gadamer describes. Not only does Montaigne write in French at the end of the sixteenth century and spend his first career before becoming an essayist as a lawyer implementing early modern French jurisprudence, but he frequently uses the word *stile*. When he does, moreover, his usage reflects not only his legal training and profession, as scholars have noted,[16] but his literary debt to such humanists as Petrarch and Erasmus. As we will see in chapters 2 and 3, their Latin discussions of *stilus* early-modernize those of their ancient authorities, who are much more likely to use the term *genus dicendi* for style, reserving the word *stilus* for the writing instrument itself.[17] Seemingly committed to defending his own style in his own terms, in other words, Montaigne actually renders into the vernacular the Latin stylistic terminology of his humanist predecessors.

Answering Gadamer's call for philological exploration while at the same time revisiting some of his claims, this study offers a fuller account of the complex history of one kind of style. Accordingly, it focuses throughout on discussions of style, both those from antiquity recovered by the humanists and those engaged in by these same humanists in response to their recover-

---

16. On Montaigne's legal career, see below, chap. 4, p. 104. On *le style de Parlement* or *stylus Parlamenti* that Montaigne turns into "une quête individuelle, et à un style personnel," see Marc Fumaroli, *L'âge de l'éloquence: Rhétorique et "res literaria" de la Renaissance au seuil de l'époque classique* (Geneva, 1980), 427–622, esp. 445. And see André Tournon, *Montaigne: La glose et l'essai* (Lyon, 1983), 185–202, esp. 195: "Le travail de Montaigne, conseiller à la Chambre des Enquêtes, était de trier, dans les documents présentés, ceux qui étaient pertinents; d'apprécier isolément leur force probante; de les remembrer pour en faire la synthèse; de les réinterpréter systématiquement, afin d'exposer à tour de rôle l'argumentation de chacune des parties. Et lorsqu'il n'avait pas été chargé du rapport, il avait à contrôler point par point la façon dont ses collègues avaient exécuté les mêmes tâches, employé les mêmes méthodes prescrites par le 'style.'"

17. See Willibald Sauerländer, "From Stilus to Style: Reflections on the Fate of a Notion," *Art History* 6 (1983): 253–70, and Thomas O. Sloane, ed., *Encyclopedia of Rhetoric* (Oxford, 2001), s.v. "style."

ies. As indicated above, the intimacy rediscovered in the wake of these discussions turns out to be a "quality of style." In Hoskyns's and Jonson's terms, as we have seen, it is a *fashion*—what Montaigne sometimes calls a *façon* (see above, p. 1, and below, chap. 4, p. 103).

But this rediscovery of intimacy also requires recovering a fuller range of meaning for other key stylistic terms, including the one Cicero bequeaths to his humanist admirers when he characterizes his favorite genre of letter as *familiare* and his own brand of letter writing as writing *familiariter*. No small part of the argument of this book, therefore, addresses the philological evidence for the history—and even the prehistory—of the cluster of words related to *familiaritas*. And an important feature of this cluster is its connection with the law.

If the term *style* in the Renaissance, as Gadamer suggests, owes its origin to legal procedure, intimate style—one that is *familiare*—may very well deserve a legal pedigree as well. For the Latin *familia*, as we will see, corresponds to the Greek *oikos*, often translated as "household" or "family"; and both are the locus of not only belonging in an affective sense—the place where I belong, among those who are near and dear to me—but also of what belongs to me, my property.[18] There is even good reason to believe, as I argue in chapter 1, that the specialized terminology designed to formulate the legality of the household as property gradually lends itself both to the affective dimensions of the household and to the quality of style developed to communicate that affection.

Owing its identity in large measure to a style that in Latin is called *familiare*, from the *familia*, intimate style in the Renaissance also shares its history with a quality of style that ancient Greek literary theorists beginning with Aristotle identify as *oikeion*, from the *oikos*.[19] Often translated

---

18. On the evolution of legal terms into psychological and especially affective terms, see, for instance, Emile Benveniste, *Indo-European Language and Society*, trans. Elizabeth Palmer (London, 1973), 273–88, and P. G. A. Pocock, "The Mobility of Property and the Rise of Eighteenth-Century Sociology," in *Theories of Property: Aristotle to the Present*, ed. Anthony Parel and Thomas Flanagan (Waterloo, Ont., 1979), 141–66.

19. On the belatedness of stylistic terminology as part of the language of literary theory, see Larue van Hook, *The Metaphorical Terminology of Greek Rhetoric and Literary Criticism* (Chicago, 1905), whose warning about the often undetected metaphorical application of such terms applies in turn to the central argument of this book: "Real literary criticism does not begin until a language is practically developed. Thus a critical vocabulary is formed more by appropriating and borrowing words and

into Latin by the rhetoricians as *proprium* and retaining in Latin as well as in Greek its affiliation with legal ownership, this quality of style sets the standard for discursive excellence both in antiquity and in the Renaissance. When Petrarch challenges every writer of his own day to write in a way that is not only intimate (*familiare*) but all his own (*proprium*), as we will see in chapter 2, the legal dimension of style is not lost on the former law student turned *literatus*.[20]

Petrarch's challenge to writers regarding their style brings us around to the second remark in Gadamer's appendix that pertains to this study. For Gadamer credits Goethe with conceptualizing style as "the individual hand that is recognizable everywhere in the works" (494). Such a style, Gadamer explains, moves beyond merely imitating to fashioning a language accommodated to self-expression. "Rare though the correspondence is between 'faithful imitation' and an individual manner (or way of understanding)," Gadamer writes, "this is precisely what constitutes style" (494).

In the argument that follows, style, and especially intimate style as an exclusive belonging, will emerge as both a source of individuation and a key marker for differentiating one writer from another. Renaissance discussions of style, as it turns out, provide one very effective forum for promoting the increasingly embraced values of individuality and difference. Finding its footing in the practice of imitation, as Gadamer reminds us, style as a concept reaches its stride in the achievement of self-expression—an achievement as productive for the developing self as for its means of expression.[21]

---

extending their uses than by the invention of terms wholly new. Many of these terms in reality metaphorical are either unconscious or faded. Thus it is difficult in our study to tell where to draw the line sharply in the selection of a strictly metaphorical terminology" (9).

20. For Petrarch on his own legal training, see the so-called Letter to Posterity (*Sen.* 18.1.7), *Petrarch: Selected Letters*, ed. Craig Kallendorf (Bryn Mawr, 2000), 26; *Letters of Old Age*, trans. Aldo S. Bernardo, Saul Levin, and Reta A. Bernardo, 2 vols. (Baltimore, 1992), 2: 674–75, and *Fam.* 9.8, quoted below, chap. 2, n. 23.

21. On the Renaissance investment in self-expression, taken up in more detail below, see, for instance, Margaret Mann Phillips, "Erasmus and the Art of Writing," in *Scrinium Erasmianum*, ed. J. Coppens (Leiden, 1969), 1: 335–50, and Terence Cave, *The Cornucopian Text: Problems of Writing in the French Renaissance* (Oxford, 1979), who argues in regard to this investment as formulated in Erasmus's *Ciceronianus*, "It is important, of course, not to attach to the phrase 'si teipsum non exprimis' the connotations which 'self-expression' acquires as the focus of a Romantic insistence on intensity of emotional experience. Nevertheless, it is a formulation virtually absent

In this study, however, the credit for inaugurating such a concept of style will go to Petrarch rather than Goethe. Some four hundred years before the German philosopher-poet, in other words, the so-called "father of humanism," also a philosopher-poet, will turn away from his fourteenth-century contemporaries and back to Roman antiquity in search of a style that can express his innermost thoughts and feelings.[22] What he discovers will stun subsequent generations of humanists, including Erasmus and Montaigne. With their help, this stunning discovery will change how early moderns expect to read and write.

---

from classical and medieval rhetoric, and marks a shift the magnitude of which it is hard to measure.... [S]ignificant utterance is now said to arise from, and to be guaranteed by, a subjective 'self.'... Erasmus places it at the centre of the problem of rhetoric, thus renewing the ancient debate on the relationship between rhetoric and truth in terms of a new and potent grammar of identity and an intensified textual self-consciousness" (42–43).

22. On Petrarch as the "father of humanism," see, for instance, B. L. Ullman, *Studies in the Italian Renaissance* (Rome, 1955), 35, 123; Theodor Mommsen, "Petrarch's Conception of the 'Dark Ages,'" *Speculum* 17 (1942): 242; and, more recently, Witt, *'In the Footsteps of the Ancients,'* 230–91, a chapter entitled "Petrarch, Father of Humanism?" Concluding that Petrarch is not the "founder of a movement" but rather "the leader of its third generation" (289), Witt nevertheless credits Petrarch with the reformation of the familiar letter: "Geri [D'Arezzo] may have been the pioneer in this endeavor, but probably his innovation, like those of other pre-Petrarchan humanists, lacked the theoretical elaboration that would have given it programmatic status. In terms of historical impact, credit for reforming the European private letter belongs to Petrarch in his *Rerum familiarium*" (265). See also Angelo Mazzocco, "Petrarch: Founder of Renaissance Humanism?" in *Interpretations of Renaissance Humanism*, ed. Angelo Mazzocco (Leiden, 2006), 215–42. On earlier influences on Goethe's concept of style, see Sloane, *Encyclopedia of Rhetoric*, 754: "Goethe's well-known distinction of *style* and *manner* in his essay *Einfache Nachahmung der Natur, Manier, Stil* (1789)—to which he adds the category of *imitation* ('Nachahmung')—is influenced by his Italian predecessors."

CHAPTER 1 A Rhetoric of Intimacy in Antiquity

If the humanists, as we will see in later chapters, rediscover a rhetoric of intimacy as part of their revival of antiquity, the ancients they revive did not themselves discover this rhetoric all at once. For the earliest rhetoricians gave their attention almost exclusively to the more public forms of oratory practiced in the law courts and the assembly and not to more private forms of communication, such as the letter. Indeed, it is not until the first century CE, as we will also see, that rhetoricians begin to address these neglected genres as part of their treatment of the *ars rhetorica*.

Among these earliest rhetoricians who lack a theory of letter writing is Aristotle, whose *Rhetoric* is arguably the Greek manual with the greatest impact on both Roman rhetorical theory and that of the Renaissance humanists. Well known to Cicero in the first century (BCE) and again to Erasmus in the sixteenth but unknown to Petrarch in the fourteenth (except perhaps in a plodding and partial Latin translation), the *Rhetoric* is, in spite of its unambiguous oratorical orientation, key to the discoveries and rediscoveries that are the focus of this book.[1] For without addressing the letter, the kind of discourse eventually associated most closely with rhetorical intimacy, the *Rhetoric* does address a fundamental feature of letter writing that establishes the groundwork for later epistolary theory: writing itself.

Countering the accusations of his teacher Plato in *Gorgias* and *Phaedrus*, Aristotle defends writing in the *Rhetoric* over and against oral discourse. And he mounts his defense in terms that will prove decisive for epistolary theory and practice. "[W]riting avoids the necessity of silence," Aristotle

---

1. For Cicero's knowledge of Aristotelian rhetoric, see *Ad fam.* 1.9.23 and *De or.* 2.115–17, 152, 160; 3.182–83; *Orator* 114, 192–94; and Jakob Wisse, *Ethos and Pathos from Aristotle to Cicero* (Amsterdam, 1989), 106–62; for Erasmus's, see especially his *De conscribendis epistolis* and my "In the Household of the Peripatetics: Aristotle and Renaissance Letters," in *Beyond the "Poetics": Aristotle and Early Modern Literature*, ed. Ullrich Langer (Geneva, 2002), 111–21. For Petrarch's unfamiliarity, see Pierre de Nolhac, *Pétrarque et l'humanisme* (Paris, 1965), 2: 147–52, and Rudolf Pfeiffer, *History of Classical Scholarship, 1300–1850* (Oxford, 1976), 13–15. And see Keith Erickson, *Aristotle's Rhetoric: Five Centuries of Philological Research* (Metuchen, N.J., 1975), 1–18.

claims (3.12.1; Kennedy 255–57), "if one wishes to communicate to others [who are not present], which is the condition of those who do not know how to write."[2] Locating the origin of writing in the problem of distance—spatial distance—Aristotle distinguishes the style appropriate to writing, a *lexis graphikē*, from an oral, agonistic style, a *lexis agōnistikē*. Again, the key factor is distance.[3]

Agonistic style, characteristic of two of the three kinds of oratory (political or deliberative and legal), is designed to accommodate audiences in the

---

2. Aristotle, *On Rhetoric*, trans. George A. Kennedy (Oxford, 1991). Here and hereafter, page numbers are in the text. For the Greek, I have used *Aristotelis Ars Rhetorica*, ed. W. D. Ross (Oxford, 1959). On the Eastern origins of writing, including letter writing, and its status among the Greeks, see Deborah Tarn Steiner, *The Tyrant's Writ: Myths and Images of Writing in Ancient Greece* (Princeton, 1994). On the origins of writing in the need to overcome distance, see Patricia Rosenmeyer, *Ancient Epistolary Fictions: The Letter in Greek Literature* (Cambridge, Eng., 2001), esp. 24–26, who quotes both Euripides' *Palamedes* (fr. 578.3–5) for the identification of writing and letter writing (26) and Diodorus Siculus (12.13.2) on the legendary Charondas, who advocated for literacy on the grounds that "men widely separated in space [could] have conversations through written communications with those who are at the farthest distance from them, as if they were standing nearby" (26). And compare the Freudian claim in *Civilization and Its Discontents*, trans. James Strachey (New York, 1961), that "[w]riting was in its origin the voice of an absent person" (43). For a different hypothesis—one that links writing to *kleos* or glory—see Jesper Svenbro, "Archaic and Classical Greece: The Invention of Silent Reading," in Cavallo and Chartier, *History of Reading in the West*, 37–63. And see Richard Leo Enos, "Ancient Greek Writing Instruction," in *A Short History of Writing Instruction: From Ancient Greece to Modern America*, ed. James J. Murphy (Davis, Calif., 2001), 9–33.

For a Renaissance reading of *Rhetoric* 3.12 that makes explicit the connection between writing and letter writing, see Edward Meredith Cope, *The Rhetoric of Aristotle with a Commentary* (London, 1877; rpt. New York, 1973), 3: 145. For Aristotle as an accomplished letter writer, see Demetrius, *On Style*, 4.223. On Aristotle's letter collection as the first, see Adolf Deissman, *Light from the Ancient East*, trans. Lionel R. M. Strachan (London, 1927), 231, and M. Luther Stirewalt Jr., *Studies in Ancient Greek Epistolography* (Atlanta, 1993), 13, 35. For Aristotle's attention to letters in the *Poetics*, see 16.6–7, 16.11, and Stirewalt, 75.

3. For the centrality of distance in rhetorical theory and practice in both antiquity and the Renaissance, see Carlo Ginzburg, *Wooden Eyes: Nine Reflections on Distance*, trans. Martin Ryle and Kate Soper (New York, 2001). For a reading of the *Rhetoric* that rejects as a point of departure Aristotle's responsiveness to Plato's criticisms, see Eugene Garver, *Aristotle's Rhetoric: An Art of Character* (Chicago, 1994).

assembly or the larger law courts where listeners are situated at some physical remove from the speaker. While such audiences require, on the one hand, an energetic delivery with all the skills of performance, they are, on the other, only distracted by intricate argument and precise detail. The listener's ear, in other words, misses the refinements appreciated by the reader's eye. Aristotle's third type of oratory, epideictic oratory, in contrast, is meant to be read rather than heard and consequently allows for more precision and detail. "Written style is most exact (*akribestatē*)," Aristotle explains, whereas

> the agonistic is very much a matter of delivery. . . . On comparison, some written works seem thin when spoken, while some speeches of [successful] orators seem amateurish when examined in written form. The cause is that [their style] suits debate. Thus, things that are intended for delivery, when delivery is absent, seem silly, since they are not fulfilling their purpose. . . . The demegoric [i.e., agonistic] style seems altogether like shadow-painting; for the greater the crowd, the further the distance of view; thus, exactness (*akribē*) is wasted work and the worse in both cases. . . . As a result, the same orators are not successful in all kinds of speeches. Where there is most need of performance, the least exactness (*akribeia*) is present. This occurs where the voice is important and especially a loud voice. The epideictic style is most like writing; for its objective is to be read. (*Rhetoric* 3.12.2–5; Kennedy 255)[4]

4. On the rhetorical and philosophical assumptions behind Aristotle's crucial distinction between oral and written style at *Rhetoric* 3.12, see the work of Wesley Trimpi, including "The Meaning of Horace's *Ut pictura poesis*," *Journal of the Warburg and Courtauld Institutes* 36 (1973): 1–34; "Horace's 'Ut pictura poesis': The Argument for Stylistic Decorum," *Traditio* 34 (1978): 29–73; "The Early Metaphorical Uses of ΣΚΙΑΓΡΑΦΙΑ and ΣΚΗΝΟΓΡΑΦΙΑ," *Traditio* 34 (1978): 403–13. On this distinction and the association of writing with sophistic education see Enos, "Ancient Greek Writing Instruction," 27–33. For these distinctions in the context of letter writing, see my "In the Household of the Peripatetics," and Baños, *El arte epistolar en el Renacimiento europeo*, 81–89. See also E. Catherine Dunn, "Lipsius and the Art of Letter-Writing," *Studies in the Renaissance* 3 (1956): 154 n. 36.

For the alliance between epistolary and epideictic writing in Isocrates, see Robert G. Sullivan, "Classical Epistolary Theory and the Letters of Isocrates," in Poster and Mitchell, *Letter-Writing Manuals and Instruction from Antiquity to the Present*, 7–20. In the later tradition, Hermogenes discusses conversational style under panegyric. See *On the Types of Style*, trans. Cecil W. Wooten (Chapel Hill, 1987), 388. For Hermogenes on Plato's as the "most beautiful of panegyric styles in prose," see *On the Types of Style*, 386.

Drawing a sharp distinction between two kinds of style that characterize his three kinds of oratory, Aristotle bases these distinctions on the perspective of the audience, how near or far they are from the source of the discourse—the speaker or the written word—and therefore on how much detail they can take in. While the one kind of style furthers the agonistic aims of debate, the other, lacking this adversarial agenda, regularly fosters the expression of more benign feelings. For this same reason, Aristotle contends, epideictic oratory also enjoys greater structural and thematic freedom (3.14.1–4). But if an epideictic speech may include elements that do not strictly speaking belong to the matter at hand—that are, in Aristotle's words, *xena* or foreign rather than *oikeia* (3.14, 1415a7; Kennedy 261)—the reader, like the single judge, can nevertheless still readily distinguish between "what pertains [i.e., belongs] to the subject (*to oikeion tou pragmatos*) and what is irrelevant" (3.12.5, 1414a13; Kennedy 256). Throughout the *Rhetoric*, as we will see shortly, Aristotle comes back to this notion of *belonging*.

A regular fixture of the rhetorical tradition by Cicero's day, Aristotle's division of oratory into three kinds corresponds roughly to an older, Platonic triad that it seems to have replaced. This replacement is worth noting because it reflects the longstanding affinity of epistolary writing with not just epideictic oratory but conversation (Gr. *dialogos*; Lat. *sermo*). With both of these, it shares structural and thematic flexibility. With the former, however, it also shares the expectation of being read. Fully in favor of a flexible discourse, Plato nevertheless prefers speaking and listening to reading and writing.

In a late dialogue not incidentally called the *Sophist* (222CD), Plato therefore identifies the third type of discourse alongside the political (*dēmēgorikē*) and the legal (*dikanikē*) as *proshomiletic* instead of *epideictic*, rejecting the sophistic display that will figure so prominently in Aristotle's rhetorical theory. Centuries later, Quintilian reminds his own readers of Plato's philosophical arguments in favor of conversation, which Quintilian Latinizes as *sermocinatrix* (*Institutio oratoria* 3.4.10–11). He will also refer in passing to the deep connection between the letter and conversation (*epistola* and *sermo*)—a connection on which Cicero, Seneca, and Demetrius, as we will see, ground their epistolary theory (9.4.19–21).[5]

---

5. See Erika Rummel, "Erasmus' Manual of Letter-Writing: Tradition and Innovation," *Renaissance and Reformation*, n.s., 13 (1989): 308. On the intersection of panegyric and the letter in the later school tradition, see Stirewalt, *Studies in Ancient Greek Epistolography*, 62–63. If epideictic oratory did indeed originate with the sophists, it is understandable that Plato would reject it for philosophical dialogue, while

Departing from his teacher in featuring epideictic oratory (at the expense of proshomiletic or conversational discourse), Aristotle characterizes its style, as we have seen, as *graphic* rather than *agonistic*. On the other hand, Aristotle looks beyond these subdivisions to a stylistic excellence applicable to all three kinds of oratory when he calls for appropriateness, *to prepon* (*Rhetoric* 3.12.6).[6] Famously translated by Cicero into Latin as *decorum* (*Orator* 70; *De officiis* 1.94), this virtue or excellence of style informs equally the argument advanced (*logos*), the emotions aroused (*pathos*), and, most important for an emerging rhetoric of intimacy, the character (*ēthos*) created by the speaker or writer (*Rhetoric* 3.7.1). As it pertains to character, moreover, Aristotle qualifies this most successful style as *oikeia* (3.7.4). Lacking this quality, a speech of any kind will fail to create either the vividness or the credibility that persuades audiences (3.7.7, 3.2.13).[7]

Routinely conflated by subsequent theorists with appropriateness or *to prepon*, as we will see in more detail later in this chapter (see below, p. 45), the stylistic quality of being *oikeion* takes the *oikos*, understood as both family and property, as its point of departure.[8] In the *Politics*, Aristotle upholds the status of family and property, famously defending these two dimensions of the *oikos*—legal and affective—against Plato's attack in the *Republic*. As witness for the defense, Aristotle invokes Hesiod's *Works and Days* (1.2, 1252b9–11; cf. *Works and Days* 405): "First and foremost a house, a wife, and an ox for the plow." In keeping with this Hesiodic pronouncement about belonging and having belongings, Aristotle emphasizes the deep psychological attachment that defines our relation to the *oikos*. Holding all things in common,

---

Aristotle, much more receptive to sophistic literary theory, would not. On this matter, see Enos, "Ancient Greek Writing Instruction," 27–33, and Luc Vaillancourt, *La lettre familière au XVIe siècle: Rhétorique humaniste de l'épistolaire* (Paris, 2003), 40. On Plato's response to temporal and spatial distance and the accommodations they demand, see *Sophist* 254BC.

6. On *to prepon*, see two articles by Wesley Trimpi: "Horace's 'Ut Pictura Poesis'" and "Reason and the Classical Premises of Literary Decorum," *Independent Journal of Philosophy* 5/6 (1988): 103–11.

7. On *to oikeion* in the *Rhetoric*, and its relation to both style and character, see Cope, *Rhetoric of Aristotle with a Commentary*, 3: 12–19, 75–76, 146–47. For Plato on the division between *logos* and *lexis* that underlies Aristotelian rhetorical theory and on the role of *ēthos* in both, see *Republic* 392C and 400DE.

8. On "family" and "property" as the two principal meanings of *oikos*, see Douglas M. MacDowell, "The ΟΙΚΟΣ in Athenian Law," *Classical Quarterly*, n.s., 39 (1989): 10–21.

including wives, children, and belongings, Aristotle argues (2.3, 1261b33–1262a13), denies the basic human need to care for what is one's own.[9]

In the first book of the *Rhetoric,* on the other hand, Aristotle assumes both private ownership and a family structure, and he builds these assumptions into his topics for argumentation. Among these topics, Aristotle includes a brief discussion of wealth as a commonly acknowledged source of happiness. This discussion includes in turn a brief survey of the various kinds of property that constitute wealth, introducing a number of distinctions that will shape centuries of both legal and literary theory. In contrast to possession (*ktēsis*), use (*chrēsis*), and enjoyment (*apolausis*), Aristotle explains, actual ownership—"whether things are *oikeia* or not"—"depends on who has the right of alienation (*apallotriōsai*), and by alienation I mean gift and sale" (1.5.7, 1361a21–22; Kennedy 59). What is *oikeion*, in this context, is what legally belongs to me and to no one else. Its opposite is *allotrion*, what belongs to somebody else and not to me.[10]

---

9. On the tradition of common ownership, see my *Friends Hold All Things in Common: Tradition, Intellectual Property and the "Adages" of Erasmus* (New Haven, 2001). For the Stoics on caring for what is one's own, see below.

10. For the legal context of *oikeion* as property that we can either give away or sell, see Cope, *Rhetoric of Aristotle with a Commentary*, 2: 286. On the editorial addition of *oikeia* at 1361a15 that goes back to the Renaissance, see William M. A. Grimaldi, S.J., *Aristotle, Rhetoric 1: A Commentary* (New York, 1980), 111–12. For *allotrion* as the opposite of *oikeion*, see *Rhetoric* 3.12.5. For Aristotle's theory of property, including his terminology, see Jill Frank, *A Democracy of Distinction: Aristotle and the Work of Politics* (Chicago, 2005), 54–80, where Frank argues for property as a characterological as well as an external good: "The language Aristotle uses is striking. He speaks of habit as a kind of holding or possession and of action as a mode of use. He speaks of virtue, in other words, in terms of property.... What is owned for proper use—things or habits—is what is proper to one, *ta oikeia*" (70–72). On the concept of *oikeion* in the sense of belonging, and its opposition to *allotrion*, see Plato, *Lysis* 221E–222C. For the *oikos* as both a legal and an economic unit, see *Brill's New Pauly: Encyclopedia of the Ancient World*, ed. Hubert Cancik and Helmuth Schneider (Leiden, 2005), s.v. *family*, esp. 335. On the relation to the Latin *familia*, see 338–39. Also see *Paulys Realencyclopädie der classischer altertumswissenschaft*, s.v. *familia*. For the correspondence between *domus* and *oikos* and the meaning of *domus* as family, see Benveniste, *Indo-European Language and Society*, 243–45. And on the *famulus* as equivalent to the *oiketēs*, the slave or servant, see Benveniste, 291: "What constitutes the *familia* is, etymologically speaking, the whole of the *familia*, the servants who live in the same house."

Whereas the first book of the *Rhetoric* features *to oikeion* as a legal concept, the second book foregrounds its affective dimension, taking into account that our emotional relations are every bit as topical for the orator as our proprietary relations (2.4.28). Among our emotional attachments is one that Aristotle identifies as *oikeiotēs*, often translated as *intimacy*. Treated at much greater length in his ethical works, *oikeiotēs* figures as a subset of the larger category of *philia*, often translated as *friendship* but pertaining more generally to the whole range of close affective attachments. In his fuller treatment in the *Nicomachean Ethics*, in fact, Aristotle acknowledges that there are degrees of *oikeiotēs* determining the claim that any attachment makes on us (9.2.9–10). Assuming that we feel closest to those with whom we live in more or less day to day physical contact, Aristotle theorizes a common humanity that renders even strangers *oikeioi* and *philoi*—near and dear (8.1.3–4). On the other hand, he concedes, it is hard to share intimately (*oikeiōs*) in the joys and sorrows of many other people (9.10.5).[11]

When in the third book of the *Rhetoric* Aristotle turns from matters of proof to matters of style, his qualification of the most excellent style as *oikeia* (3.7.4) retains both legal and affective dimensions.[12] For Aristotle begins by reminding his readers not only that style provokes deep feelings but also that these feelings are aptly analogized to our affective responses to either those with whom we belong, that is, our fellow citizens, or those with whom we do not belong, namely, strangers (3.2.2–3).[13] Prose style in general is less strange or "foreign" than poetry and so uses, alongside metaphor, words that are at once *kyria* and *oikeia* (3.2.6, 3.7.7).[14] Language so qualified contributes

---

11. Another term for close relations or intimacy in the *Ethics* is *synētheia*, sometimes translated into Latin as *consuetudo* (see below). As the etymology of the word suggests, it too depends on character. See *Nicomachean Ethics* 8.4.1–2 and 9.5.2. On the influence of Aristotelian *oikeiotēs* on Stoic *oikeiōsis*, discussed below, see C. O. Brink, "Οἰκείωσις and οἰκειότης: Theophrastus and Zeno on Nature in Moral Philosophy," *Phronesis* 1 (1956): 123–44.

12. On the division in the art of rhetoric between matters of proof and matters of style, see Friedrich Solmsen, "The Aristotelian Tradition in Ancient Rhetoric," *American Journal of Philology* 62 (1941): 35–50, 169–90, and my *Hermeneutics and the Rhetorical Tradition*, 10–12.

13. "for people feel the same in regard to *lexis* as they do in regard to strangers (*pros tous xenous*) compared with citizens (*pros tous politas*)" (Kennedy 221). Both what is *xenon* and what is *allotrion* contrast with what is *oikeion*.

14. As a stylistic term, *kyrios* is often translated as *proper* and so rendered indistinguishable from *oikeios*. In this regard, I remind the reader of Larue van Hook's warn-

to the credibility of the speech because it effectively establishes the speaker's character (3.7.4, 3.7.7). For Aristotle, in fact, the stylistic quality of *intimacy* or *belonging* fosters the expression of character as the singularly most compelling source of persuasion.[15]

A key factor in Aristotelian rhetorical theory, where it is closely aligned with style, and especially a style that is *oikeia,* character or *ēthos* may also figure prominently in the prehistory of rhetorical and hermeneutic intimacy because of its own prehistory. Denoting physical location before it becomes a psychological construct, *ēthos* pertained first to the place or habitat most natural for an animal — its "haunt" — and only thereafter to the place where a person feels most at home.[16] In keeping with this early meaning, Homer, for instance, refers to the return of the sows to their *ētheia* (*Odyssey* 14.411) and to the absent Odysseus as *ētheios* (*Odyssey* 14.147). In this second reference, the term is applied affectionately by the loyal servant Eumaeus to a master he believes is far away. Such an application indicates that the affection that attaches to those who belong with us is not eradicated by physical distance. Indeed, as it applies to animals as well as to humans, *ēthos* in its earlier sense demarcates what one scholar of the term calls "the center of belonging."[17] Rooted etymologically in Indo-European **swedh,* root of Latin *suus* and *suesco* — "one's own" — *ēthos* may also retain some-

---

ing, cited in the introduction, about the belatedness of the specialized terminology of literary criticism (above, pp. 8–9). For *kyrios* as a legal term, see Douglas M. MacDowell, *The Law in Classical Athens* (Ithaca, 1978), 84–92, and A. R. W. Harrison, *The Law of Athens: The Family and Property* (Oxford, 1968), 200–205.

15. On the key role of *ēthos* in persuasion according to Aristotle, see Garver, *Aristotle's Rhetoric,* 172–205. For the confusion regarding Aristotelian *ēthos,* see Wisse, *Ethos and Pathos from Aristotle to Cicero,* 60–65. See also William M. Sattler, "Conceptions of *Ethos* in Ancient Rhetoric," *Speech Monographs* 14 (1947): 55–65.

16. See Charles Chamberlain, "From 'Haunts' to 'Character': The Meaning of Ethos and Its Relation to Ethics," *Helios* 11 (1984): 97–108. On the term *oikos* as "a word for habitat," see Benveniste, *Indo-European Language and Society,* 253.

17. Chamberlain, "From 'Haunts' to 'Character,'" 101: "This localization of *ēthos* in the soul is no doubt the natural culmination of its development as the center of belonging." Whereas Chamberlain treats the relation between *ēthos* and belonging philologically, Martin Heidegger treats it philosophically. See his "Letter on Humanism" in *Basic Writings,* ed. David Farrell Krell (New York, 1977), 189–242, which holds that "*Ethos* means abode, dwelling place" (233), "the sphere of the familiar" (234). See also Michael J. Hyde, ed., *The 'Ethos' of Rhetoric* (Columbia, S.C., 2004).

thing of a proprietary sense: what belongs to me, in the sense of my property, as well as to where I belong.[18] In this sense, then, *ēthos* is conceptually aligned with the *oikos,* an alignment reinforced, as we will see, by the eventual translation of what is *oikeion* in Greek by what in Latin is *suum* (see below, p. 26).

In the *Poetics,* meanwhile, Aristotle exploits this alignment between *ēthos* and *oikos* to explain the diversity of poetic styles.[19] Whereas the dramatic agents occupying the very heart of Aristotle's argument undertake their tragic actions as a consequence of their choices and their choices as a consequence of their ethical and intellectual qualities, the tragic poet himself, we learn in the *Poetics* (chapter 4), also makes a choice, only his is between the higher and the lower verse forms—the heroic, for instance, rather than the satiric (4, 1448b24) or the tragic rather than the comic (4, 1449a2–6); and he does so as a consequence of *his* character.[20] Aristotle first attributes this choice of style to not just the poet's *ēthos* but the more intensified *oikeion ēthos.* Then, later in the same chapter, Aristotle substitutes this telling phrase with an equally striking variation: *oikeia physis* (4, 1449a3–4), the poet's innermost nature. For Aristotle, in other words, artistic expression

---

18. Chamberlain, "From 'Haunts' to 'Character,'" 104 n. 8. On the relation between *suus* and *philos,* suggesting the link between the affective and the possessive, see Benveniste, *Indo-European Language and Society,* 273–88, esp. 276: "From the fact that *suus,* a possessive pronoun, gave rise to such expressions as *sui* 'his own people' and *aliquem suum reddere* 'to make somebody his friend' . . . it is easy to pass from a possessive relationship to one of friendship. This would impel us to seek the etymology of *philos* no longer as meaning 'dear,' but as an ancient possessive."

19. It is worth remembering that style (*lexis*) and character (*ēthos*) are prominent elements of the arts of both poetry and rhetoric. In the *Poetics,* Aristotle includes these two among the six constituent parts; in the *Rhetoric, ēthos* constitutes one of the sources of persuasion alongside *logos* and *pathos* and forms the focus of the first two books, while *lexis,* along with *taxis,* or arrangement, is the subject of book 3. While Aristotle divides these elements for the sake of organization, it is one of the intentions of my argument to demonstrate their inseparability, an inseparability epitomized in the famous apophthegm attributed to Socrates—"Speak that I may see you"—discussed below, p. 38.

20. On the relation between action, choice, and character in the argument of the *Poetics,* see my *Poetic and Legal Fiction in the Aristotelian Tradition* (Princeton, 1986), 36–54, and "Aristotle's *Poetics*: A Defense of Tragic Fiction," in *A Companion to Tragedy,* ed. Rebecca Bushnell (Oxford, 2005), 41–50.

through style is inevitably "intimate" or *oikeia*; its haunt is the character of the poet.[21]

Without offering an explicit theory of either letter writing or rhetorical intimacy, then, Aristotle lays the groundwork for a theory of style that will in time further the aim of the letter writer to express his innermost thoughts and feelings. As we have seen, this Aristotelian style is *graphic,* responsive to distance, and designed for nonadversarial exchange. It not only allows for structural and thematic flexibility but actively calls for intricate detail. Alongside *to prepon* but distinct from it, *to oikeion* is oratory's chief stylistic virtue—one that retains the legal and affective dimensions of belonging as well as its deepest roots in the character or *ēthos* of the writer.[22]

Like Aristotle, Cicero has no place for epistolary rhetoric in his rhetorical manuals. Not even those newly recovered and highly revered by the humanists, such as *De oratore,* the *Orator,* and *Brutus,* include letter writing in their treatments of the art.[23] Also like Aristotle, Cicero divides oratory into three kinds and associates epideictic oratory with reading (*De or.* 2.341). Unlike Aristotle, however, Cicero, through Antonius in *De oratore,* registers some disdain for these display pieces—mere entertainments on which the Greeks lavish attention but for which the Romans have little time or patience. On the other hand, Cicero does have Antonius acknowledge the opportunity in such speeches not only to uphold virtue but to express character (2.343).[24]

---

21. For a different reading of these important phrases, *oikeion ēthos* and *oikeia physis,* see Gerald F. Else, *Aristotle's Poetics* (Cambridge, Mass., 1957), 135–49. It is worth noting that Aristotle's discussion of a style that belongs to one's character takes place in the context of a chapter about the human impulse to imitate. See below for the Renaissance treatment of imitation and individual style. On *oikeia physis,* see George L. Kustas, *Studies in Byzantine Rhetoric* (Thessaloniki, 1973), 30.

22. On the other hand, Aristotle credits the discovery of the appropriate meter, the *oikeion metron* (4.18), for each of these two kinds of poetry to the demands of stylistic *decorum.*

23. On the role of Cicero's later rhetorical works in the work of the humanists, see, for instance, R. Sabbadini, "Guarino Veronese e le opera rettoriche di Cicerone," *Rivista di filologia e d'istruzione classica* (1885): 425–34, and Pierre Blanc, "Pétrarque lecteur de Cicéron. Les scolies pétrarquiennes du *De oratore* et de *l'Orator*," *Studi petrarcheschi* 9 (1978): 109–66.

24. At *Orator* 37–42, Cicero expands the category of epideictic to include *descriptiones* and *historiae.* See Elaine Fantham, *The Roman World of Cicero's "De oratore"* (Oxford, 2003), 136.

Throughout the rhetorical works of his maturity, Cicero focuses on this expression of character. For nothing helps an orator's case like the ability to—in Antonius's words—*exprimere mores* (*De or.* 2.184).

Yet again like Aristotle, in other words, Cicero includes character among what Antonius calls the three principles or *rationes* underlying the art of rhetoric (2.128).[25] In *De oratore,* Antonius routinely gives the *ratio* of character first place, though he finds various ways to describe it.[26] On one occasion, for instance, he insists that "nothing in oratory ... is more important than to win for the orator the favour of his hearer (*ut faveat oratori is, qui audiet*)" (2.178).[27] On others he prefers some form of the verb *conciliare* (2.128, 2.182–84). "A potent factor in success," he advises,

> is for the characters (*mores*), principles, conduct and course of life, both of those who are to plead cases and of their clients, to be approved ... and for the feelings of the tribunal to be won over, as far as possible, to goodwill (*conciliari quam maxime ad benevolentiam*) towards the advocate and the advocate's client as well. Now feelings are won over (*conciliantur*) by a man's merit, achievements or reputable life.... [A]ll the qualities belonging to men who are upright, unassuming and not given to haste, stubbornness, strife or harshness are powerful in winning good-

---

25. See James M. May, *Trials of Character: The Eloquence of Ciceronian Ethos* (Chapel Hill, 1988), 3: "As Aristotle's tripartite theory of *pisteis* lost currency, *ēthos* (along with *pathos*) as an efficacious tool of persuasion was either omitted from the discussion or, at best, relegated to a less prominent position. Thus, in the two early works of Roman rhetoric that sprang from Hellenistic sources, the *Rhetorica ad Herennium* and Cicero's *De inventione,* the role of ethos was subsumed under the *partes orationis*. It was not until Cicero's mature works, and specifically the *De oratore,* that ethos (and pathos with it) would be restored on a par with logos."

26. On Cicero's efforts to forge new terminology, see *De finibus,* trans. H. Rackham (Cambridge, Mass., 1914; rpt. 1971), 3.15: "Indeed my own practice is to use several words to give what is expressed in Greek by one, if I cannot convey the sense otherwise. At the same time I hold that we may fairly claim the license to employ a Greek word when no Latin word is readily forthcoming." See also *De finibus* 3.4–5 and Jill Kraye, "Cicero, Stoicism and Textual Criticism: Poliziano on ΚΑΤΟΡΘΩΜΑ," *Rinascimento,* n.s., 23 (1983): 79–110. And see William M. Sattler, "Conceptions of Ethos in Ancient Rhetoric," 55–65. For Cicero on the distinction between written and oral style, see *Brutus* 24.91–93 and 31.118.

27. All quotations are from *De oratore,* trans. E. W. Sutton (Cambridge, Mass., 1942), and are cited in the text.

will (*valde benevolentiam conciliant*) while the want of them estranges it from such as do not possess them (*abalienantque ab eis in quibus haec non sunt*). (2.182)²⁸

Whereas the more humane qualities attract us (*conciliare*) to the character being expressed, the harsher qualities alienate (*alienare*) us.

In another late work, the *Orator*, Cicero uses not only *conciliare* but *commendare* to indicate the effects of the expression of character on the listener (124); in this same work, moreover, Cicero reverts to Greek terminology to stabilize a shifting Latin usage:

> There are, for instance, two topics which if well handled by the orator arouse admiration for his eloquence. One, which the Greeks call ἦθος or "expressive of character," is related to men's nature and character, their habits and all the intercourse of life (*Quorum alterum est quod Graeci ἦθος vocant, ad naturas et ad mores et ad omnem vitae consuetudinem accommodatum*).... The former is courteous and agreeable, adapted to win good will (*Illud superius come, iucundum, ad benevolentiam conciliandam paratum*).²⁹

If Cicero's revision here more straightforwardly aligns his theory with Aristotelian rhetoric, it nevertheless obscures the degree to which Cicero's application of Aristotle has acquired a Stoic orientation. Cicero's more oblique formulations of Aristotelian *ēthos*, on the other hand, highlight this orientation.³⁰

---

28. In "Ciceronian *Conciliare* and Aristotelian Ethos," *Phoenix* 27 (1973): 262–75, Elaine Fantham argues persuasively for an identification of *conciliare* with the stimulation of friendly or favorable emotions and with the Ciceronian confidence in style (267, 273–75), but she rejects the possibility that Cicero's choice of terminology relies on "any philosophical distinction" (268). Indeed, it is Cicero's "professional love of, and faith in style" (273), she suggests, that motivates his move from *conciliare* to *delectare*. For a concern, contemporary with Cicero's, with winning the goodwill (*benivolentia*) of the audience through the *persona* of the speaker without any recourse to Stoic language, see *Ad Her.* 1.5.8. On the opposition of *conciliare* and *alienare* for the rhetorician, see Quintilian, *Institutio oratoria* 4.1.14–16, 4.1.23, 11.1.8–9, and cf. 11.1.6.

29. All quotations are from Cicero, *Orator*, trans. H. M. Hubbell (Cambridge, Mass., 1939; rpt. 1971) and are in the text. On this shifting usage, see Quintilian, *Institutio oratoria* 12.10.59.

30. On Cicero's attempts to integrate rhetoric and philosophy, especially Stoic philosophy, see Seigel, *Rhetoric and Philosophy in Renaissance Humanism*, 19–30. For Crassus against the Stoics, see *De oratore* 3.65–66, quoted by Seigel, 23–24, and compare *De finibus* 4.21–22.

For the Stoics, in their effort to understand how human beings relate to the world, including their most intense and intimate relationships with other human beings, take as their point of departure how the human being relates to himself—a relationship that begins at birth and continues to develop throughout his life. From beginning to end, human life is a process of self-development—what one recent student of Stoicism describes as "the search for personal identity."[31] In *De finibus,* where Cicero stages the philosophical debate of his day concerning the ultimate aims of human experience, he puts in the mouth of the elder Cato this signature bit of Stoicism. "It is the view of those whose system I adopt," Cato explains,

> that immediately upon birth (for that is the proper point to start from) a living creature feels an attachment for itself and to feel affection for its own constitution (*ipsum sibi conciliari et commendari ad se conservandum*); while on the other hand it conceives an antipathy (*alienari*) to those things which appear to threaten destruction. (*De fin.* 3.16)

It is human nature, then, to respond to the world according to a binary distinction between whatever preserves us and whatever destroys us. Toward the instruments of our preservation we experience attachment and affection—*conciliatio* and *commendatio*—while toward those of our annihilation, we experience antipathy or *alienatio.* Chief among the instruments of preservation is the self, the earliest focus of our attachment and affection.[32]

In the *Academica* (2.131), Cicero tells us that this theory of natural attachment—*conciliatio naturae*—originates with Zeno, "founder and first head" (*inventor et princeps*) of the Stoic school; what he does not say in the course of Romanizing this Greek philosopher is that Zeno referred to his foundational concept as *oikeiōsis,* derived, like the term so crucial to Aristotle's rhetorical and ethical theory, from *oikeion* and the *oikos.* Indeed, recent scholarship on Stoic philosophy seems to agree on two points that underscore the importance of this derivation: first, "had there been no *oikeiosis,* there would have been no Stoa"; and second, the best rendering of this no-

---

31. G. B. Kerferd, "The Search for Personal Identity in Stoic Thought," *Bulletin of the John Rylands University Library of Manchester* 55 (1972): 177–96. See also Christopher Gill, *The Structured Self in Hellenistic and Roman Thought* (Oxford, 2006), 29–46, 129–59.

32. Compare Diogenes Laertius 7.85 and see Kerferd, "Search for Personal Identity in Stoic Thought," 190–96, and Troels Engberg-Pedersen, *The Stoic Theory of Oikeiosis* (Aarhus, 1990), 71, and Gill, *Structured Self in Hellenistic and Roman Thought,* 36–39.

toriously untranslatable term is "belonging."³³ In the earliest stages through simple perception and only later through higher forms of cognition, humans are wired psychologically to discriminate between what belongs to them—and where they belong—and what does not, what is alien. If the earliest Stoics formulate this psychological discrimination, with its clear affective dimension, by the fundamentally legal opposition *oikeion/allotrion,* Cicero often (if not always) translates their formulation from Greek into Latin with *commendare, conciliare/alienare.*³⁴ So he has Cato offer this further explanation:

> From this impulse is developed the sense of mutual attraction (*commendatio*) which unites human beings as such; this also is bestowed by nature. The mere fact of their common humanity requires that one man should feel another man to be akin to him (*non alienum*). (*De fin.* 3.63)

Recalling Aristotle's similar acknowledgment in the *Nicomachean Ethics* cited above (p. 17), Cato extends the scope of human belonging from its primary focus on the self to its relations first with those who constitute the household or family and eventually with the human race, understood as the larger family of humankind.³⁵

---

33. See S. G. Pembroke, "*Oikeiosis*," in *Problems in Stoicism*, ed. Anthony A. Long (London, 1971), 114–15, and Engberg-Pedersen, "Discovering the good: *oikeiōsis* and *kathēkonta* in Stoic ethics," *The Norms of Nature: Studies in Hellenistic Ethics*, ed. Malcolm Schofield and Gisela Striker (Cambridge, Eng., 1986), 145–83, and *Stoic Theory of Oikeiosis*, 68–69 and 99: "From start to end the process of *oikeiosis* should be understood in terms not of good but of belonging. At its end, however, something is apparently seen as belonging with such a character that the person will at that stage come to grasp the *notion* of what is genuinely *good* and to identify what he has come to see as belonging as good." In *The Structured Self in Hellenistic and Roman Thought*, Gill, who rejects Engberg-Pedersen's case for the subjectivity of the Stoic self (359–70), prefers "appropriation" to "belonging" (37), a translation that indicates as well the proprietary dimension of the concept.

34. See Pembroke, "*Oikeiosis*," 118: "Moral awareness is, to use the Stoic term, the most highly articulated form of perception possible, but what is proper (*oikeion*) and what is alien (*allotrion*) are at all levels of consciousness not only the terms in which perception operates but the conditions without which it could not arise." And see Kerferd, "Search for Personal Identity in Stoic Thought," 193.

35. See Cicero, *De finibus* 5.65; Kerferd, "Search for Personal Identity in Stoic Thought," 195–96; and Pembroke, "*Oikeiosis*," 124–25. And see Richard P. Saller,

Like Aristotelian rhetorical theory in passing over the letter in silence, Cicero's mature rhetorical works, especially *De oratore* and the *Orator*, nevertheless promote a rhetoric grounded in the expression of character; and they do so through the specialized terminology they share with Cicero's version of Stoicism. This terminology indicates just how much the philosopher's concern with self-development informs the orator's task of self-expression—or at least self-presentation. For the orator must present himself (that is, his character), Cicero insists, in a way that stimulates attachment and affection rather than alienation. The audience must be made to feel the *oikeiōsis* or *conciliatio*—the belonging—between themselves and the speaker. To affirm merely that the orator must please his listeners and gain their good will grossly undervalues the force that successful speakers marshal by tapping into a psychological process that activates our deepest instincts not only for self-preservation but for intimate attachment and affection. Without addressing epistolary composition per se in his rhetorical works, Cicero reinforces the alliance between *ēthos* and *to oikeion* or *belonging*—an alliance that underwrites a rhetoric of intimacy.

In contrast to Cicero's rhetorical works, *De officiis*, his most successful attempt at popularizing Stoic philosophy, does address intimate discourse, but not before rehearsing the case for both private property and "personal identity" or self-development. Recalling Aristotle's telling phrase (*oikeia physis*) in the *Poetics* (see above, p. 19), Cicero refers to the self as not only *persona* and *mores* but *propria natura* (1.30.107–1.31.110).[36] Indeed, what is

---

"'Familia, Domus,' and the Roman Conception of the Family," *Phoenix* 38 (1984): 336–55.

36. See on this issue two articles by Christopher Gill: "Personhood and Personality: The Four-*Personae* Theory in Cicero, *De officiis* 1," *Oxford Studies in Ancient Philosophy* 6 (1988): 169–99, and "The Question of Character-Development: Plutarch and Tacitus," *Classical Quarterly* 33 (1983): 469–87, where Gill argues that in the context of Tacitus's writings, "there is no special contrast between *mores* and *ingenium* of a kind that would justify our reading the first as acquired or developed qualities and the second as innate ones" (485). See also C. J. de Vogel, "The Concept of Personality in Greek and Christian Thought," in *Studies in Philosophy and the History of Philosophy*, ed. John K. Ryan (Washington, D.C., 1963), 20–60, esp. 30–33.

For both the link between character and action and the reduced status of character in Roman rhetorical theory, see Andrew M. Riggsby, "The Rhetoric of Character in the Roman Courts," in *Cicero the Advocate*, ed. Jonathan Powell and Jeremy Paterson (Oxford, 2004), 165–85. For the interchangeability, as opposed to the indi-

proprium in Latin routinely corresponds to what is *oikeion* in Greek, complete with legal pedigree. So in a letter to Manius Curius, Cicero playfully parries the language of the law courts, including the term *proprius* as a legal designation for one's property, to differentiate the intimate bond Curius enjoys with Atticus from the one this same correspondent shares with Cicero himself. "When you write that you belong (*proprium te esse*) to [Atticus] by right of ownership and legal bond (*mancipio et nexu*)," Cicero quips, "but to me in usufruct (*usu et fructu*), I am quite satisfied with that arrangement; for it is just that of which he has the enjoyment and profit (*quo quisque fruitur atque utitur*), which constitutes a man's property (*Id enim est cuiusque proprium*)" (*Ad fam.*7.30.2).[37] In *De officiis,* Cicero couples what in the legal sense is *proprium* with what is *suum* to advocate a psychological individuality conducive to rhetorical intimacy.

Striking a lawyerly balance between the claims of the community and those of the individual, *De officiis* promotes the cause of private property. The commonwealth itself, Cicero stresses repeatedly (1.20–21, 2.73, 2.78–79, 2.85), owes its reason for being to the private wealth it is there to protect. The principal justification for *res publica,* he insists, is *res sua* (2.73).[38] Justice itself holds among its most sacred tasks the fair and stable demarcation between what belongs to someone and what does not—between what is *sua* (and *propria*) and what is *aliena* (2.83–84). For Cicero defines the closest (if not, as we will see, the noblest) bond among the gradation of attachments that constitutes society as that between husband and wife as the nucleus of the household or *domus* (1.54), the locus of property and the seedbed or *seminarium* of *res publica.*

But if the *domus* constitutes the foundational community based on natural affection, it also constitutes the individual standing or status of the *dominus,* the property owner, within the larger society—a status tied to the value of his personal property. Looking to moderate if not to completely overturn

---

viduality, of friends for the Stoic sage, see Glenn Lesses, "Austere Friends: The Stoics and Friendship," *Apeiron* 26 (1993): 57–75, who concludes: "The basis of friendship among the sage has nothing to do with unique, personal traits" (74).

On the epistolary elements of *De officiis,* see Roy K. Gibson and A. D. Morrison, "What Is a Letter?" in *Ancient Letters: Classical and Late Antique Epistolography*, ed. Ruth Morello and A. D. Morrison (Oxford, 2007), 1–16, esp. 9 n. 28.

37. Cicero, *Letters to His Friends,* trans. W. Glynn Williams (Cambridge, Mass., 1928; rpt. 1995).

38. For *res familiaris* as an alternative term for property in *De officiis,* see 1.25, 1.92, 2.64, 2.87.

this valuation, Cicero exhorts the *dominus* or householder not to rely on the magnificence of his house to increase his worth but rather through his own conduct to ennoble his house(hold). "One's standing ought to be enhanced by one's house," Cicero concedes, "but not won entirely because of it; the master should not be made honorable by the house (*domo*), but the house (*domus*) by the master (*domino*)."[39] The character of the property owner, in other words, bestows ultimate value on the property owned.

If Cicero formulates the individual's affective relations in legal terms, and especially in terms of the law regarding private property, he also makes the case for psychological individuality with the help of these same terms. Like Aristotle, moreover, Cicero aligns *to prepon* with *to oikeion,* without erasing the distinction between them. For it is an act of *decorum* (Gr. *to prepon*), Cicero maintains, to nurture what is peculiarly our own (Gr. *oikeion*), what belongs to us. Whatever is *suum* and *proprium* is most fitting. "Everybody," Cicero insists, "must resolutely hold fast to his own peculiar gifts (*sua*), insofar as they are peculiar (*propria*). . . . For we must so act as not to oppose the universal laws of nature (*contra universam naturam*), but, while safeguarding those, to follow the bent of our own particular nature (*propriam nostram*)" (*De off.* 1.31.110). In psychological as well as in legal matters, moreover, whatever is not *suum* and *proprium* is *alienum*. So Cicero warns his son Marcus against the hazards to the developing self of indecorously taking for one's own what rightfully belongs to someone else:

> it is each man's duty to weigh well what are his own peculiar traits of character (*quid quisque habeat sui*), to regulate these properly, and not to wish to try how another man's would suit him (*nec velle experiri, quam se aliena deceant*). For the more peculiarly his own a man's character is the better it fits him (*id enim maxime quemque deceat, quod est cuiusque maxime suum*). (1.31.113)

In keeping with the stress on individual property throughout *De officiis,* what belongs to one man does not belong to another, whether personal

---

39. Cicero, *On Duties*, ed. M. T. Griffin and E. M. Atkins (Cambridge, Eng., 1991; rpt. 2002), 54 (1.139). On the status of the house, see Susan Treggiari, "The Upper-Class House as a Symbol and Focus of Emotion in Cicero," *Journal of Roman Archeology* 12 (1999): 33–56. On the correspondence of the *domus,* which "always signifies 'house' in the sense of family" (243), to the Greek *oikos* rather than *domos*, see Benveniste, *Indo-European Language and Society*, 242–61. In addition, Benveniste highlights the semantic correspondence in Latin between "having something at home" and "possessing" it (245).

character or legal ownership; and no one achieves the goal of living decorously by appropriating what belongs to someone else while disregarding what is his own (1.31.111).[40]

What is true for living, moreover, is true for speaking and writing. Without completely discrediting the *genera dicendi* so fundamental to the oratory practiced in the law courts and assembly, Cicero's mature rhetorical works at the very least acknowledge the kind of individuality in style that his philosophical work recognizes in human psychology. So in *De oratore*, Cicero has Crassus not only sum up the demands of stylistic *decorum* with the recognition that there are almost as many styles of oratory as there are orators (*nonne fore ut quot oratores, totidem paene reperiantur genera dicendi?*) (*De or.* 3.34) but also appreciate Caesar's style (*genus dicendi*) as very nearly unique (*prope singulare*) (3.30).[41] Appropriating the language of property law, then, Ciceronian stylistic theory inherits in the bargain the *propriety* of individual ownership.

Complementing its focus on private property with an equally keen eye to the differences between one character and another, *De officiis* also addresses both the kinds of human relations that unite individuals, encouraging their cooperation, and the kind of discourse that best promotes these relations. Among men of compatible (though not identical) characters, intimacy or *familiaritas* is the strongest and most honorable bond (*De off.* 1.55). Elsewhere—in a letter to Atticus, in fact—Cicero observes that this same in-

---

40. In *A Commentary on Cicero, "De Officiis"* (Ann Arbor, 1996), Andrew R. Dyck considers the treatment of *decorum* the most difficult section of the essay: "The subject itself is not an easy one; for here a term from the aesthetic sphere (τὸ πρέπον) is adapted to ethical uses and made to subsume the older virtue σωφροσύνη. At the same time the attempt to distinguish this new virtue from the *honestum* as a whole proves to be difficult. Moreover, the subject is bedeviled by the lack of a fully adequate Latin translation for τὸ πρέπον and other terminological difficulties. Finally the order of presentation is confusing" (241).

41. See George A. Kennedy, *Quintilian* (New York, 1969), 121. On the Stoic insistence on both individual differences and individuality, see Catharine Edwards, "Self-Scrutiny and Self-Transformation in Seneca's Letters," *Greece and Rome* 44 (1997): 27: "There is a strong sense . . . of the different qualities of different individuals. Thus in Stoicism there is a preoccupation with the disposition of the individual which, at least from the time of Panaetius, might attend particularly to an individual's distinctive character traits. Yet, as has often been noted, this potential for a focus on self-examination is not seriously developed until the first century C.E." For Seneca on these differences, see below.

timacy surpasses by far political alliances, the mere *amicitiae* that attach themselves to success (*Ad Att.* 1.18.1). While numerous *amici* may court a man in his home and accompany him to the forum, only very few *familiares*—and in Cicero's case maybe only one—can share the unguarded joke (*iocari libere*) or the intimate sigh (*suspirare familiariter*) (*Ad Att.* 1.18.1; cf. 4.17.1).[42] Only very few can really appreciate the kind of communication that Cicero identifies in *De officiis* as *sermo*.

One of the two principal discursive forms of a rhetoric of intimacy, *sermo* had yet in Cicero's day to receive theoretical attention (*De off.* 1.132).[43] In an effort to redress this neglect, Cicero enumerates the suitable occasions and establishes some preliminary rules of engagement, including the distinction between playful and serious conversation and the procedures for offering mild correction (1.132, 1.134–36). Specifically setting *sermo* apart from the oratory of debate, he identifies it with the process of *conciliatio* discussed above, wondering to what extent "an approachable manner of conversation will win over men's hearts" (*conciliet animos comites affabilitasque sermonis*) (2.48). The other discursive form identified with intimacy is the letter, which Cicero characterizes in his correspondence with Atticus as *scribere familiariter* (*Ad Att.* 9.4.1). To write intimately is to write letters.

---

42. For Cicero's *Letters to Atticus*, I have used the text and translation by D. R. Shackleton Bailey, 7 vols. (Cambridge, 1965–70). On the place of *amicitia* in Roman politics see J. Hellegouarc'h, *Le vocabulaire latin des relations et des partis politiques sous la république* (Paris, 1963); David O. Ross Jr., *Style and Tradition in Catullus* (Cambridge, Mass., 1969), 83–84; and David Konstan, *Friendship in the Classical World* (Cambridge, Eng.,1997), 122–48. See also P. A. Brunt, "'Amicitia' in the Late Roman Republic," *Proceedings of the Cambridge Philological Society* 191, n.s., 11 (1965): 1–20, who insists on the affective as well as the political dimensions of the term. On the *familiaritas* between Cicero and Atticus that motivates not only the letters but also his dialogue on friendship, see *De amicitia* 1.4 and *Cicero's Letters to Atticus*, ed. Shackleton Bailey, 1: 3–59. On the manuscript order of the *Letters to Atticus* and the advantages of reading them in this order, see Mary Beard, "Ciceronian Correspondences: Making a Book out of Letters" in *Classics in Progress: Essays on Ancient Greece and Rome*, ed. T. P. Wiseman (Oxford, 2002), 103–44, esp. 116–30.

43. On Cicero's role in establishing the genre in Rome see Fantham, *Roman World of Cicero's "De oratore,"* 136. For its importance to Cicero, see *Ad Atticum* 3.12.2: "ego etiam nunc eodem in loco iaceo sine sermone ullo, sine cogitatione ulla." On the relation between *sermo* and *epistola* see, for instance, Wolfgang G. Mueller, "Der Brief als Spiegel der Seele," *Antike und Abendland* 26 (1980): 138–157; Baños, *El arte epistolar*, 43–44. And see Trimpi, *Ben Jonson's Poems*, 60–75.

Like conversation, the letter in Cicero's day remained undertheorized.[44] Also like conversation, it came in two varieties, the playful (*familiare et iocosum*) and the serious (*severum et grave*) (*Ad fam.* 2.4.1). Throughout his letters Cicero refers to his epistolary writing not only as composed in an intimate, conversational style but as conversation itself: in one instance as *sermo plebeius* (*Ad fam.* 9.21.1) and in another as *sermo familiaris* (*Ad Att.* 1.9.1; cf. *Ad fam.* 7.32.3).[45] He also describes the letter as a replacement for conversation when physical distance separates the two interlocutors (*Ad Att.* 7.15.1, 9.10.1). Whereas Aristotle identified writing in general with distance, in other words, Cicero identifies distance more narrowly with writing letters, the kind of writing developed specifically to inform the absent. "Letter-writing was invented," Cicero suggests, "just in order that we might inform those at a distance if there were anything which it was important for them or for ourselves that they should know" (*Ad fam.* 2.4.1; cf. *Ad Quint.* 1.1.37).[46]

If the need to communicate information over space occasions the letter's invention, it is rather the need to communicate feeling, especially the feeling of closeness or intimacy, that accounts for the letter's development. On several occasions, Cicero confesses to his most intimate correspondent Atticus that he writes daily not because he has anything new to report but because he needs to express his feelings. "Since I left Rome," he confides to Atticus, "I have not let a day pass so far without sending you some sort of letter, not that I have had a great deal to write about but just to talk to you in absence (*sed ut loquerer tecum absens*). Nothing gives me greater pleasure

---

44. On this neglect see Malherbe, *Ancient Epistolary Theory*, 3; Baños, *El arte epistolar en el Renacimiento europeo*, 37–39, and James J. Murphy, *Rhetoric in the Middle Ages: A History of Rhetorical Theory from St. Augustine to the Renaissance* (Berkeley, 1974), 195–97. And see Carol Poster, "A Conversation Halved," in Poster and Mitchell, *Letter Writing Manuals and Instruction from Antiquity to the Present*, who may underestimate the Ciceronian contribution: "Literary letters, such as those of Cicero or Seneca, are probably what first come to mind when most rhetoricians think of ancient epistolarity, but contribute little to our knowledge of ancient epistolary theory" (39).

45. On the letter as written conversation, see, most recently, Baños, *El arte epistolar en el Renacimiento europeo*, 43–44, and Vaillancourt, *La lettre familière au XVIe siècle*, 54–55.

46. On the importance of writing in oratorical training, see *De oratore* 1.150–53 and *Brutus* 24.92. On writing in *De oratore* as the means to commemorate and glorify, see Fantham, *Roman World of Cicero's "De oratore,"* 138.

than that, when I can't do it face to face" (7.15.1). Elsewhere Cicero shares a similar confidence:

> I have nothing to write about, having heard no news and having replied to all your letters yesterday. But since my distress of mind is such that it is not only impossible to sleep but torment to be awake, I have started this scrawl without any subject in view, just in order as it were to talk to you (*ut quasi loquerer*), which is my only relief. (9.10.1; cf. 8.14.1)

Sometimes Cicero even repeats information he knows that Atticus will have already heard from someone else, just so that his dearest friend will understand how he, Cicero, experiences events:

> I am sure you are dying to know what's afoot here, and also to know it from me—not that news of what goes on in full public view is any more reliable from my pen than when it comes to you from the letters or reports of others, but I should like you to see from a letter of my own how I react to developments, and my attitude of mind and general state of being at the present time. (4.3.1)

Engaged most deeply by those letters that express his thoughts and feelings, Cicero explains to his friend Curio that this kind of writing is not always suitable. Under some circumstances, he cautions, not writing at all is the only alternative because "I dare not write what I feel, and I am not inclined to write what I don't feel" (*Ad fam.* 2.4.1; cf. *Ad Att.* 9.4.1).

Like the intimate, face-to-face exchanges that it replaces, then, familiar letter writing promotes itself as an expression of the letter writer's deepest feelings. Whereas Aristotle, as we have seen, drew a sharp distinction between the styles of oral and written discourse, Cicero, who preserves the stylistic differences between the letter and a speech in court or public assembly (*Ad fam.* 9.21.1; cf. *Ad Her.* 3.23–25), nevertheless insists on the closest affinity between at least one kind of writing and one kind of speaking—*epistola* and *sermo*. Indeed, Cicero routinely writes to Atticus and a few others with all the spontaneity and abruptness that would characterize his most unrestrained and informal conversations (e.g., *Ad Att.* 7.11.1, *Ad Quint.* 1.3.1).

Letters such as these go well beyond Aristotelian epideictic oratory in their thematic and structural flexibility. In a long letter to Atticus responding to a number of loosely arranged topics (6.1), Cicero applauds the meandering quality of Atticus's epistolary composition. "If my arrangement of topics (*oikonomia*) is rather confused," he chides Atticus, "you must blame yourself. I am following your impromptu (*schediazonta*)" (6.1.1). Later in the same letter, Cicero captures this extemporaneous quality with another quirky Greek phrase—*ō pragmatōn asugklōstōn* (6.1.17)—that evokes those loose ends that the Fates have not bothered to weave together. Less allusively in another letter, Cicero encourages spontaneity in Atticus's correspondence, telling him to record "whatever comes into [his] head" (1.12.4; cf. 12.1.2, 14.7.2).[47]

Like conversation in being loosely structured, the Ciceronian *epistola* nevertheless differs from the more specialized category of philosophical *sermo*. For the philosophical plain style must avoid, for instance, the repetitions that simulate strong emotion (*Orator* 85), while epistolary style, in an effort to communicate emotional intensity, relies on just such strategies.[48] "Brother, brother, brother," begins a letter to Quintus,

> were you really afraid that some fit of anger prompted me to send my men to you without a letter? Or that I did not want to see you? I be angry with *you*? *Could* I be angry with you? (1.3.1)

To similar effect, Cicero weaves into a letter to Atticus an agitated conversation with Curio, who wonders if Cicero has heard the latest news:

> I said no. "Publius," he says, "is standing for Tribune." "No, really." "Yes, and as Caesar's deadly enemy, and means to undo everything they've done." "What about Caesar?" "Says he had nothing to do with proposing Publius' adoption." (2.12.2)

Thoroughly conversational in tone, this letter does more, however, than deftly incorporate the intense give and take of everyday talk—Cicero's *quotidiana verba* (*Ad fam.* 9.21.1). It also converts the alliance between these two intimate forms of communication—*epistola* and *sermo*—into a competition.[49] For Cicero claims that at the exact moment of his face-to-face

---

47. On the long afterlife of this expression, see below, p. 78. On the flexible structure of the letter see *Ad Quint.* (trans. W. Glynn Williams [Cambridge, Mass., 1953]), 2.11.1: "But just as when we are together it is not often that we are at a loss for something to talk about, so our letters ought occasionally to ramble at random." On Cicero's use of Greek in the letters to Atticus, see G. O. Hutchinson, *Cicero's Correspondence: A Literary Study* (Oxford, 1998), 13–16.

48. This distinction is perhaps confirmed by Quintilian, *Institutio oratoria*, trans. Donald A. Russell, 5 vols. (Cambridge, Mass., 2001), 6.2.17: "There is also a sort of intermediate emotion, arising out of the love and longing of friends and close connections; this is less than *pathos* and more than *ēthos*."

49. For the inclusion of dialogue in the letters, see Hutchinson, *Cicero's Correspondence*, 113–38, and Peter White, *Cicero in Letters: Epistolary Relations of the Late Republic* (Oxford, 2010), 18–23.

exchange with Curio, he received letters from Atticus detailing the same news—only doing so more effectively. "What nonsense that is about the living voice!" Cicero writes to Atticus; "I got an infinitely better idea (*quanto magis vidi*) from your letter (*ex tuis litteris*) than from his talk (*ex illius sermone*) of what is going on" (2.12.2). Sometimes, in other words, epistolary writing surpasses conversation in its power to express the full force of events and the emotional reactions they provoke (see *Ad Att.* 2.11.1).

In yet another letter to a friend, Cicero makes the same point (*Ad fam.* 3.11.1–2). For he assures Appius Pulcher, his predecessor as governor of Cilicia, that none of the public discussion concerning Appius's recent court acquittal can compete with the clarity and vividness of Appius's own epistolary account of the ordeal. Cicero then adds to this assurance the admission that he was so moved by the intensity of Appius's written account that, frustrated by the letter writer's absence, he succumbed to an impulse to kiss the letter (3.11.2).[50]

If Cicero follows Aristotle in keeping the oration—at least the deliberative and forensic oration—with its oral, agonistic orientation, at the very center of his rhetorical manuals, his letters nevertheless provide both directions for and models of a different kind of rhetoric, a rhetoric of intimacy. As we have seen, this rhetoric shares some key features with epideictic oratory: it enjoys a thematic and structural flexibility that the more highly structured oration lacks; it is benign—even affectionate—rather than agonistic; and it is not only essentially written rather than oral but written in a style responsive to distance and dependent on detail. Like the other two branches, epideictic oratory aims at a stylistic excellence that Aristotle calls *oikeia*—a quality that, deriving from the *oikos* or household and corresponding to the Roman *familia,* retains both the proprietary relation between an owner and his belongings and his affective relation to where and with whom he belongs.[51]

---

50. On the language of kissing and Cicero's use of it, see Philippe Moreau, "Osculum, basium, sauium," *Revue de philologie, de littérature et d'histoire ancienne* 104 (1978): 87–97. On such letter kissing as a commonplace motif, see White, *Cicero in Letters*, 184 n. 31. On the correspondence with Appius Pulcher, see White, 52–53.

51. For the legal origins of the Roman *familia*, including its early association with *pecunia*, its correspondence to the Greek *oikos*, and its possible etymological link with not only the proprietary concept of the Oscan *famel* but the legal-religious concept of *fas*, see two articles by Roger Henrion: "Des origins du mot *familia*," *L'antiquité classique* 10 (1941): 37–69 and 11 (1942): 253–87. And on the collective noun *familia* from *famulus*, see Benveniste, *Indo-European Language and Society*, 291.

In his philosophical works, as we have also seen, Cicero extends the proprietary dimension of belonging to character formation by holding up for approval the cultivation of what is *suum* and *proprium,* while in his rhetorical works he addresses the oratorical challenge of fostering this belonging through the expression of character. Whereas Aristotle's orator undertakes the challenge with the credibility of his arguments in mind, Cicero's orator (whether he knows it or not) expresses himself with the recognizably Stoic agenda of *conciliating*—rather than *alienating*—his audience. Cicero's letter writer, on the other hand—or at least the Cicero who writes letters to Atticus—takes self-expression as the mark of intimacy and the belonging it fosters as an end in itself.[52]

Like the rhetorical treatises of both Aristotle and Cicero, Demetrius's *On Style* (*Peri hermēneias*), as the title indicates, features style as a matter of central importance to the orator.[53] Unlike these other treatises, however, *On Style* addresses head on the topic of letter writing, identifying it explicitly with the expression of character, identified here in turn with the *psychē* or soul:

> The letter, like the dialogue (*ho dialogos*), should abound in glimpses of character (*to ēthikon*). It may be said that everybody reveals his own soul (*psychēs*) in his letters. In every other form of composition it is possible to discern the writer's character (*to ēthos*), but in none so clearly as in the epistolary. (4.227)[54]

---

52. For a reading of Cicero's letters as essentially persuasive, see Hutchinson, *Cicero's Correspondence*, esp. 20–22. In *Cicero in Letters*, Peter White, on the other hand, entertains the possibility that at least some of Cicero's letters express "a desire for contact for its own sake" (77), although White does caution against thinking "that the corpus reveals to us the real Cicero" (170).

53. Whereas Aristotle does not divide *lexis* into a set number of kinds and Cicero here and there acknowledges three *genera dicendi*, Demetrius discusses four *charaktēres*. In addition, Demetrius has a number of words that are fairly translated as *style*, including *charaktēr* (4.223, 235), *lexis* (4.228), and *hermēneia* (4.228, 230, 235). At 4.226, Demetrius invokes both *to prepon* and *oikeion*, but it is hard to grasp in this context any distinction between the two terms.

54. Demetrius, *On Style*, trans. W. Rhys Roberts (Cambridge, Mass., 1927; rpt. 1973). For discussion of this treatise, including author and date, see Pierre Chiron, *Un rhéteur méconnu: Démétrios* (Paris, 2001), and *Démétrios, Du style*, ed. Pierre Chiron (Paris, 2002), xiii–xl. And see Dirk Marie Schenkeveld, *Studies in Demetrius "On Style"* (Amsterdam, 1964). For the place of Demetrius's treatise in the history of letter

If the letter goes beyond the dialogue in its attention to psychology, and especially to expressing character, it also differs in being written rather than oral. On this point Demetrius follows Aristotle (*Rhetoric* 3.12), preserving the distinction between discourse that is designed to be read and discourse that depends on delivery (4.193). In following Aristotle, moreover, Demetrius departs from Artemon, the little-known epistolary theorist responsible for editing Aristotle's letters. Whereas Artemon considers the letter one half of a conversation, Demetrius insists that because it is written or *graphic*, the letter is necessarily more studied than what is spoken extemporaneously (4.224).

Graphic by nature, the letter is also, according to Demetrius, a plain-style genre. In keeping with this generic affiliation, the letter should exhibit the quality of intimacy that Demetrius calls not *oikeiotēs* but *synētheia*. Thoroughly appropriated by Stoic literary theory, this quality, like so much else in Demetrius, nevertheless looks back to Aristotle.[55]

In the third book of the *Rhetoric,* as we have seen, Aristotle identifies the best style as *oikeia* and the language of everyday speech as *oikeia* and *kyria* (3.2.13). Demetrius replaces *oikeia* with *synēthēs* (2.77, 3.190; cf. 2.86–87), not only a term used throughout the *Nicomachean Ethics* to indicate, like *oikeiotēs*, a relation of intimacy, but one that sets in high relief the alliance between intimacy and character. Whereas *oikeiotēs* preserves the sense of belonging associated with the *oikos*, *synētheia* incorporates the concept of *ēthos*.[56] Linked to this quality of *synētheia*, moreover, is another term, *idiotēs*, that figures in Aristotle's and Demetrius's recommendations for rhetorical success. For the best proofs are those that make use of *ta idia*—that is, de-

---

writing up through the Renaissance, see Baños, *El arte epistolar en el Renacimiento europeo*, 30–33, and Vaillancourt, *La lettre familière au XVIe siècle*, 43–46. For Demetrius on character, see Vaillancourt, 45: "On aurait tort cependant d'y voir autre chose qu'une stratégie rhétorique visant à établir la crédibilité et l'autorité morale de l'auteur, c'est-à-dire son *ethos*. Il ne s'agit pas de parler de soi avec complaisance, mais de rendre manifestes ses vertus à des fins persuasives."

55. For the Peripatetic influence on Demetrius, see *Du style*, ed. Chiron, ix; for the Stoic influences on Demetrius, see Chiron, *Un rhéteur méconnu*, 336–43. Whereas Aristotle attributes some of the thematic and stylistic flexibility later to be associated with the letter with epideictic oratory, as we have seen, Demetrius, perhaps following Aristotle, identifies the letter itself with *epideixis* (4.225).

56. On the Stoic virtue of *synētheia* (Lat. *consuetudo*), see Chiron, *Un rhéteur méconnu*, 299–302.

tails that belong uniquely to the subject under consideration, in contrast to others that are more common or *koina*. So Aristotle recommends that the orator faced with the task of praising Achilles do so in terms of those particular details (*ta idia*) that belong to him alone—that he killed Hector, that he was the youngest warrior to go to Troy, and that only he had not taken the oath to defend Menelaos's right to Helen—rather than in terms of the more common characteristics (*ta koina*) he shares with several other heroes, like Diomedes (*Rhetoric* 2.22.11–12).

Like Aristotle's orator, Demetrius's plain stylist is advised that the writing or speaking that lacks this quality of being *idiotikos* will fail (4.208). Demetrius also makes clear that this quality—like that of being *oikeion*—is grounded in the legal concept of private property. Comparing the two most widely read historians of ancient Greece in terms of their imitative practices, Demetrius claims to prefer Thucydides to Herodotus. For whatever Thucydides steals from others, Demetrius observes, "he uses . . . in his own way (*idiōs*) and so makes . . . his own property (*idion*)" (2.113). What is *idios*, in contrast once again to what is either *allotrios* or *koinos* (somebody else's property or common property), is one's own.

Without *synētheia*, then, the letter will fail to persuade (4.221); and this failure is critical, according to Demetrius, because alongside vividness (*enargeia*), persuasiveness (*to pithanon*) distinguishes epistolary style. Vividness, moreover, depends on the *akribeia* of detail (4.209), which the plain style shares with the only other of the four stylistic kinds or *charakteres* that figures prominently in letter writing, the "graceful" (4.235). Indeed, it is the kind of detailed finish or *akribeia* characteristic of the graceful style that renders it incompatible with the forceful style (4.274; cf. 1.8), while it is the regular use of wit that gives to this style its ethical quality. For there is "some indication of a man's character (*ēthous*)" in his humor (3.171). And both finish and humor lend to the graceful style its special power to please.[57] For Demetrius, in other words, detail and character are at the very heart of letter writing, which nevertheless resembles other forms of discourse, oral as well as written, in aiming to please and to persuade.

For Seneca, in contrast, the letter writer, like Cicero in his correspondence with Atticus, rejects persuasion altogether for the more intimate aim of expressing his own feelings (ep. 115.1), concentrating his efforts on having "you

---

57. On the correspondence between Demetrius's distinction between forceful and graceful styles and Panaetius's between *contio* and *sermo*, see Chiron, *Un rhéteur méconnu*, 340–43. On humor in Cicero's letters, see *Ad fam.* 2.4 and Hutchinson, *Cicero's Correspondence*, 172–99.

know what pleased him, rather than that he should please you" (ep.100.11).[58] For like the philosophical and even the oratorical Cicero, Seneca appreciates the related demands of experiencing psychological attachment and expressing character—of *conciliare* and *mores exprimere*. Even more explicitly than Cicero, however, Seneca links these demands to epistolary writing.[59]

Although most of Seneca's 124 letters to Lucilius serve "to correct and regulate character" ([*mores*] *corrigunt et ordinant*), epistle 121, largely unavailable to readers before the Renaissance, "investigates its nature and origin" (121.2; see ep. 11);[60] and it does so on the grounds that Lucilius's efforts at developing his own character will be aided by understanding how each human nature, his included, responds to the first, most pressing demand of universal nature: self-preservation (121.3). In the service of this understanding, Seneca explains in some detail the very principle of *conciliatio* that Cicero, as we have seen, attributed to Zeno and discussed in his philosophical works.

---

58. Seneca, *Ad Lucilium Epistulae Morales*, trans. Richard M. Gummere, 3 vols. (Cambridge, Mass., 1917; rpt. 1979). All English translations are from this volume. On Seneca's attentiveness to this Ciceronian letter collection in particular, see Aldo Setaioli, "On the Date of Publication of Cicero's Letters to Atticus," *Symbolae Osloenses* 51 (1976): 105–20; Marcus Wilson, "Seneca's *Epistles* Reclassified," in *Texts, Ideas, and the Classics: Scholarship, Theory, and Classical Literature*, ed. S. J. Harrison (Oxford, 2001), 164–87, esp. 186–87, and Daniel G. Gambet, "Cicero in the Works of Seneca Philosophus," *TAPA* 101 (1970): 175: "A comprehensive analysis of Seneca's citations from Cicero reveals that no portion of the orator's works is referred to more often than the correspondence with Atticus." And see epp. 21.4–5 and 97.3. For Seneca on the difference between his letters to Lucilius and Cicero's to Atticus, see ep. 118.1–2. See also Beard, "Ciceronian Correspondence," 116–17.

59. On Seneca's role in transforming the letter into an instrument of self-scrutiny, see Edwards, "Self-Scrutiny and Self-Transformation in Seneca's Letters," 23–38, esp. 25: "Although there was a strong philosophical tradition of concern with the well-being of the soul in the works of Plato, the Epicureans, and Stoics particularly, there is very little in the way of what might be termed self-scrutiny in any extant philosophical letters from before Seneca's time. Seneca by contrast makes extensive use of the potential of the letter form to explore the notion of the self." For Seneca's self-expression as characteristic of epistolary writing, see Brad Inwood, *Reading Seneca: Stoic Philosophy at Rome* (Oxford, 2005), 345–46, where he emphasizes "the importance of literary factors for generating this sense of self in Seneca's corpus." In *Fam.* 24.5, Petrarch dubs Seneca *preceptor morum incomparabilis*. See below, chap. 2.

60. On the reception of Seneca's letters, see L. D. Reynolds, *The Medieval Tradition of Seneca's Letters* (Oxford, 1965), esp. 112.

As we have also seen, this principle, called *oikeiōsis* in Greek, motivates the individual's intense interest in and attachment to the self (36.8, 82.15, 116.3).

Whereas the Ciceronian orator directs this self-interest and attachment to the rhetorical aim of a self-presentation that conciliates his audience, Seneca concentrates instead on the two kinds of discourse, *sermo* and *epistula*, that express this innermost self, the speaker's or writer's soul (epp. 40.1, 67.2, 114.3).[61] And whereas Cicero in *De officiis* focused attention on the *domus* as a man's principal belonging, Seneca redirects that focus to the soul or *animus* as by far one's most valuable possession. Neither a handsome family (*familia formosa*) nor a beautiful house (*domus pulchra*), Seneca insists, can substitute for the soul as the single piece of property that is really one's own (*quod proprium hominis est*) (ep. 41.7–8).

Throughout the letters to Lucilius, moreover, Seneca champions the conversational features of epistolary style as singularly well suited to do what, in effect, all style does for better or worse: reveal the soul (75.4–5, 114.2).[62] "You have been complaining that my letters to you are rather carelessly written," Seneca chides Lucilius:

> Now who talks carefully (*accurate*) unless he also desires to talk affectedly (*putide*)? I prefer that my letters (*epistulas*) should be just what my conversation (*sermo*) would be if you and I were sitting in one another's company or taking walks together,—spontaneous and easy: for my letters have nothing strained or artificial about them. If it were possible, I should prefer to show, rather than speak my feelings. Even if I were arguing a point, I should not stamp my foot, or toss my arms about, or raise my voice; but I should leave that sort of thing to the orator, and should be content to have conveyed my feelings to you without having either

---

61. On ep. 121, see Jacques Brunschwig, "The Cradle Argument in Epicureanism and Stoicism," in Schofield and Striker, *Norms of Nature*, 113–44, esp. 135–39; and see Gill, *Structured Self in Hellenistic and Roman Thought*, 43–46.

62. For Cicero on this same proverbial insight—*talis hominibus fuit oratio qualis vita*—see *Tusc. disp.* 5.47 and the introduction, above, p. 6; and compare ep. 114.2 and 6.6 and Quintilian 11.1.30. And see Frank Ivan Merchant, "Seneca the Philosopher and His Theory of Style," *American Journal of Philology* 26 (1905): 47: "[Seneca] adopts as an expression of his own view the Greek proverb, modernized by Buffon, that a man's speech corresponds to his life, that the style is the man." For the central role of this proverb in the history of the plain style, see Trimpi, *Ben Jonson's Poems*, 53–59. See also Ginzburg, "Style: Inclusion and Exclusion," in *Wooden Eyes*, 228, and Leo Spitzer, *Linguistics and Literary History: Essays in Stylistics* (Princeton, 1948), 11.

embellished them or lowered their dignity. I should like to convince you entirely of this one fact,—that I feel whatever I say, that I not only feel it, but am wedded to it. (75.1)

Whereas the orator uses the skills associated with delivery to stir the emotions of his audience, the letter writer focuses instead on getting his correspondent to understand his own deepest feelings.[63] Echoing the Ciceronian distinction, noted above, between a letter and a speech in court or *contio* (*Ad fam.* 9.21.1), which in turn echoes the Aristotelian distinction in the *Rhetoric* (3.12) between *graphic* and *agonistic* style, Seneca endorses the softer, more conversational genres at the expense of the more rousing *contiones*.[64] For these speeches in the courtroom and the schoolroom lack the very stylistic quality that wins Seneca's endorsement: *familiaritas* or intimacy. "Lectures (*disputationes*) prepared beforehand and spouted in the presence of a throng," Seneca instructs Lucilius, "have in them more noise but less intimacy (*familiaritatis*)" (ep. 38.1). For this quality, Lucilius must look to epistolary writing.

But *familiaritas* captures more than an essential quality of effective writing, according to Seneca; it is also the mark of sound reading—and not just letter reading but all reading. Seneca complements his advice to Lucilius on rhetorical matters, in other words, with a corresponding hermeneutics. In the second letter of the collection, Seneca introduces three models of reading with long and prosperous afterlives in the Renaissance.[65] Among them, as we will see, is reading *intimately*.

After an opening letter that uses legal language to foreground temporality as a chronic condition of loss, Seneca turns in the second letter of the collection to the best reading practices as a partial remediation, if not a remedy, for this condition.[66] One of these three practices, exemplified in the way Sen-

---

63. On the need to communicate one's feelings in speaking and in writing, see epp. 24.19, 75.4, and 115.1.

64. On the different demands of the eye and the ear in regard to detail—differences that recall Aristotle's treatment above—see ep. 100.2–3.

65. For Seneca on the two activities of reading and writing, see ep. 84.2: "We ought not to confine ourselves either to writing or to reading; the one, continuous writing, will cast a gloom over our strength, and exhaust it; the other will make our strength flabby and watery. It is better to have recourse to them alternately."

66. The very opening of the first letter—*vindica te tibi*—invokes the legal procedure of *vindicatio* and then goes on to characterize time as our only valuable possession (ep. 1.3), which, like material property, must be carefully husbanded (1.4–5). For

eca claims to read Epicurus, is compared to entering enemy territory, not in order to take up residence but to effect a quick and cautious reconnaissance. "[F]or I am wont to cross over even into the enemy's camp," Seneca admits, regarding books he only peruses but does not thoroughly absorb, "not as a deserter, but as a scout" (*soleo enim et in aliena castra transire, non tamquam transfuga, sed tamquam explorator*) (ep. 2.5–6).[67] Also held up for approval is a second practice: the reader who, like the eater with a healthy appetite, derives nourishment from a slow and thorough reading, digesting some one matter fully rather than satisfying his finicky tastes (*fastidiens stomachus*) with sampling (*degustare*) a variety of dishes (2.4–5). "Food does no good and is not assimilated into the body," Seneca warns, "if it leaves the stomach as soon as it is eaten" (2.3). Acting sometimes like a consumer and at other times like an enemy, the right kind of reader, at still other times, acts like a friend. Seneca applauds this third practice by discrediting its opposite.

Like the itinerant traveler who makes many acquaintances but forgoes real friendship, the superficial and indiscriminate reader inevitably fails to understand the mind or *ingenium* of any of the many authors he reads because he fails to read them intimately or *familiariter*:[68]

> Be careful, however, lest this reading of many authors and books of every sort may tend to make you discursive and unsteady. You must linger among a limited number of master thinkers (*certis ingeniis*). . . . Everywhere means nowhere. When a person spends all his time in foreign travel, he ends by having many acquaintances, but no friends. And the same thing must hold true of men who seek intimate acquaintance with no single author (*qui nullius se ingenio familiariter applicant*), but visit them all in a hasty and hurried manner. (ep. 2.2)

Later in his correspondence with Lucilius, Seneca returns to the digestion metaphor and to the likeness between reading and traveling. Once again, both reinforce the need for reading *intimately*.

---

the intense interest of the humanists beginning with Petrarch in this letter, see Letizia A. Panizza, "Textual Interpretation in Italy, 1350–1450: Seneca's Letter I to Lucilius," *Journal of the Warburg and Courtauld Institutes* 46 (1983): 40–62.

67. For a somewhat different treatment of the reader as enemy see my *Friends Hold All Things in Common*. For Petrarch's appropriation of this passage, see below, p. 62.

68. For the longstanding relation between reading and traveling, see my *Hermeneutics and the Rhetorical Tradition*.

In keeping with the second letter of the collection, epistle 84, the ancient document most often identified with humanist literary theory, compares readers to travelers; it does so, however, not with an eye to the kinds of friendship made but rather on the grounds that both activities overcome distance. Seneca even implies that reading is the lazy man's traveling—taking "exercise by deputy" (*aliena opera exerceor*) (84.1). In addition, both activities, reading and traveling, offer refreshment to the weary mind, feeding it after the depletion of long labor. The nourishment offered the reader, however, must be fully digested for the restorative power of reading to work. Such digestion, Seneca reports, has traditionally been associated with the productivity of bees. Their actual method of production, on the other hand, is the subject of some dispute. While there are those who maintain that honey is the product of the straightforward process of collecting pollen (*sucum*) from a number of flowers (84.4), there are others, including Seneca himself, who credit the bee with a power to transform the mixture through "a certain property of their breath" (*proprietate spiritus sui*) (84.5). This *proprietas* or property corresponds to the *ingenium* of the individual reader (84.5), who in his writing similarly changes his reading material into something new and different.

With this transformation in mind, Seneca challenges Lucilius to read thoroughly and in detail (epp. 33, 39). Extracts and summaries cannot do justice to the carefully crafted design of a literary text worth the effort. Reading *summatim* instead of *familiariter*, with the help of *commentaria, breviaria, summaria* (39.1), and even *flosculi* (33.7), can offer a taste of a writer's *ingenium* but no real understanding (33.5–7, 39.1), even though it is this understanding of his mind, including his thoughts and feelings, which should define the reader's goal. Anything worth reading, Seneca insists, is an *opus ingenii* (33.5). And a writer's *ingenium*, like everybody else's, is woven into the very fabric of his soul (114.3). "Examine the separate parts, if you like," Seneca concedes regarding such an *opus*, "provided you examine them as parts of the man himself" (33.5).[69]

Offered most programmatically in the second letter and confirmed here and there throughout the collection, the philosopher's advice to his correspondent about the best reading practices does not rely exclusively on the idea of intimacy or *familiaritas* but includes, as we have seen, both the digestive metaphor so closely identified with Senecan hermeneutics and the routinely recycled figure of the bee. Renaissance humanists regarded these

---

69. On ep. 33, see Wilson, "Seneca's *Epistles* Reclassified," 181–87.

figures as worthy of practically endless repetition.[70] And yet, as we will see in the pages that follow, both the rhetoric and the hermeneutics of some of the most influential humanists will settle on the notion of intimacy—a notion grounded in the legal concept of *belonging*—as key to both writing and reading.[71]

Throughout his letters to Lucilius, Seneca makes his stand against Ciceronian rhetoric by replacing the oration with not only *sermo*—replacing, that is, one oral form with another—but also its written counterpart, the letter. In the *Institutio oratoria,* a complete curriculum in twelve books for the aspiring orator, Seneca's near contemporary (and critic) Quintilian, virtually ignoring both *sermo* and letter, restores the centrality of the oration;[72] at the same time, he insists on the importance of reading and writing for speaking well. For writing, he claims, provides the very roots (*radices, fundamenta*) of oratory (10.3.1–3; cf. 10.1.3). Quintilian also insists, in contrast to Aristotle, that the orator must speak the way he writes, even though the reader can linger over and therefore appreciate details that would escape the listener (10.1.17–19, 12.10.51).

Like Seneca, however, Quintilian advocates thorough and repeated readings of a carefully crafted list of authors (*Institutio oratoria* 10.1.37; cf. 2.5.18). "For a long time," he advises,

> the only authors to be read should be the best and the least likely to betray our trust, and they should be read thoroughly, with almost as much care as we devote to writing. We must do more than examine everything bit by bit; once read, the book must invariably be taken up again from the beginning. (10.1.20)

Elsewhere Quintilian recommends reading that is deep rather than wide (*multa magis quam multorum lectione*) (10.1.59). Of course, Quintilian intends such recommendations for the advanced student approaching the end

---

70. On this Senecan figure and its afterlife in the Renaissance, see Martin L. McLaughlin, *Literary Imitation in the Italian Renaissance: The Theory and Practice of Literary Imitation in Italy from Dante to Bembo* (Oxford, 1995), 25–27, and G. W. Pigman III, "Versions of Imitation in the Renaissance," *Renaissance Quarterly* 33 (1980): 1–32.

71. For a different approach to Senecan hermeneutics, one that features the distinction between grammatical and philosophical reading, see Emily E. Batinski, "Seneca's Response to Stoic Hermeneutics," *Mnemosyne* 46 (1993): 69–77.

72. For Quintilian's criticism of Seneca, see 10.1.125–31; for his mention of the letter, see 1.1.29 and 9.4.19–21.

of his curriculum rather than for the beginner, whose reading and writing exercises he outlines in the first two books (e.g., 1.8.1–21).[73]

Among these writing exercises is one called variously *ethologia* (*Institutio oratoria* 1.9.3–4), *prosopopoiia* (1.8.3, 3.8.49, 6.1.25–27, 6.2.17, 9.2.29, 9.2.37, 11.1.41), and *ethopoiia* (9.2.58, 9.3.99). Adapted, like reading, to each stage of the curriculum and crucial throughout, this exercise in its various forms first develops the skill of the schoolboy and eventually refines that of the accomplished orator at accommodating (as the various names imply) style to character (*ēthos, prosōpon*), and especially to someone else's character.[74] Showcasing Cicero's mastery of this skill, Quintilian deems it

---

73. For Quintilian's use of *familiariter* in regard to how an orator should know a case or *causa* rather than a single author, see 5.7.7. For Quintilian on reading, see George A. Kennedy, *Quintilian*, 44–45, 49–50, 102–3.

74. What Quintilian calls *ethopoiia*, the author of the *Ad Herennium* calls *narratio in persona* : "A narrative based on the persons should present a lively style (*sermonis festivitatem*) and diverse traits of character (*animorum dissimilitudinem*), such as austerity and gentleness, hope and fear, distrust and desire, hypocrisy and compassion, and the vicissitudes of life, such as reversal of fortune, unexpected disaster, sudden joy, and a happy outcome. But it is in practice exercises that these types will be worked out" (trans. Harry Caplan [Cambridge, Mass., 1954; rpt. 1989], 1.8.13).

For a practice of *ēthopoiia* as old as the Athenian orator Lysias, see Dionysius of Halicarnassus's essay on the orator (*The Critical Essays*, trans. Stephen Usher, 2 vols. [Cambridge, Mass., 1974], 1: 33–39), who is said to have deployed a *lexis* that is *oikeia* in the interest of giving the speaker a voice or *phōnē* that is *oikeia* so that he can communicate with the audience *oikeiōs* (chaps. 8–9).

On the place of this exercise in the schoolrooms of late antiquity, including their connection with epistolary writing, see the collections of *progymnasmata* by Hermogenes, Aphthonius, and Theon in *Progymnasmata: Greek Textbooks of Prose Composition and Rhetoric*, trans. George A. Kennedy (Atlanta, 2003). See also Lanham, "Freshman Composition in the Early Middle Ages," and Dirk M. Schenkeveld, "The Intended Public of Demetrius's *On Style*: The Place of the Treatise in the Hellenistic Educational System," *Rhetorica* 18 (2000): 29–48, esp. 44–45. Not surprisingly, these textbooks continue to use such terms as *oikeion, idion*, and, in their Latin versions, *proprium*. See my "Literary Property and the Question of Style: A Prehistory," In *Borrowed Feathers: Plagiarism and the Limits of Imitation in Early Modern Europe*, ed. Hall Bjørnstad (Oslo, 2008), 21–38, esp. 34–35.

In *Hermogenes' On Types of Styles* (trans. Cecil W. Wooten [Chapel Hill, 1987]), moreover, Hermogenes reinforces the growing individuality of style by offering, all told, twenty stylistic types that combine in various ways to produce an author's "peculiar style" (5). On this proliferation of styles, Wooten comments: "The most

as difficult as it is necessary (3.8.49–50). Indeed, Cicero himself, Quintilian reports (9.2.29–32), gave special attention to this particular strategy, finding it indispensable for displaying the inner thoughts of his adversaries, introducing conversations into his narratives—like the one cited above with Curio (p. 32)—and routinely animating his speeches with words of "advice, reproach, complaint, praise or pity" put into the mouths of others (9.2.29–31). Throughout not only his education but his professional career, then, Quintilian's orator is expected to approach the question of style from the perspective of character—a perspective that, focusing on the demands of public speaking, nevertheless reinforces the agenda of the epistolary writer to express himself.

Accordingly, Quintilian, following Cicero, feels compelled to clarify the

---

obvious advantage that Hermogenes' system has over Cicero's or Dionysius' is that it is considerably more subtle and hence more capable of bringing out various nuances of style that their systems do not pick up. Where they see three kinds of style he sees seven, four of which are divided into subtypes, producing a total of twenty. Admittedly these types could be grouped into clusters that correspond to the plain, the middle, and the grand. But Hermogenes' system still conceptualizes and classifies several varieties of these three types of style that do not exist in Cicero and Dionysius" (133). On the "split personality" of Hermogenes' theory of style, which aims to accommodate the psychology of the individual while gauging "stylistic value preeminently out of one model," see Kustas, *Studies in Byzantine Rhetoric*, 17. Referring to the comments of a sixth-century critic, possibly Phoebammon, Kustas both characterizes the delicate negotiation in matters of style between the practice of imitation and the pressure to express one's individuality and reminds us of the continuity in terminology beginning with Aristotle: "It is quite possible, we are told, to emulate an ancient author and at the same time preserve one's own identity (οἰκεία φύσις) [Prol. Syll., 382.1ff.].... By cultivation through formal training of his natural bent, an author brings himself in line with the ancient standard without abjuring his own talent. The premium which a text such as this places on individuality and the explicit connection which it draws between character and style are inspired in part, we must not forget, by a reading of Hermogenes and can also be fruitfully regarded in the light of evolving Christian patterns of emphasis on the personal" (30). On the continued importance of Hermogenes, see Annabel M. Patterson, *Hermogenes and the Renaissance: Seven Ideas of Style* (Princeton, 1970). On the continued importance of *ēthopoiia* as a rhetorical exercise, see Lorna Hutson, "Ethopoeia, Source-Study and Legal History: A Post-Theoretical Approach to the Question of 'Character' In Shakespearean Drama," in *Post-Theory: New Directions in Criticism*, ed. Martin McQuillan, Graeme Macdonald, Robin Purves, and Stephen Thomson (Edinburgh, 1999), 139–60.

Greek concept of *ēthos*, which, lacking a Latin equivalent, also lacks transparency (*Institutio oratoria* 6.2.8). Drawing an initial distinction between *ēthos* and *pathos*, Quintilian explains that the former is translated into Latin by *mores*,

> and the "ethical" division of philosophy is therefore called "moral" (*philosophiae moralis*). But looking at the nature of the thing, I think *ēthos* means not so much *mores* as a certain special aspect of *mores* (*non tam mores significari videntur quam morum quaedam proprietas*), because *mores* itself covers all mental attitudes. More cautious writers have preferred to express the sense rather than translate the word. (6.2.8–9)

To resolve the controversy that borders on confusion concerning this concept considered key to the rhetorical art, Quintilian departs from the traditionally sanctioned plural *mores* in favor of the singular *morum quaedam proprietas*: not some generalizable set of attitudes or habits but rather the particular ethical *property* (or *propriety* as distinct from *decorum*) that belongs to the individual speaker. For what is *proprius* in the Roman rhetorical manuals, whether in matters of proof or matters of style, is routinely *oikeion* in the Greek.[75] And what is *oikeion*, as we have seen, is what belongs, first in a legal and then in a psychological sense, to someone but not to anyone else.

As part of his extended treatment of style, Quintilian confirms not only the pressure on the orator to individualize both his character and the style that expresses it but also the centrality of *proprietas*, with its legal pedigree, to the rhetorical art. For Quintilian credits *proprietas* with fostering clarity as the preeminent excellence of style even as he cautions that the term itself can be understood in more than one way. Its primary sense in a rhetorical context is calling a thing by the name that belongs to it (*primus enim intellectus est sua cuiusque rei appellatio*) (*Institutio oratoria* 8.2.1), while a secondary sense "occurs when there are a number of things all called by the same name: in this case the original term from which the others are derived is styled the *proper* term (*proprium*)" (8.2.7). But the rhetorical sense of *proprietas* is itself a derivation understood in a secondary sense because the *proper* context of the term is legal.[76]

---

75. See *Ad Her.* 4.12.17 and Caplan trans., 270 n. d, and cf. *De or.* 3.37.149. But for Quintilian's association of *ēthos* with the middle style, see 6.2.19. On the continued relation between *prepon* and *oikeion* in Byzantine rhetoric, see Kustas, *Studies in Byzantine Rhetoric*, 41 n. 1.

76. Earlier in the treatise (5.10.58), Quintilian makes a similar point about *proprietas* that clarifies its legal origins: "A property (*proprium*) is either (a) that which be-

Although advocating a style at odds with Quintilian's emphasis on the oration, as we have seen, Seneca points up the legal context of Quintilian's terminology when he bemoans the human impulse, noted without disapprobation by Aristotle, to favor what is one's own. It is "the foolish greed of mortals," Seneca laments, that "makes a distinction between possession (*possessionem*) and ownership (*proprietatem*), and believes that it has ownership in nothing in which the general public has a share" (ep. 73.7–8).[77] If Seneca the Platonizing philosopher laments the exclusivity of legal *proprietas*, however, Seneca the stylist fully endorses such "ownership" when applied in a secondary sense to the writer, figured in epistle 84, as we have seen, as the bee. For in literary production, as in making honey, Seneca insists, what matters most is what belongs exclusively to the producer. Like Seneca's writer, then, Quintilian's orator must observe a *propriety* that retains its fundamentally legal dimension of belonging.[78]

In his complete curriculum for the orator, Quintilian stresses both the importance of individual character and its impact on style. If he alludes at the beginning and at the end to the traditional three *genera dicendi* (*Institutio oratoria* 1.10.24, 11.1.6, 12.10.58–65), Quintilian nevertheless plays down this theory to play up the enormous variety and individuality of style (12.10.66–67), insisting, like Cicero's Crassus before him, that "if we turn

---

longs to one object alone (as speech or laughter to man) or (b) that which necessarily belongs to something, but not to this alone (as heat to fire). The same thing may have several properties (*plura propria*), as fire itself has those of light and heat."

77. In the plea for common ownership that follows, Seneca illustrates how misleading the language of *individuality* can be in that the goods that are *individua*—that cannot be divided—are those that belong to everyone in common and not to individuals or *singuli*: "But our philosopher considers nothing more truly his own than that which he shares in partnership with all mankind. . . . These goods, however, are indivisible [i.e., *individua*],—I mean peace and liberty—and they belong in their entirety to all men just as much as they belong to each individual (*At haec individua bona, pax et libertas, et tam omnium tota quam singulorum sunt*)" (ep. 73.7–8).

78. *Proprietas* also figures in the fundamentally legal distinction between *scriptum* and *voluntas* as an element in both (8 Proem 10, 12.2.9). On this division see my *Hermeneutics and the Rhetorical Tradition*, 7–19. In "The Mobility of Property and the Rise of Eighteenth-Century Sociology," P. G. A. Pocock notes the "fascinating and elusive relationship between the notions of right and ownership" and a "world of language in which 'property'—that which you owned—and 'propriety'—that which pertained or was proper to a person or situation—were interchangeable terms" (142).

our attention to the various styles of oratory, we shall find almost as great variety of talents (*ingeniorum*) as there are of personal appearance (*corporum*)" (12.10.10).[79] Wrapping up the treatment of style in the twelfth and final book of the treatise, this insistence repeats a key point introduced much earlier, in book 2 (2.8.1), where Quintilian further asserts that no two oratorical styles are alike (2.8.2). At this preliminary stage of education, Quintilian directs his advice to the teacher (rather than to the orator himself), who should take full account of the individual bent—the *ingenium* or *natura*—of each of his students. Even if, in deference to current pedagogical practice, he is not prepared to give carte blanche to youthful predisposition, the teacher must acknowledge the *propriety* of each student's talent—that *proprietas ingeniorum* (like the *proprietas morum* noted above) that is his own:

> It is certainly necessary to distinguish special types of talent (*proprietates ingeniorum*); no one can persuade me not to make these part of the basis for the choice of study.... On the other hand, a pupil who is destined for the courts must make great efforts not only in one department but in everything that belongs to his profession, even the things which seem particularly difficult to the learner. If nature (*natura*) were sufficient on her own, learning (*doctrina*) would be altogether unnecessary! (2.8.6–9)

When addressing the orator himself, on the other hand, Quintilian is careful to qualify this advice (10.2.19–20), leaving it up to the individual to cultivate his own particular talent.

In keeping with this advice (which recalls Cicero's to son Marcus), Quintilian, who is not especially given to recounting anecdotes, rehearses an exchange between two orators, the young Julius Secundus before he becomes a leading orator of his day and his uncle Julius Florus, already at the height of an equally renowned career. Finding his nephew suffering from what we would call "writer's block," the elder Julius relieves the younger's anxiety by encouraging him to bring his expectations in line with his abilities—or, in other words, to accept his limitations. Quintilian responds to this encouragement with a wholehearted approval that Petrarch, as we will see in the next chapter, reads in turn as an injunction to own one's individual style (*Institutio oratoria* 10.3.15). In the final book of his major letter collection, the so-called *Familiares* (*Fam.* 24.7), Petrarch even writes to Quintilian to thank him for this and all his other advice regarding the practice of eloquence. Petrarch also takes the opportunity of this single correspondence

---

79. For the limitations of the traditional *genera dicendi* according to Quintilian, see George A. Kennedy, *Quintilian*, 121.

to lament the mutilated state of his manuscript of Quintilian's great work, which, Petrarch speculates, may exist somewhere in its entirety, giving him hope that he might someday read it not in fragmentary form but from beginning to end. Although Petrarch was right in his speculation, as it turns out, his hope was never fulfilled.[80]

With the gradual recovery of the ancient texts treated in this chapter, from Aristotle's *Rhetoric* to Quintilian's *Institutio oratoria,* Renaissance readers and writers will rediscover the rhetorical and hermeneutical intimacy that these same ancient texts took centuries to hammer out. To further complicate this rediscovery, as Petrarch's letter to Quintilian drives home, Renaissance readers and writers will have access to these texts not according to the orderly chronology presented in this chapter but according to the random offerings of chance. They will encounter Aristotle's treatment of a stylistic excellence with deep roots in the legal and affective dimensions of belonging, for instance, only after—considerably after—Seneca's letters to Lucilius on reading and writing *familiariter.* In fact, they seem to pay very little attention to this aspect of Seneca's advice, despite its availability, until they discover that Cicero endorses the same *familiaritas*—a discovery offered very much by chance in 1345 in the cathedral library of Verona.

80. On Poggio Bracciolini's discovery of the complete text of the *Institutio oratoria* in 1416 at St. Gall, see Sabbadini, *Le scoperte dei codici latini e greci ne' secoli XIV e XV*, 1: 77–78.

CHAPTER 2 A Rhetoric and Hermeneutics of
Intimacy in Petrarch's *Familiares*

In 1345 in the cathedral library of Verona, Petrarch first encounters the intimate Cicero in the form of a lost collection of letters to his best friend Atticus.¹ By his own report, Petrarch is amazed. Although he had been on the lookout for these very letters for some time (*Fam.* 24.3), nothing in Cicero's extant works prepared Petrarch for what he found: the letter writer, it turned out, bore little resemblance to either the larger-than-life lawyer-politician, whose thundering accusations in the forum terrified opponents and enthralled audiences, or the dispassionate philosopher, whose measured advocacy of the life of virtue Romanized Greek Stoicism.² In stark contrast to both of these profiles, the

---

1. For the details of this discovery, see ibid., 2: 213; Giuseppe Billanovich, *Petrarca letterato* (Rome, 1943), 3–5; Rudolf Pfeiffer, *History of Classical Scholarship 1300–1850* (Oxford, 1976), 9–11; and Ernest H. Wilkins, *Studies in the Life and Works of Petrarch* (Cambridge, Mass., 1955), 170–81. On its importance for the rediscovery of intimacy, see Nancy Struever, "Rhetoric of Familiarity." On Petrarch's familiarity with medieval letter writing through his ownership of a thirteenth-century collection (MS Par. Lat. 2923), see Jean LeClercq, "L'amitié dans les lettres au moyen âge," *Revue du moyen âge latin* 1 (1945): 391–410, and Daniela Goldin Folena, "Pluristilismo del *Familiarium rerum liber*," in *Motivi e forme della "Familiari" di Francesco Petrarca*, ed. Claudia Berra (Milan, 2003), 263.

2. On Petrarch's hunt for books by Cicero, see *Seniles* 16.1. See also *Fam.*7.4. in *Letters on Familiar Matters*, trans. Aldo S. Bernardo, 3 vols. (Albany, 1975–1985; rpt. New York, 2005), 1: 343–44. All English translations of the *Familiares* will refer in the text to this edition by volume and page number. Quotations in Latin, also in the text by volume, page, and line number, refer to *Le Familiari*, ed. Vittorio Rossi, 4 vols. (Florence, 1933–42). For Seneca's letters (ep. 21.3) as Petrarch's first introduction to Cicero's letters, see *Fam.* 3.18.

On the Ciceronian nature of Petrarch's passion for books, see *Fam.* 18.7 (Bernardo 3: 55): "If I have a passion for books, this will not astonish anyone who has ever read Cicero's letters; for from his intellect issued as from a pure and overflowing fount nearly all the celebrated works in which ancient Latin culture glories, yet he nonetheless seems not only to yearn but burn for works by others." In "Reading, Writing,

| 49

great man as revealed in his own correspondence wavered in his judgments, capitulated to social pressure, complained bitterly about his misfortunes, and blamed others for his mistakes.

Widely recognized as an early milestone in the humanist project of recovering ancient texts, this famous encounter between Petrarch and the epistolary Cicero sets the primal scene for the Renaissance rediscovery of intimacy. For in response to his lucky find, Petrarch takes three decisive steps: first, he decides to write *like* the intimate Cicero; second, he decides to write directly *to* Cicero; and third, following Cicero, he decides to include this letter along with many others in a single letter collection, the *Familiares*.[3] Taken together, as we will see, these steps thoroughly transform the cultural landscape of early modern Europe insofar as they reinvigorate a genre—the familiar letter—that will come to dominate the histories of education, literature, and printing, thereby changing the way the humanists and their successors read and write. As a consequence of his discovery in Verona, in other words, Petrarch bequeaths to future writers and readers not only an intimate Cicero but, as I will argue, a rhetoric and hermeneutics of intimacy.

---

and the Self: Petrarch and His Forerunners," *New Literary History* 26 (1995): 717–30, Brian Stock asserts that Petrarch's "much discussed 'modernity' and 'individuality' are best understood in the context of his search for the manuscripts of ancient authors and his accompanying reflections on his own literary activities" (717).

On Petrarch's Stoicism see Seigel, *Rhetoric and Philosophy in Renaissance Humanism*, 31–62; Norman Nelson, "Individualism as a Criterion of the Renaissance," *Journal of English and Germanic Philology* 32 (1933): 316–34, esp. 324 and 333; Ugo Dotti, *Petrarca e la scoperta della coscienza moderna* (Milan, 1978), 129–38.

3. On the important consequences of this discovery, see Ernest H. Wilkins, *Life of Petrarch* (Chicago, 1961), 51, and Pierre Mesnard, "Le commerce épistolaire comme expression sociale de l'individualisme humaniste," *Individu et société à la Renaissance* (Brussels, 1969), in whose words, Petrarch's discovery "allait engendrer presque une révolution culturelle" (20). On the recovery of ancient manuscripts as a defining feature of the Renaissance, see, for instance, Ullman, "Some Aspects of the Origin of Italian Humanism," in *Studies in the Italian Renaissance*, 27–40. Ullman concludes his essay in the same volume entitled "Petrarch's Favorite Books" with the claim that "[Petrarch] was no mere book collector, nor was he an ordinary reader of the books he so eagerly gathered about him. Perhaps the secret of his humanism may be found in the fact that he read over and over again with intense zest these few favorite books" (137). On Petrarch's rediscovery of the "Ciceronian model for the relations between rhetoric and philosophy," see Seigel, *Rhetoric and Philosophy in Renaissance Humanism*, 31.

As his own letters record, Petrarch's devotion to Cicero predates his discovery by many years. Even in childhood, Petrarch recalls, he preferred the antique Roman to all other writers—a preference that blinded him temporarily to Cicero's all-too-human vulnerability to error (*Fam.* 22.10, 24.2; Bernardo 3: 187, 3: 315; cf. *Sen.* 16.1). Unlike some of his acquaintances, however, Petrarch outgrows this more extreme form of Ciceronianism, with its leanings toward idolatry (24.2), in part at least as a consequence of reading Cicero's letters. On the other hand, Petrarch never stops either considering himself a Ciceronian or insisting that there is no incompatibility between this affiliation and a sincere profession of Christianity. "I have no fear of being any less a Christian for being a Ciceronian," he asserts, "for to my recollection Cicero never said anything against Christ." "I confess that they are different," he continues, "but I deny that they are in conflict" (*Fam.* 21.10; Bernardo 3: 186).[4]

Maturing with him, Petrarch's early preference for Cicero is also recorded in 1333 or 1334, about a decade before his discovery, in Petrarch's own hand in a list of favorite books—*mei libri peculiares*—written on the flyleaf of one of his manuscripts of Augustine and Cassiodorus. At the very top of this list of favorites Petrarch puts Cicero's works of moral philosophy, including those featured in the previous chapter.[5] Below these are Cicero's rhetorical works, including *De oratore,* where Petrarch would have discovered Cicero's Stoicized version of Aristotelian *ēthos*.[6] As we have seen, this Ciceronian version replaced credibility with *belonging*. In second place on

---

4. See, in addition, *Fam.* 2.9, Bernardo 1: 100: "What obstacle does either Plato or Cicero place in the way of the study of truth if the school of the former not only does not contradict the true faith but teaches it and proclaims it, while the solid books of the latter deal with the road leading to it?" On Petrarch's Ciceronianism, see McLaughlin, *Literary Imitation in the Italian Renaissance,* 32–33, 40–44, and Maria Accame Lanzillotta, "Le pastille del Petrarca a Quintiliano (Cod. Parigino Lat. 7720)," *Quaderni Petrarcheschi* 5 (1988): 87. On his Christian humanism, see Witt, *'In the Footsteps of the Ancients,'* 248–60, 289–91.

5. See Ullman, "Petrarch's Favorite Books," 117–37. For Petrarch's ownership of the Troyes manuscript containing most of Cicero's philosophical works, see Sabbadini, *Le scoperte dei codici latini e greci ne' secoli XIV e XV,* 1: 115–21, and Nolhac, *Pétrarque et l'humanisme,* 1: 226–48. And on Petrarch's library, see also Nolhac, *Pétrarque et l'humanisme,* 1: 33–85, and *Petrarch and the Ancient World* (Boston, 1907), 43–94.

6. For Petrarch's familiarity with the *Orator* as well as *De oratore,* where he would encounter the *stilus familiaris,* see Blanc, "Pétrarque lecteur de Cicéron," esp. 126–30.

the list of favorites is Seneca, especially the collection of letters to Lucilius. When it comes time to announce his own letter collection, however, Petrarch proclaims Cicero rather than Seneca his model.[7] For Petrarch considers Cicero the standard for intimate writing—a standard, Petrarch recalls in the programmatic opening letter of his collection, that Seneca rejected in his own letter writing (*Fam.* 1.1; Bernardo 1: 10; cf. *Fam.* 12.10; Bernardo 2: 157).[8]

Whereas "Seneca chided Cicero" (*Fam.* 1.1; Bernardo 1: 10) for his inclusion of personal matters or *familiaria* in his epistolary writing (cf. *Fam.*12.10), Petrarch finds himself drawn to this very aspect of the Ciceronian letter. "I shall for the most part follow the example of Cicero," he announces,

> more than that of Seneca in these letters. As you know, Seneca collected in his letters all the morality that he had interspersed [*sic*] in almost all his books; Cicero restricted his philosophical concerns to his books and included in his letters accounts of the highly personal (*familiaria*), un-

---

7. If Petrarch is, by his own account, a letter writer after the Ciceronian rather than the Senecan fashion, he is a Ciceronian, also by his own account, after the Augustinian rather than the Hieronymian fashion (*Fam.* 2.9). On the history of Ciceronianism, see Remigio Sabbadini, *Storia del ciceronianismo e di altre questioni letterarie nell' età della Rinascenza* (Turin, 1885); Izora Scott, *Controversies over the Imitation of Cicero in the Renaissance* (1910; rpt. Davis, Cal., 1991), and McLaughlin, *Literary Imitation in the Italian Renaissance*. I will return below to Seneca as Petrarch's model for reading intimately.

8. On Seneca's rejection of Cicero's epistolary style, see ep. 118.1 and ep. 21. On Cicero as the source of all successful writing, see *Fam.* 24.4; Bernardo 3: 319; Rossi, IV, 228, 19–25: "O Great father of Roman eloquence (*O romani eloquii summe parens*), not I alone but all who bedeck themselves with the flowers of Latin speech are grateful to you; for it is with the waters from your wellsprings that we irrigate our fields, frankly admitting that we are sustained by your leadership, aided by your judgments, and enlightened by your radiance. In a word, under your auspices, so to speak, we have achieved whatever writing skills and principles we possess." For Petrarch's special attachment to Cicero and Seneca, whom he singles out as *nostri*, see *Fam.* 3.10; Bernardo 1: 140; Rossi, I, 124, 79. On the Senecan elements of Petrarch's formation, see Aurelia Bobbio, "Seneca e la formazione spirituale e culturale del Petrarca," *La Bibliofilia* 43 (1941): 224–91. On Seneca and Cicero as the two ancient sources behind Petrarch's view of friendship, see Claude Lafleur, *Pétrarque et l'amitié: Doctrine et pratique de l'amitié chez Pétrarque à partir de ses textes latins* (Paris, 2001), 33–50.

usual and varied goings-on of his time. (*Fam.* 1.1; Bernardo 1: 10; Rossi I, 10, 220–25)⁹

Petrarch also claims in the opening letter to have learned from Cicero that "the true characteristic of an epistle is to make the recipient more informed about those things that he does not know" (*Fam.* 1.1; Bernardo 1: 11). Chief among these things is the writer's "state of mind" (*animi status*) (*Fam.* 1.1; Bernardo 1: 11, Rossi I, 11, 233).¹⁰ So closely aligned is his letter writing with *familiaria*, Petrarch recalls, that he eventually decides to call the collection *Familiarium rerum liber*. Whereas an earlier choice for the title advertised the collection's epistolarity—*Epistolarum mearum ad diversos liber*—this one advertises its intimacy (*Fam.* 1.1; Bernardo 1: 11).¹¹ And if intimacy or *familiaritas* charac-

---

9. On the difference between books and letters see *Fam.* 1.5. At *Ad Att.* 1.19.1, Cicero remarks to Atticus with tongue in cheek that he never sends a letter without some *argumentum* or *sententia*.

10. See also *Fam.* 4.1; Bernardo 1: 180: "See . . . how I wish that nothing of me be hidden from your eyes, having carefully opened not only my entire life to you but even my simple thoughts." For Cicero's similarly revealing his thoughts and feelings in his letters, see, for instance, *Ad Att.* 4.3.

11. On the change of title, see Billanovich, *Petrarca letterato*, 46–47; Rossi, I, xi and Bernardo 1: xxiii. On Petrarch's "scoperta della *familiaritas*" as the "condizione della scrittura epistolare," see Daniela Goldin Folena, "*Familiarium Rerum Liber*: Petrarca e la problematica epistolare" in *Alle lettere: Teorie e pratiche epistolari dai greci al novecento*, ed. Adriana Chernello (Milan, 1998), 62.

For a somewhat different appreciation of *familiaritas* as the "titular principle" of the entire collection, one that "creates a sense of virtual community across time and space" (160), see Stephen Hinds, "Petrarch, Cicero, Virgil: Virtual Community in *Familiares* 24, 4," *Materiali e discussioni per l'analisi dei testi classici* 52 (2004): 157–75; also see his "Defamiliarizing Latin Literature, from Petrarch to Pulp Fiction," *TAPA* 135 (2005): 49–81, esp. 50–58.

While Poliziano, following Petrarch, opens his collection with a programmatic letter, his opening features writing *communiter* rather than *familiariter*. See Angelo Poliziano, *Letters. Volume I*, ed. and trans. Shane Butler (Cambridge, Mass., 2006), 6–7 (1.1). On Poliziano's familiarity with the *Familiares*, see his "Survey of Early Italian Poetry" in *The Three Crowns of Florence: Humanist Assessments of Dante, Petrarca and Boccaccio*, trans. David Thompson and Alan F. Nagel (New York, 1972), 105, where he refers to the programmatic opening letter; and see McLaughlin, *Literary Imitation in the Italian Renaissance*, 209–16, and Vladimír Juřen, "Les notes de

terizes the subject matter and determines the title, it also defines the style. So Petrarch alerts his reader to expect to find "many things in these letters written *familiariter*" (*Fam.* 1.1; Bernardo 1: 10; Rossi I, 11, 229)—written, that is, in the same intimate style that characterized Cicero's letters.[12]

Indeed, Petrarch follows Cicero (often if not always) in trying to invest his letter writing with the immediacy and intensity of direct communication. The opening words of the programmatic first letter—and so of the entire collection—set the tone. Petrarch's abrupt question to his "Socrates"— "What are we to do now, dear brother?"—draws the reader unceremoniously into an ongoing conversation between intimate friends.[13] So does a later lament, "Oh brother, brother, brother" (*Fam.* 8.7; Bernardo 1: 415), to this same correspondent—a strategy that Petrarch openly acknowledges as "a new kind of beginning for a letter, indeed an ancient one used by Marcus Tullius almost fourteen hundred years ago."[14] And so do Petrarch's admis-

---

Politien sur les lettres de Cicéron à Brutus, Quintus et Atticus," *Rinascimento*, n.s., 28 (1988): 235–56. On the innovation of the programmatic opening letter, see Paolo Cherchi, "Petrarca (*Familiares* I, 1) e Plinio il Giovane (*Epistolae* I, 1)," *Rassegna europea di litteratura italiana* 24 (2004): 101–5. On the difference between Petrarch's opening letter and those of Pliny or Peter of Blois, see Goldin Folena, "*Familiarium Rerum Liber*," 51–82, esp. 53: "Tali precedenti rimangono lontano dalla *Praefatio* delle *Familiari* proprio per le motivazioni sostanzialmente interiori e per i nuovi criteri sottesi alla *collatio in unum* petrarchesca." On the collection of Peter of Blois, see R. W. Southern, "Peter of Blois: A Twelfth Century Humanist?" in *Medieval Humanism and Other Studies* (Oxford, 1970), 105–32.

On the social dangers of *familiaritas* see *Fam.* 1.2 and Cicero, *Ad Quint. fr.* 1.1. On a disingenuous *familiaritas*, see *Ad Att.* 6.1.

12. On the attitude of the next two generations of Italian humanists to Petrarch's Ciceronianism, see Fumaroli, *L'âge de l'éloquence*, 77–83, and James Hankins, "Petrarch and the Canon of Neo-Latin Literature," online at http://nrs.harvard.edu/urn-3:HUL.InstRepos:3342975; for Erasmus's assessment, see below, chap. 3, p. 83.

13. On Petrarch's two friends, Ludwig van Kempen and Lello Stefano dei Tosetti, known in the letters by their ancient pseudonyms—Socrates and Laelius—see Wilkins, *Life of Petrarch*, 9, and Jan Papy, "Creating an 'Italian' Friendship: From Petrarch's Ideal Literary Critic 'Socrates' to the Historical Reader Ludovicus Sanctus of Beringen," in *Petrarch and His Readers in the Renaissance*, ed. Karl A. E. Enenkel and Jan Papy (Leiden, 2006), 13–30; on their falling out (*Fam.* 20.13), see Lafleur, *Pétrarque et l'amitié*, 53, 71–76.

14. On this Ciceronian strategy of the abrupt beginning, see chap. 1, p. 32. Petrarch similarly closes this letter (*Fam.* 8.7) with a quotation from the *Letters to At-*

sion that he has on more than one occasion in his letters followed Cicero's advice to "write whatever comes into [his] mind" (*Fam.* 1.5; Bernardo 1: 31), and his insistence elsewhere that "whatever I say to friends is in large measure spontaneous" (*Fam.* 18.8; Bernardo 3: 56).[15]

In contrast to a studied elegance, this spontaneity better suits the hesitation and uncertainty that Petrarch freely shares with his friends as if he were deliberating with himself. Reflecting the twists and turns of a mind in flux and anticipating the signature style of the anti-Ciceronian Montaigne (see chap. 4, p. 98), this early modern form of self-expression has its roots not only in epistolary writing, according to Petrarch, but in a style of letter writing identified with Cicero. "I shall offer my friends not only my deliberations," Petrarch explains:[16]

> but the thoughts and movements of my mind, which are called spontaneous (*primos*); nor will I write merely summaries and conclusions (*rerum summas atque exitus*), but the particulars of their beginnings and their progress (*particulas atque primordia et progressus*); to the friends whom I meet I shall relate early in the morning whatever occurred to me during the night. If upon sitting at table I change my mind, upon arising I shall tell my friends, and I shall take pleasure in seeing my opinions struggle until the better wins.... As I was saying this and similar things in defense of my daily routine, I happened by chance to come upon Cicero's letters, a magnificent book replete with great variety and with this kind of friendly discourse (*familiaribus colloquiis*). In it I read a similar defense and was delighted that, whether because of similar reasoning—which I would like to believe but dare not hope for—or simply because of similar subject matter, I had expressed what that great man had long ago stated without my knowing until that moment.... To make this still clearer, I shall cite Cicero's very words; while writing to Atticus, he changes his mind many

---

ticus. For the abrupt, conversational beginning, see *Ad Atticum* 7.11 and 9.2a. In *Fam.* 18.8, Bernardo 3: 59, Petrarch admits to finding "myself more effective when speaking with rousing words than when speaking with restraint."

15. On the intimacy and spontaneity of Petrarch's letters, see Nancy S. Struever, *Theory as Practice: Ethical Inquiry in the Renaissance* (Chicago, 1992), 6–9, and Goldin Folena, "*Familiarium Rerum Liber*," 66.

16. For Petrarch on the flux see *Fam.* 19.16; Bernardo 3: 106: "You express the desire to hear about my state; yet if the word *state* derives from *standing still*, man does not have here on earth a single state but perpetual motion and slipping, and ultimate collapse." See also *Fam.* 24.1.

times and then adds, as if speaking to himself, "Don't you change your opinion as often?" And he replies as I said: "I speak with you as with myself. And who would not be in disagreement with himself in such an important matter?" (*Fam.* 18.8; Bernardo 3: 58–59; Rossi III, 290–91, 105–28)

In a scene of reading reminiscent of his transformative encounter with Augustine's *Confessions* on Mount Ventoux (and of Augustine's own conversion-inducing encounter with Paul's Letter to the Romans in the *Confessions*) (*Fam.* 4.1; cf. 18.2), Petrarch narrates discovering a likemindedness with his favorite ancient. This mind, like his own, both reflects intensely upon its thoughts and feelings and undertakes in writing to communicate these to a friend in the role of another self.[17] With his discovery of Cicero's *Letters to Atticus*, in other words, Petrarch discovers Cicero's rhetoric of intimacy.

One hallmark of this rhetoric, as we have seen, is spontaneity. Another, also featured in the long passage just quoted, is particularity—the particular details (noted in the previous chapter as part of *graphic* style) that make a difference. Throughout his letters, in fact, Petrarch returns to these two related features of an intimate style: particularity and difference. In defense of the details that crowd his own epistolary descriptions, Petrarch reminds his friend and benefactor Giovanni Colonna of his request when they parted that Petrarch not "[spare] my pen nor . . . strive for brevity or ornamentation, nor [select] only the most interesting things, but rather [cover] them all" (*Fam.* 1.5; Bernardo 1: 31); and at the forefront of his programmatic opening letter, Petrarch introduces the Ciceronian theme of difference, including the difference between men, whose minds, despite their likemindedness, are no "more alike than the shapes of their foreheads" (*Fam.* 1.1.; Bernardo

---

17. On intimate communication as the product of this likemindedness, see Petrarch to his Socrates: "My Socrates has always been worthy of authority and of trust in whatever he discusses, but especially in speaking of the secret thoughts of his friend; and what is more, one listens to many things more favorably coming from the mouth of a friend than from one's own mouth" (*Fam.* 7.6; Bernardo 1: 348). See also *Fam.* 8.5; Bernardo 1: 409: "I ask you, what life is happier or gayer than the one spent with friends whose perfect love and mutual affection make all feel as one, bound as if with an indissoluble knot and a single mind in all things; with whom there is no disagreement, no secrets, but instead harmonious accord, serene brows, and a truthful and unstudied conversation, as well as a perfectly open mind?" For Petrarch's "preoccupation with the problems of authentic self-expression," see Carol Everhart Quillen, *Rereading the Renaissance: Petrarch, Augustine and the Language of Humanism* (Ann Arbor, 1998), 145.

1: 9). This diversity among men, moreover, engenders a diversity of styles, any one of which may find favor with one reader but not with another, and even with the same reader on some occasions but not on others.[18]

In the same letter, Petrarch also acknowledges variations in his own style. While some of these variations have unintentionally crept in over time (*Fam.* 1.1; Bernardo 1: 11–12), others are intentional stylistic shifts that accommodate differences in audience and subject matter. As we saw in the previous chapter, Cicero is the chief spokesman not only for this accommodation to difference but for the so-called *genera dicendi* that help to effect this accommodation. In a letter to Francesco Nelli, the friend called "Simonides" to whom he will dedicate the *Seniles,* Petrarch rehearses these Ciceronian *genera*:

> We know that according to Cicero there are really three kinds of styles (*stilos*) that he calls figures (*figuras*): the sublime (*grandiloquum*), which he calls serious (*gravem*), the moderate (*moderatum*), which he calls ordinary (*mediocrem*), and the humble (*humilem*), which he calls tenuous (*extenuatum*).... In my opinion, if I appropriately turn to a humble style in writing a letter, it is a good thing. (*Fam.* 13.5; Bernardo 2: 190; Rossi III, 69, 119–29)

But even the humblest style, Petrarch insists, is different from no style at all. Whereas his own letter writing falls readily into the plain style, "stylelessness" better describes the way his unskilled contemporaries, including his would-be employers at the Roman Curia, not only write their own letters but expect him to write his. "Certainly what they order me to use," he complains, "what they themselves call style, is not style (*stilus*)" (*Fam.* 13.5; Bernardo 2: 190; Rossi III, 69, 133–34).[19] In the programmatic opening let-

---

18. *Fam.* 1.1; Bernardo 1: 9: "And as one particular sort of food not only does not appeal to different stomachs but does not even appeal always to a single one, so it is impossible to nourish a single mind at all times with the same style." On the metaphor of digestion, see below, p. 108. In "Pluristilismo del *Familiarium rerum liber*," Goldin Folena cites Boncompagno da Signa's comparison between the diversity among faces and that among narrations (270).

19. On this discussion of style, see Riccardo Fubini, "La coscienza del latino negli umanisti," *Studi medievali* 2 (1961): 520. For Petrarch's preoccupation with style, see Giuseppe Mazzotta, *The Worlds of Petrarch* (Durham, N.C., 1993), 93–98. And see Goldin Folena, "Pluristilismo del *Familiarium rerum liber*," 261–90, who, despite her title, concludes as follows: "Ma se consideriamo le singole lettere nella loro unità compiuta, non ci sfuggerà la suggestione esercitata sul loro autore dal nuovo modello epistolare ciceroniano, rilevabile sopratutto nella corrispondenza del Petrarca con gli amici più intimi; e certo nelle ripetute revisioni del proprio *corpus* epistolare

ter, moreover, Petrarch adjusts the Ciceronian categories to suit his own epistolary style, which he describes on this occasion as not only *mediocre,* invoking Cicero's middle style, but *domestice* and *familiare,* foregrounding its intimacy (*Fam.* 1.1; Bernardo 1: 6–7; Rossi I, 6, 114–15).[20]

For Petrarch as for Cicero, then, intimacy is a matter of style. Aligned with epistolary theory and practice, and especially with the theory and practice of the Ciceronian letter, intimate style captures the spontaneity and

---

egli tende a far prevalere complessivamente il tono della colloquialità derivante dalla *familiaritas* che egli considera peculiare del Cicerone epistolografo." On Petrarch's labors over his epistolary style, despite his claim that it is spontaneous, see, for instance, *Fam.* 7.13; Bernardo 1: 368: "I could show you three or four beginnings of letters different in styles and in almost any other way called for by the variety of events which my serious state of mind gave birth to. How I felt about these efforts may be seen by the oblique lines that my pen drew across them like so many wounds inflicted by their author and chastiser." For Petrarch's attempt to "weave artfully from nothing a friendly letter (*familiaris epystola*)" based on a Ciceronian maxim, see *Fam.* 9.11; Bernardo 2: 30; Rossi, II, 242, 9–11.

On the centrality of style to Petrarch's rhetorical agenda, which differed considerably from those of his contemporaries, see Leonardo Bruni, "Life of Petrarca," in *The Three Crowns of Florence: Humanist Assessments of Dante, Petrarca and Boccaccio,* ed. and trans. David Thompson and Alan F. Nagel (New York, 1972), 77, where Petrarch's contemporaries were thought to lack "judgment for any fine style" while he is credited with "a talent sufficient to recognize and call back to light the antique elegance of the lost and extinguished style." And see Witt, "Medieval '*Ars Dictaminis*' and the Beginnings of Humanism," 33: "No one reading Petrarch's correspondence or his other writings could of course consider his letters uninformed by the teachings of classical rhetoric. The creation of the 'domestic' style, a *stilus humilis,* surely demanded a deep knowledge of the art and a superb gift for sensing appropriateness of style. His writings reflect an expanded understanding of the functions and complex character of rhetoric. Nevertheless, in at least three respects he is anti-rhetorical. He rejected the practice of contemporary rhetoric of treating all letters oratorically. Moreover, a subjective element pervading his thought tended to undercut the rhetorician's aim of moving the audience toward a specific end. Finally, his breadth of interests and the depth to which he pursued them testify to his rejection of the narrow technical approach to rhetoric prevailing among the *dictatores.*" While Witt foregrounds the "domestic" and "humble" aspect of Petrarch's *stilus,* this chapter focuses instead on the *familiaris* in an effort to account for what Witt calls the "subjective element pervading [Petrarch's] thought." See also his '*In the Footsteps of the Ancients,*' 230–91.

20. On the relation between *domus* and *familia,* see chap. 1, p. 33.

particularity of our most personal communications. Intending to express the innermost thoughts and feelings of the letter writer, it not only reflects but in turn strengthens the bond of intimacy or *familiaritas*—the deep sense of belonging—between him and his letter reader. In the previous chapter, I traced this intimate style back to the *lexis oikeia* of Aristotle's *Rhetoric* and noted its origin in the legal concept of property ownership. Whatever is *oikeion* belongs to someone and not to anyone else. I noted further that one standard Latin translation for *oikeion* is *proprium*, a term, as we will see shortly, that figures prominently in Petrarch's thinking about style. As we will also see in both this and subsequent chapters, *proprietas* as a stylistic matter continues to reflect its deep connection to *proprietas* as a legal matter.

But the concept of intimacy or *oikeiotēs* in Greek also corresponds to *familiaritas* in Latin, with its roots in the *familia*, the Roman counterpart of the *oikos*; and this correspondence, as we have seen in chapter 1, includes the legal as well as the affective dimensions of the household, the center of belonging. A distinguishing feature of intimate style, as Petrarch inherits it, is that it belongs to the speaker or writer only, serving thereby as an effective instrument of self-expression. In the opening letter and elsewhere, as we have already seen, Petrarch describes his peculiar style as *familiare*. In keeping with Cicero's advice to his son in *De officiis*, which Petrarch read as an extended letter, this same style is characterized in the language of property law as *sua* and *propria*.[21] Applying the ethical theory of Cicero's treatise to

---

21. The continued pairing of *sua* and *propria* in regard not only to legal property but to the Latin translation of Greek *oikeion* is clear from the earliest printed Latin commentaries and vernacular translations of Aristotle's *Rhetoric*. See, for instance, Pietro Vettori's commentary on *Rhetoric* 1.5.7 (Florence, 1548), 83, and Bernardo Segni's translation of the same passage (Florence, 1549), 24–25. On the epistolary elements of *De officiis*, see Roy K. Gibson and A.D. Morrison, "What Is a Letter?" 9–13. When in his programmatic opening letter to the *Familiares* (1.1; Bernardo 1: 7; Rossi, I, 7, 139), Petrarch notes that Cicero wrote letters not only to Brutus, Atticus, and his brother Quintus but also to his son Marcus, he must have had *De officiis* in mind (unless he is referring to Lactantius's reference to such a letter in *The Divine Institutes* [3.14, 17], cited in Seigel, *Rhetoric and Philosophy in Renaissance Humanism*, 29–30). On Petrarch's use of *De officiis*, see Witt, "Medieval '*Ars Dictaminis*' and the Beginnings of Humanism," 30: "Significantly, Petrarch's new approach to the letter derived inspiration from Cicero's actual correspondence, and only after appreciating the style did he understand Cicero's remark in the *De officiis*, I, I.3, cited in the dedicatory letter." For the singular popularity of this classical text with Renaissance humanists, including Petrarch, see Dyck, *Commentary on Cicero, "De officiis,"*

the discursive agenda of his epistolary project, Petrarch uses legal language (as did Cicero) to approve a unique style—one that belongs entirely to the individual writer.

Petrarch's approval of this kind of style receives its fullest treatment in three letters, two of them to Boccaccio (22.2, 23.19) and a third to Tommaso da Messina (1.8).[22] In the first of the two letters to Boccaccio (22.2), Petrarch formulates in legal terms not only the goal of an individual style but the obstacles it encounters. For it is precisely the style of those authors a writer knows best that—as it were "through long usage and continual possession" (*longo usu et possessione continua*)—he is most likely to "adopt . . . and for some time regard as [his] own" (*praescripserim diuque pro meis habuerim*) (*Fam.* 22.2; Bernardo 3: 213; Rossi IV, 106, 80–83).[23] Lesser-known authors present no such hazard because their writing retains the status of "common property" (*comunia*). "I quickly recognize that they are not mine," Petrarch explains, "and recall whose they are; these really belong to others, and I have them in my possession with the awareness that they are not my own" (Bernardo 3: 212; Rossi IV, 106, 68–72). And if the failure to forge an individual style is understood in the legal terms of ownership, possession, and use, so

---

44–45. In his letter to Bembo (*Ciceronian Controversies*, ed. Joanna Dellaneva, trans. Brian Dwick [Cambridge, Mass., 2007], 102–5 [5.12]), Pico quotes at some length the pertinent passages in *De officiis* (1.31.110–13), indicating their relevance to humanist discussions of style.

22. On these three letters, see McLaughlin, *Literary Imitation in the Italian Renaissance*, 25–34.

23. On *usus* and *possessio* as legal terms, see *Justinian's Institutes*, trans. and ed. Peter Birks and Grant McLeod (Ithaca, 1987), s.vv., and Alan Watson, *The Law of Property in the Later Roman Republic* (Oxford, 1968), 81–90 and 203–21, and for *praescriptio*, see *Gai Institutiones or Institutes of Roman Law by Gaius*, trans. Edward Poste and Rev. E. A. Whittuck (London, 1904), s.v. For Petrarch's use of legal language elsewhere to further his epistolary agenda, see *Fam.* 9.8; Bernardo 2: 26; Rossi, II, 237, 1–7: "From our youth to the present time, fortune has begrudged me your face. You were nonetheless always present in my thoughts and—to use the words of our once common studies—I had private rights (*civiliter te possedi*) to you, something which neither distance of place nor passage of time was able to take away from me, nor will death, I believe. I address you then with that youthful intimacy (*familiaritate*) of ours and, with my former privilege restored, as they say, I pick up my pen once again."

On Seneca on Epicurus on common property, see *Fam.* 1.8, Bernardo 1: 41, and Seneca, ep. 12.11; and see Wilson, "Seneca's *Epistles* Reclassified," 176–86, and my "Literary Property and the Question of Style," 21–38.

is the prospect for success, since every writer, Petrarch insists, recalling Cicero's words to his son Marcus, possesses a style that is his own—something *suum* and *proprium* that deserves cultivation:

> Surely each of us naturally possesses something individual and personal (*suum ac proprium*) in his voice and speech as well as in his looks and gestures that is easier, more useful, and more rewarding to cultivate and correct than to change. (*Fam.* 22.2; Bernardo 3: 213; Rossi IV, 107, 110)

In the second letter to Boccaccio (23.19), Petrarch returns to this formulation in praising the style of his young protégé Giovanni Malpaghini—a style that is on its way to achieving individuality. "I am confident that he will strengthen his thought and expression," Petrarch says of Malpaghini, "forging a personal style (*unum suum ac proprium*) from his extensive reading, not necessarily avoiding imitation but concealing it so that his work will not resemble anyone else's" (Bernardo 3: 301; Rossi IV, 205, 10). Malpaghini's style, in other words, will eventually belong to him alone.

Whereas his goal of stylistic individuality echoes the language—and especially the legal language—of Cicero's *De officiis,* Petrarch's confidence in certain reading and writing practices to effect this goal relies on two of Seneca's letters to Lucilius examined in chapter 1. In the letter to Tommaso (1.8), Petrarch foregrounds the Senecan pedigree of this advice regarding the best writing practices. "If after a trial you discover that it is ineffectual," he counsels Tommaso, "you must blame Seneca. But if you find it effective you must render thanks to him and not to me" (Bernardo 1: 41).[24] The advice itself features the Senecan figure of the bee as the model for imitation because it creates something new from a combination of elements gathered from elsewhere. Petrarch faults Macrobius for merely repeating this advice (without attribution, no less) and thereby failing to practice it. Petrarch himself, in contrast, models the practice for his own readers by introducing the novel figure of the silkworm. For the bee makes honey by borrowing from others, while the silkworm not only creates something of even greater beauty and value but does so out of material that is entirely its own (Bernardo 1: 42). In

---

24. In his letter to Seneca (*Fam.* 24.5; Bernardo 3: 322), Petrarch admits that "I daily listen to your words with more attention than one could believe." And only Seneca, along with Cicero, is referred to with the intimate designation *noster* (3.10.12; Bernardo 1: 140; Rossi, I, 124, 12). On the formative influence of Seneca on Petrarch, see Nolhac, *Pétrarque et l'humanisme*, 2: 115–26, and Carla Maria Monti, "Seneca 'Preceptor morum incomparabilis'? La posizione di Petrarca (*Fam.* XXIV, 5)," in Berra, *Motivi e forme delle 'Familiari' di Francesco Petrarca,* 189–228.

addition to highlighting what is individual in imitative practice, then, Petrarch distinguishes between two processes that demand different degrees of talent or *ingenium*; and this attention to difference provokes Petrarch to quote the advice that the accomplished orator Julius Florus, as we have seen in chapter 1, gives to his nephew Julius Secundus in Quintilian (Bernardo 1: 43–44)—advice regarding the need always to take one's own individual talent or *ingenium* into account (see above, p. 47).[25] Those who may not be up to imitating the silkworm, in other words, can at least imitate the bee, whose practice Petrarch also invokes in the two letters to Boccaccio, once with attribution to Seneca (*Fam.* 23.19; Bernardo 3: 302) and once without (*Fam.* 22.2; Bernardo 3: 213).[26] In the first of these two letters (22.2), moreover, Petrarch figures the practice of reading as well as that of writing in Senecan terms.

In the second letter to Lucilius, as we have seen in chapter 1, Seneca figures the reader as consumer, as enemy, and as friend. Long before discovering Cicero's letters to Atticus in 1345, Petrarch associated his own reading practices with this Senecan letter, even quoting directly from it on the same flyleaf that lists his favorite books, mentioned above (p. 51). Pertaining to the way Seneca claims to read Epicurus ("for I am wont to cross over even into the enemy's camp,—not as a deserter but as a scout" [ep. 2.5–6]), this quotation distinguishes between those books read with caution and for reconnaissance purposes only and those read and reread continuously.[27]

---

25. For the influence of Quintilian, see Nolhac, *Pétrarque et l'humanisme*, 2: 83–94; Lanzillotta, "Le postille del Petrarca a Quintiliano," 100–101. And see McLaughlin, *Literary Theory in the Italian Renaissance*, 23–25.

26. On the apian metaphor, McLaughlin concludes, "What is significant here is not so much Petrarch's literal knowledge of apiculture, as the priority accorded on a figural level to the contribution of the individual," noting that Petrarch adds individuality to Seneca's emphasis on unity (*Literary Imitation in the Italian Renaissance*, 26).

27. In *On His Own Ignorance and That of Many Others* (in *Invectives*, ed. and trans. David Marsh [Cambridge, Mass., 2003]), a late work of the 1360s, Petrarch uses a different figure of the reader as enemy to justify his own reading of classical, especially Platonic and Ciceronian, works. This figure, as Petrarch himself makes clear, has Augustinian rather than Senecan roots: "When Augustine was about to leave Egypt, he filled his pockets and bosom with the gold and silver of the Egyptians. This man, who would become a great fighter for the Church and a great champion of the faith, arrayed himself with the arms of the enemy before he went into battle" (333). As Ullman notes in *Studies in the Italian Renaissance* (36), Augustine is the only Christian writer on Petrarch's list of favorites. Ullman also notes (119) that both Ben Jonson and a medieval prior (c. 1150) made good use of Seneca's distinction between

In the letter to Boccaccio (*Fam.* 22.2), Petrarch echoes this distinction when he contrasts the works of Ennius, Plautus, and Apuleius, which he claims to have read only once—"hastily and quickly, brooking no delay except as one would in unknown [i.e., enemy] territory (*alienis in finibus*)"— with those of Virgil, Horace, and Cicero, here and elsewhere, as we will see, figured as friends (Bernardo 3: 212; Rossi IV, 105, 11).[28] These authors Petrarch recalls not just reading but, again following Seneca, fully digesting. Only Petrarch complicates his source by highlighting the temporal dimension. "I ate in the morning," Petrarch remembers, "what I would digest in the evening, I swallowed as a boy what I would ruminate upon as an older man" (*Fam.* 22.2; Bernardo 3: 212). Read at leisure and pondered with the full force of his mental powers over the course of a lifetime, these works were lodged *intimately* (*familiariter*) in the deepest recesses of his mind (Rossi IV, 106, 13).

If Cicero's letters to Atticus teach Petrarch the art of *writing* intimately (*familiariter*), in other words, Seneca's to Lucilius issue the directive for *reading* intimately (*familiariter*). Following Seneca in figuring the reader as not only consumer and enemy but friend, Petrarch tightens the bond between writer and reader by forging the link between a rhetoric of intimacy and its corresponding hermeneutics. Using his letter collection to feature an intimate, epistolary style, as we have seen, Petrarch also pushes the limits of the letter itself, transforming it from an instrument designed to bridge spatial distance into one equally preoccupied with temporal distance. And this preoccupation with distance, and especially temporal distance, signals the beginnings of an early modern understanding of the past that students of the period have identified as one of Petrarch's signature contributions.[29]

---

the scout and the deserter. Concerning the latter's reference to Seneca to distinguish between classical, especially Ciceronian, and Christian literature, Ullman concludes: "Nothing brings out in more striking fashion an essential difference between the Middle Ages and the Renaissance than the different way in which the medieval prior and the first modern man adapt the quotation from Seneca" (119). On the *spoliatio Aegyptiorum*, see my *Friends Hold All Things in Common*, 8–32.

28. On Petrarch's list of authors, see McLaughlin, *Literary Imitation in the Italian Renaissance*, 28–29.

29. For Petrarch's preoccupation with time, see, for instance, *Fam.* 24.1, and Witt, *'In the Footsteps of the Ancients,'* 276–89; Teodolinda Barolini, "The Making of a Lyric Sequence: Time and Narrative in Petrarch's *Rerum vulgarium fragmenta*," *Modern Language Notes* 104 (1989): 1–38; Arnaut Tripet, *Pétrarque ou la connaissance de soi* (Geneva, 1967), 75–87; and Timothy Kircher, *The Poet's Wisdom: The Humanists,*

Without fully acknowledging its hermeneutical implications, ancient rhetoric did not completely ignore the impact of distance on an audience's understanding. As we saw in the previous chapter, Aristotle both defended writing and distinguished written from oral style on the basis of distance. Whereas Aristotle assumed that all writing was designed to compensate for the spatial divide between reader and writer, however, Cicero held this compensation for distance in reserve for the writing of letters. Promoting an epistolary tradition that features Cicero, Petrarch claims for the letter the power to mitigate if not entirely erase temporal as well as spatial distance. For reader and writer, the letter nurtures the affective bond of intimacy that separation threatens.

In keeping with this claim, Petrarch, throughout his letters, both justifies his own zeal in letter writing and encourages a comparable zealousness in his friends on the grounds that epistolary exchange substitutes for face-to-face conversation and so provides the surest remedy against the erosion of intimacy occasioned by prolonged absence. To one of his dearest friends in the Colonna family he first acknowledges that "distance between places separates us from the conversations (*conversatio*) of friends" and then enjoins this same friend

> to remember not how far you may be from someone . . . but rather how far it is in your power through reflection to be present with absent ones. Here, therefore, is one way in which you can continually see us together: show yourself repeatedly by the frequent interchange of letters. (*Fam.* 2.6; Bernardo 1: 89–91)[30]

Wrapping up a theme that resonates throughout, Petrarch concludes the *Familiares* with an admission to his Socrates that living is unimaginable without letter writing and that because of his letters even death will not stifle his efforts to communicate intimately with those he holds dear. "What other

---

the Church, and the Formation of Philosophy in the Early Renaissance (Leiden, 2006), 145–228. For the power of eloquence to bridge time as well as space, see *Fam.* 1.9, Bernardo 1: 49, and of reading to collapse time ("to read in an hour what happened in a day"), see *Fam.* 4.1, Bernardo 1: 175.

30. On the relation between *conversatio* and *familiaritas* in the context of reading, see *Fam.* 4.2; Bernardo 1: 182; Rossi, I, 162, 41–44: "While others may disagree with me on how best to achieve such peace, it is my considered opinion that nothing contributes more than familiarity with noble talents, and conversation with outstanding men (*nobilium ingeniorum familiaritas et clarorum virorum conversatio*)." Compare *Fam.* 7.5; Bernardo 1: 345.

end can I expect for my conversations with friends but the end of life?" he asks. "Or how could I possibly remain silent with them while still alive if I plan to speak to them with my cold lips from the grave?" (*Fam.* 24.13; Bernardo 3: 351).[31]

Throughout his collection, moreover, Petrarch includes his favorite ancient authors among those whose absence causes him most distress (cf. *Seniles* 9.2). So he admits to carrying Augustine around with him as a constant traveling companion (*Fam.* 4.1; Bernardo 1: 177–78; cf. *Seniles* 15.7), to keeping his David by him when he sleeps (*Fam.* 22.10; Bernardo 3: 233), and to welcoming Cicero not only into his country house in Vaucluse but into one of its most intimate recesses, his library (*Fam.*12.8; Bernardo 2: 153–54). There, as an honored guest (Petrarch writes to a friend and fellow bibliophile), Cicero passes his time in relaxed conversation with friends, including Atticus, Brutus, Varro, Scipio, and Laelius. "With these and other such companions," Petrarch recalls, "my rural sojourn was certainly peaceful, pleasant, and happy" (*Fam.* 12.8; Bernardo 2: 154).[32]

---

31. See *Fam.* 1.1; Bernardo 1: 13: "for me writing and living are the same thing and I hope will be so to the very end."

32. If Petrarch had access to Cicero's letter to Varro (*Ad fam.* 9.1.2), he would have found there the ancient version of this favorite trope: "For you must know that since I came to the City, I have become reconciled with my old friends (*amicis*), in other words, with my books. And yet it was not because I was a little angry with them that I had put them away, but because they made me a little ashamed of myself. For it seemed to me that when, thanks to my utterly untrustworthy associates (*sociis*), I plunged into the seething cauldron of affairs, I had not quite obeyed their instructions. They forgive me, and invite me back to the old intimacy (*consuetudinem*), and say that you are wiser than I, because you remained true to it." On the significance of this trope in distinguishing the humanist Petrarch from his book-loving predecessors, such as Richard de Bury, Carol Quillen, in *Rereading the Renaissance*, writes: "In the *Philobiblon*, Richard characterizes books not as friends, guests, or family, metaphors used by Petrarch, but as teachers or, more tellingly, as vessels of wisdom, priceless packages of knowledge manufactured during a smarter age, now to be guarded, used, and transmitted to posterity. *Libros novos scribere* means for him not just to compose new books but to recopy the old ones" (67). See, in addition, Quillen, 106–47. See also Loredana Chines, "Loqui cum libris," in Berra, *Motivi e forme delle 'Familiari' di Francesco Petrarca*, 367–84, esp. 380, where Chines claims that "[l]a lezione petrarchesca che raffigura i morti come vivi, gli antichi come persone presenti avrà straordinaria vitalità nell'umanesimo successivo, anzi ne può divenire imagine paradigmatica." Among those mentioned as under the influence is Montaigne. On the

Mindful of the ancient proverb that everything is common among friends, including their other friends, Petrarch also recalls how on an earlier occasion Cicero introduced him to those who would in time become *his* friends.[33] "Cicero's *Academicus* made Marcus Varro dear and attractive to me," Petrarch recounts,

> and the name of Ennius I heard in his books on *Offices*; from a reading of the *Tusculan Disputations* I first felt my love for Terence; from the book *On Old Age* I became acquainted with the *Origins* of Cato and the *Economics* of Xenophon and I learned that the same book was translated by Cicero in his same *Offices*. (*Fam.* 3.18; Bernardo 1: 157)

No wonder, then, that on discovering the manuscript of Cicero's letters to Atticus, Petrarch feels compelled to share with his ancient correspondent not only the excitement of finding such personal communications but also the shock and disappointment at finding revealed in them a Cicero given to bouts of pettiness, ingratitude, and inconstancy.[34]

In the first of two letters to Cicero (*Fam.* 24.3), in other words, Petrarch chastises his ancient friend for his weaknesses. The second letter then prevails on their friendship to excuse such frankness (24.4). By way of excuse, moreover, Petrarch insists on the very rights and privileges of friendship that Cicero himself outlined in his dialogue on the topic, *De amicitia* (also called *Laelius*).[35] Indeed, not only does Petrarch use the occasion of the second letter to express his mind freely so that Cicero may come to know his thoughts and feelings by reading; he also claims in turn to know Cicero's

---

formative role of Augustine in shaping Petrarch's collection, see Roberta Antognini, *Il progetto autobiografico delle "Familiares" di Petrarca* (Milan, 2008).

33. On this proverb see *Fam.* 9.9, Bernardo 2: 27, to his Socrates: "I am not a friend unless I share with you my most precious possessions; nothing is more precious than a friend; therefore I am not a friend unless I share a friend. This is an old saying: 'Everything is held in common among friends.'" On this proverb, see my *Friends Hold All Things in Common*.

34. Exercising an epistolary freedom to reveal contradictory responses, Petrarch admits to feeling at once offended and enticed by Cicero's unfiltered expressions of his own feelings (*Fam.* 1.1; Bernardo 1: 12). And it is this complex reaction that motivates Petrarch to write. On Lactantius as the source for Petrarch's rebukes of both Cicero and Seneca, see Monti, "Seneca 'Preceptor morum incomparabilis'?" 195. And for another possible Lactantian influence, see above, n. 21.

35. On Petrarch's preference for frankness, even blunt censure, over praise in letters, see *Fam.* 7.16.

mind from what he himself has read—that is, as he writes directly to Cicero, "to know your mind from your works, which I do seem to know as though I had lived with you" (*Fam.* 24.4; Bernardo 3: 320).[36]

For Petrarch, then, the same standard of *familiaritas* that applies to writing letters applies to reading them. Like letter *writing,* letter *reading* is rooted in the intimacy associated with friendship. "Every friend's language," Petrarch reckons in a letter about his own epistolary style, "I truly understand as though it were my own" (*Fam.* 18.8; Bernardo 3: 56).[37] Looking back on his exchange with Cicero in the programmatic opening letter of the collection, Petrarch records that "I wrote to him as if he were a friend living in my time with an intimacy (*familiaritas*) that I consider proper because of my deep and intimate acquaintance with his thought" (*Fam.* 1.1; Bernardo 1: 12; cf. *Fam.* 18.4; Bernardo 3: 49)—an intimacy, not incidentally, fostered exclusively through reading.

Elsewhere Petrarch reaffirms the same *familiaritas* as the goal of not just letter reading but of all reading that culminates in understanding. In the same letter that credits Cicero with sharing his circle of friends, Petrarch extends the traditional association between conversation and the letter to books more generally, and especially to those of the ancients; for their books "speak with us, advise and join us together with a certain living and penetrating *familiaritas*" (*Fam.* 3.18; Bernardo 1: 157; Rossi I, 139, 22; cf. *Fam.* 4.2; Bernardo 1: 182; cf. also *De vita solitaria* 2.14). In his letters to Boccaccio and others, as we have seen, Petrarch includes Virgil and Horace among those he understands intimately through his reading (e.g., *Fam.* 22.10, 22.2; Bernardo 3: 233, 3: 212).[38] In his letter to Homer (24.12), in contrast, Petrarch likens his

---

36. On "living together" as the standard of intimacy, see *Fam.* 9.2; Bernardo 2: 4; Rossi, II, 215, 62–63: "We are really separated by too great a distance of place and time (*nimiis equidem seu locorum seu temporum intervallis*), thereby losing the one choice fruit of good fortune and the one remedy for adversity—living together (*simul vivere*)."

37. On the disappointment at not being understood by a friend, here Boccaccio, see *Fam.* 21.15; Bernardo 3: 202: "Hence nothing in your apologetic letter disturbed me except that I am still so little understood by you, whom I thought knew me so well." On Cicero's confidence that he will be understood by Atticus even when he "veils his meaning" or uses *allegoriai*, see *Ad Atticum* 2.19 and 2.20. On the need for rereading, see *Fam.* 1.9, Bernardo 1: 50; and on reading whole texts and even whole letter collections rather than bits and pieces, see *Fam.* 24.2, Bernardo 3: 316.

38. On the humanist program—inaugurated by Petrarch—to know the ancients through their writings as if they were alive and engaged in friendly communication,

understanding of this greatest of Greek poets, known to him only through Latin epitomes, to the faint recognition of a distant friend spied across a great divide (Bernardo 3: 342).[39]

But it is not only the ancients who need to be read and so understood in this way. Even some modern writers deserve the kind of attentiveness that the letter reader gives to a personal correspondence from a sorely missed friend. Some modern writers even demand such attention. "I wish my reader, whoever he may be," Petrarch admits to Francesco Nelli, his "Simonides,"

> to consider me alone, and not his daughter's marriage or a night with a lady friend, not the wiles of his enemy, not his security or his home, not his land or his money. Even as he reads me, I want him to be with me; if he is pressed by affairs, let him defer his reading. When he decides to read what I write, he must lay aside the burden of his affairs and the anxieties of his home life in order to direct his attention to what is before his eyes. If these conditions do not please him let him stay away from my useless writings. I refuse to have him simultaneously carry on his business and study; I refuse to allow him to learn without labor what I wrote with labor. (*Fam.* 13.5; Bernardo 2: 191)

Whether engaged with the *Familiares* or with another of Petrarch's literary efforts, the reader is held to the epistolary standard of overcoming absence, of being with the writer through the act of reading.[40]

To read *intimately,* then, is to engage in a practice that promises the kind

---

see Eugenio Garin, *Italian Humanism: Philosophy and Civic Life in the Renaissance,* trans. Peter Munz (New York, 1965), 14, who notes that Ermolao Barbaro, for example, "at the opening of the course on Aristotle which he held in Padua at sunrise, felt it necessary to say that it was his purpose to make Aristotle come back to life and to make him take part in a human conversation: *ut cum ipso vivo et praesente loqui videamur.* Aristotle was to be a man living and present, loved in all his limitations."

39. On Petrarch's knowledge of Homer, see also *Fam.* 10.4, Bernardo 2: 73–74; and on the Homeric precedent of twenty-four books, see Bernardo 2: xviii. See also Manlio Pastore Stocchi, "Riflessioni sull'epistola a Omero," in Berra, *Motivi e forme delle 'Familiari' di Francesco Petrarca,* 119–47.

40. Even at the summit of Mount Ventoux, Petrarch figures the intensity of the reading experience in epistolary terms, regarding the words of Augustine's text as though they were a personal correspondence written for his eyes alone (*Fam.* 4.1; Bernardo 1: 178). On Petrarch's reading Plautus with personal application to himself, see *Fam.* 5.14, Bernardo 1: 267. And see Hackel, *Reading Material in Early Modern England,* 17.

of understanding that defines the closest friendships; and that understanding constitutes the hermeneutical counterpart to the rhetorical practice of expressing oneself in writing—of expressing, that is, one's innermost thoughts and feelings.[41] If Petrarch recovers in Cicero's letters to Atticus an ancient writing practice accurately characterized as a *rhetoric of intimacy,* he transforms that rhetoric, at Seneca's direction, into a way of reading, a *hermeneutics of intimacy;* and he effects this transformation at least in part by turning the so-called familiar letter into an instrument responsive to temporal as well as spatial distance. For Petrarch's openly acknowledged goal as a reader is to understand his favorite ancient authors, whom he figures in epistolary terms as absent friends occupying not only a different space but also—and more urgently—a different time.

Determined to write *like* the epistolary Cicero and to write *to* him, Petrarch also decides, following Cicero, to fashion his letters into a collection—one, in his case, arranged for the most part "not according to subjects but chronologically," so that the reader might "follow my progress and the course of my life" (*Fam.* 24.13; Bernardo 3: 351).[42] Petrarch is soon followed, in turn, by the next wave of Italian humanists, among them Coluccio Salutati, Leonardo Bruni, Poggio Bracciolini, Francesco Filelfo, Aeneas Silvius

---

41. For Petrarch's "development of the theme of the self within the literary activities of the reader and the writer," see Stock, "Reading, Writing, and the Self," 717–30, esp. 724. For a different account of Petrarch's hermeneutics, a hermeneutics of subreading, described as "a central activity of Petrarch's mind, an activity that can be distinguished from medieval hermeneutics and that [Petrarch] bequeathed to his humanist heirs," see Thomas M. Greene, *The Light in Troy: Imitation and Discovery in Renaissance Poetry* (New Haven, 1982), 93–103. For the centrality of style to this hermeneutic, see 95–100.

42. On the formation of the collection, see Hans Baron, *From Petrarch to Leonardo Bruni: Studies in Humanistic and Political Literature* (Chicago, 1968), 9: "Only a little less than a quarter of the *Familiares* letters have also been preserved in their original texts as actual missives. The vital part of the revision took place between 1351 and 1353, but Petrarch continued to make alterations and to add new letters until 1366." See also Antognini, *Il progetto autobiografico delle "Familiares" di Petrarca,* whose aim is to discover "il principio architettonico profondo delle *Familiares*" (119). And see Karl A. E. Enenkel, "Die Grundlegung humanistischer Selbstpräsentation im Brief-Corpus: Francesco Petrarcas *Familiarium rerum libri XXIV,*" in *Self-Presentation and Social Identification: The Rhetoric and Pragmatics of Letter Writing in Early Modern Times,* ed. Toon Van Houdt, Jan Papy, Gilbert Tournoy, and Constant Matheeussen (Leuven, 2002), 367–84.

Piccolomini, Marsilio Ficino, Pico della Mirandola, and Angelo Poliziano, all of whom leave behind letter collections, many of which are compiled, like Petrarch's, by the authors themselves.[43]

There was, in other words, no shortage of letter writers in the Italian Renaissance. And if the history of incunabula is any indication, there were even more readers. By 1500 Piccolomini's two letter collections, first printed in 1473 and 1475, had been either reprinted or reedited nineteen times, roughly half of these in Italy.[44] Eighty years later, Montaigne will admit to owning one hundred different letter collections from Italian presses alone.[45] One of these may very well have been Piccolomini's. And another may have been the *Familiares,* first published in 1492 in Venice by the Aldine Press.[46] Still others may have been whole collections of fictitious letters; for this type was also popular. Among the most widely read was Gasparo Barzizza's *Liber epistolarum.*[47] One of the first texts printed in Paris (1470), it enjoyed

---

43. On the letter collections of the humanists following Petrarch, see Cecil H. Clough, "The Cult of Antiquity: Letters and Letter Collections," in *Cultural Aspects of the Italian Renaissance: Essays in Honor of Paul Oskar Kristeller,* ed. Clough (New York, 1976), 33–67, esp. 38–43. On Petrarch's actual influence, Clough offers a somewhat conflicting account: "Moreover the first printed edition of Petrarch's letters did not appear until 1492, which further underlines the insignificant part his actual letter collections played in stimulating those of the humanists. This, of course, is not to deny that his idea of editing his own letters was widely known and seen by the humanists as confirming the rightness of their editing their own letters" (38). In *Letters and Letter-Collections* (Turnhout, 1976), Giles Constable denies altogether the impact of Petrarch's discovery of Cicero's letter collection, calling it "an event of personal rather than general significance" (39). On the importance of the letter for Renaissance humanism, see Paul Oskar Kristeller, *Renaissance Thought and Its Sources,* ed. Michael Mooney (New York, 1979), 94 and 249.

44. See Clough, "Cult of Antiquity," 43.

45. See *Essays* 1.40, "A Consideration upon Cicero," which takes up the topic of epistolary style. For the essay as the culmination of humanist epistolary practice, see Marc Fumaroli, "Genèse de l'épistolographie classique: Rhétorique humaniste de la lettre, de Pétrarque à Juste Lipse," *Revue d'histoire littéraire de la France* 78 (1978): 886–905, and chap. 4, below.

46. The first eight books of the *Familiares* with selected letters to the ancients from book 24 were also printed in Venice in 1501 and 1503, where Erasmus would have had easy access to them during his stay with Aldus. See Rossi, xcii–xciv.

47. See Clough, "Cult of Antiquity," 40–41; Judith Rice Henderson, "On Reading the Rhetoric of the Renaissance Letter," in *Renaissance-Rhetorik/Renaissance*

eleven reprintings before the century's end. And this taste for fictional letters accounts as well for the twenty printings between 1473 and 1500 of Piccolomini's epistolary novel, *A Tale of Two Lovers* (*De duobus amantibus historia*). First written in 1444, this early example of a genre that will come into its own over the next three hundred years was soon available in German, Italian, French, and Spanish translation.[48]

Readers and writers of letters, in other words, found a friend in the printing industry; and this included readers and writers of ancient letters. First brought to the world's attention by Coluccio Salutati, Cicero's other great letter collection, *Letters to Friends* (*Epistolae ad familiares*), very probably received its title from an early sixteenth-century editor in response to Petrarch's *Familiares*. Ranked among the first and most widely circulated incunabular editions, it racked up an astonishing fifty-two printings between 1467 and 1500, thus putting into circulation, according to one estimate, about five thousand copies a year.[49] Only slightly less popular were the letters attributed to Phalaris, the sixth-century Greek tyrant, whose Latin translations saw thirty-two printings and two Italian translations by 1475 and whose original text was published in 1499 in the Aldine *Epistolae Diversorum Philosophorum Graecorum*. As part of this letter collection, Phalaris

---

Rhetoric, ed. Heinrich F. Plett (Berlin, 1993), 143–62; Scott, *Controversies over the Imitation of Cicero in the Renaissance*, 112–13. On the fictitious letters in Petrarch's collection, see Bernardo 1: xxv–xxxi.

48. See Clough, "Cult of Antiquity," 45.

49. See ibid., 43, and *Collected Works of Erasmus*. (Toronto, 1974–), 25: 8 (hereafter *CWE*); on the granting of the first privilege in Venice to Johann von Speyer in 1469 for Cicero's *Ad familiares*, see Evelyn May Albright, "Notes on the Status of Literary Property, 1500–1545," *Modern Philology* 17 (1919): 65–95, esp. 79–80. On Salutati's association with this collection (1389) and its title, see Nolhac, *Pétrarque et l'humanisme*, 1: 254–56, and Hinds, "Defamiliarizing Latin Literature," citing P. L. Schnidt, "Die Rezeption des römischen Freundschaftsbriefes (Cicero-Plinius) im frühen Humanismus (Petrarca-Coluccio Salutati)," in *Der Brief im Zeitalter der Renaissance*, ed. F. J. Worstbrock (Weinsheim, 1983), 25–59, esp. 53. Concerning the title *Epistolae ad familiares*, Hinds asserts that "the likeliest hypothesis is that it actually derives *from* Petrarch's *Familiarium rerum libri*; in other words, in a splendid instance of reverse-chronological influence, some Renaissance scholar gives to this second trove of Ciceronian letters a title back-formed from the title of Petrarch's own Cicero-influenced correspondence. A careless observer might assume that Petrarch's *Familiares* got their title from Cicero's; but the probability is that Cicero's got their title from Petrarch's" (53).

kept company with such actual or supposed ancient letter writers as Demosthenes, Plato, Aristotle, Hippocrates, Democritus, Heraclitus, Euripides, Philostratus, Basil of Caesarea, Libanius, Apollonius of Tyana, and Julian the Apostate.[50] Also in demand were the letter collections of Seneca and Pliny, each printed about ten times between 1471 and 1501.[51]

A best-seller by 1470, as noted above, Cicero's *Letters to Friends* had already—half a century earlier—become a standard school text, providing models of good Latin for young boys to follow. Both the choice of text—an ancient letter collection—and the use to which it was put—teaching rhetorical imitation—helped to define humanist education, which in turn defined the movement as a whole in opposition to scholasticism, and especially to the scholastic curriculum.[52] When Erasmus encounters the Italian literary scene sometime in the 1490s, then, the cultural landscape is marked by a widespread fascination with both the Ciceronian genre that Petrarch recovered in the cathedral library at Verona and the reading and writing practices that he made an intrinsic part of that recovery. In spite of not only differences in their literary sensibilities but also Erasmus's near silence about his Italian predecessor, it is Petrarch's rhetoric and hermeneutics of intimacy, as we will see in the next chapter, that the Dutch humanist imports to northern Europe.[53]

---

50. See Clough, "Cult of Antiquity," 44.

51. Ibid., 43–44.

52. On the use of Cicero's letters in the schools see William Harrison Woodward, *Vittorino da Feltre and Other Humanist Educators* (Cambridge, Eng., 1897; rpt. New York, 1963), 212, 232; Clough, "Cult of Antiquity," 36; Paul F. Grendler, *Schooling in Renaissance Italy: Literacy and Learning, 1300–1600* (Baltimore, 1989), 121–24; and below, chap. 3, n. 1. On the humanists' opposition to the scholastic curriculum, see, for instance, Kristeller, *Renaissance Thought and Its Sources*, 85–105; Benjamin G. Kohl, "Humanism and Education," in Rabil, *Renaissance Humanism*, 3: 5–22; and Garin, *Italian Humanism*, 2–17.

53. Whereas Petrarch favors Augustine over Jerome, Erasmus is outspoken about his preference for the desert father over the bishop. On comparisons between Augustine and Jerome, see, for instance, Petrarch, *Fam.* 2.9 and 4.16, and Erasmus, epp. 844 and 2088; and see Carol Quillen, *Rereading the Renaissance*, 100–101, 127–29, and Eugene F. Rice Jr., *Saint Jerome in the Renaissance* (Baltimore, 1985), 137–40. And whereas Petrarch preferred reading Cicero even from childhood (*Sen.* 16.1), Erasmus favored Seneca over Cicero until he was twenty (ep. 1390). See Albert Rabil Jr., "Cicero and Erasmus' Moral Philosophy," *Erasmus of Rotterdam Society Yearbook* (*ERSY*) 8 (1988): 70–90.

CHAPTER 3 *Familiaritas* in Erasmian Rhetoric and Hermeneutics

Early in his career, Erasmus assumes his office in the republic of letters as an educational reformer, grounding his agenda for reform, following his Italian predecessors, in the complementary activities of not only reading and writing but reading and writing familiar letters, especially Cicero's.[1] As part of this reform, as we will see,

1. On the place of Cicero's letters in the curriculum, see Robert Black, "Cicero in the Curriculum of Italian Renaissance Grammar Schools," *Ciceroniana*, n.s., 9 (1966): 105–20, and *Humanism and Education in Medieval and Renaissance Italy: Tradition and Innovation in Latin Schools from the Twelfth to the Fifteenth Century* (Cambridge, 2001), 352–60; Joseph S. Freedman, "Cicero in Sixteenth- and Seventeenth-Century Rhetoric Instruction," *Rhetorica* 4 (1986): 227–53. On Erasmus's following his Italian predecessors, especially Poliziano, in his own epistolary style, see Charles Fantazzi, "The Evolution of Erasmus' Epistolary Style," *Renaissance and Reformation*, n.s., 13 (1989): 263–88.

For Erasmian humanism as an extension of the Petrarchan variety, see Sem Dresden, "Erasme et les belles-lettres," *Colloque Erasmien de Liège* (Paris, 1987), 3–16; Charles Béné, "Erasme et Cicéron" *Colloquia erasmiana turonensia*, ed. Jean-Claude Margolin (Toronto, 1972), 2: 571–79; Fumaroli, "Genèse de l'épistolographie classique"; Mark Vessey, "Erasmus' Lucubrations and the Renaissance Life of Texts," *ERSY* 24 (2004): 23–51, esp. 30–35; and Kircher, *Poet's Wisdom*, 37. Although Witt does not address northern humanism in his *'In the Footsteps of the Ancients,'* his contrast between the profound Christianity of Petrarchan humanism, "based on the assumption of the compatibility of Christianity with pagan culture" (291), and the secular variety of Petrarch's Italian successors reinforces the Petrarchan dimension of Erasmian humanism.

In the introduction to *De copia* (LB I 4A; *CWE* 24: 297), Erasmus echoes Petrarch's letter to Cicero (*Fam.* 24.4) without attribution, upholding the Roman orator as the "great father of all eloquence" (*omnis eloquentiae parens*). In view of this echo and Erasmus's laudatory reference to Petrarch in a list of Ciceronian letter writers (*Ciceronianus, Opera omnia Desiderii Erasmi Roterodami* [Amsterdam, 1969–], I-2, 661 [hereafter ASD]; *CWE* 28: 414), Etienne Wolff's conclusion in "Pétrarque et le genre épistolaire: Réflexions sur *Familiares* I, 1," *Epistulae Antiquae II: Actes du IIe Colloque International: Le genre épistolaire antique et ses prolongements européens*, ed. Léon Nadjo and Elisabeth Gavoille (Louvain, 2002), 385, that "Erasme ... ne

Erasmus imports into northern Europe the very rhetoric of intimacy that Cicero labeled writing *familiariter* and Petrarch sought to revive in his *Familiares*. As we will also see, this importation is least in evidence where we might expect to find it, in Erasmus's epistolary theory. Instead, it leaves its mark elsewhere: on his composition manuals that are not obviously epistolary, on his satiric intervention in the Ciceronian debate of his day, and, perhaps most surprisingly, on his program for spiritual reform. Taking up the call of religious reformer somewhat later in his career, Erasmus enjoins both the right kind of Christian writer and the right kind of Christian reader to take the schoolboy's training in reading and writing letters as a point of departure. Of course, rhetorical intimacy as an Erasmian import from south of the Alps also leaves its mark on Erasmus's own letter writing.

By the end of his career, Erasmus the educational and religious reformer had become Erasmus the consummate correspondent, spending half of every day reading and writing letters and using the occasion both to secure the prestige of the genre and to associate it with *familiaritas*.[2] Admitting to a special aptitude for epistolary writing (ep. 909; *CWE* 6: 217–18), which he claims to consider a singularly useful skill (ep. 117; *CWE* 1: 233–34), Erasmus follows the theorists examined in previous chapters by characterizing this kind of writing in terms of its opposition to the *contiones* of the orator. "In spite of the very great utility, and to some extent, the attractiveness, of the kind of prose (*orationis genus*) that deals with struggle and conflict," Erasmus explains in a very early letter to Cornelis Gerard (1489?), "I take much more pleasure in what is called the familiar kind (*familiare*); for while the latter is gentle and peaceable, the former is somewhat too agitated, and whereas the latter is cheerful and friendly (*amicum*), the former frequently verges on ill-will" (ep. 27; *CWE* 1: 49; Allen 1: 116). Opting for the letter's

---

connaissait pas les lettres de Pétrarque, et considère celui-ci surtout comme un poète italien" is hard to sustain. See also ep. 337 and Theodor Mommsen, "Rudolf Agricola's Life of Petrarch," *Traditio* 8 (1952): 367–86, which demonstrates that Erasmus's most esteemed northern predecessor prized Petrarch for his achievements as a Latin prose stylist.

2. See ep. 1985 (1528) to Henry Botteus, *Opus epistolarum Desiderii Erasmi Roterodami*, ed. P. S. Allen et al., 12 vols. (Oxford, 1906–1958), 8: 376, and J. W. Binns, "The Letters of Erasmus," in *Erasmus*, ed. T. A. Dorey (Albuquerque, 1970), 56. Unless otherwise indicated, references to Erasmus's correspondence in Latin are to the Allen edition. His other works in Latin are to ASD. All works in English, unless otherwise indicated, are to *CWE*.

conciliatory over the oration's agonistic quality, Erasmus tightens even further the identification of epistolary writing with *familiaritas* when he insists, at a later point in his correspondence (1521), that "letters which are deficient in true feeling and do not reflect a man's actual life do not deserve to be called letters"; on the contrary, he points out, the letter should display "the writer's character and fortunes and sentiments, and the state of affairs both public and private" (ep. 1206; *CWE* 8: 219–20; Allen 4: 500–501). Also following his Italian predecessors in collecting his letters, this accomplished and prolific correspondent, as I hope to show, ties first his educational and then his religious reform to the fate of the letter and the *familiaritas* on which it relies.[3]

Taking its cue everywhere else from Quintilian, who, as we have seen, has next to nothing to say about epistolary writing (e.g., *Institutio oratoria* 1.1.28–29, 9.4.19–20), *De ratione studii*, Erasmus's manual for the schoolmaster, deviates from its ancient source by adjusting its exercises to the demands of epistolary composition. To hone the students' skill in translation, for instance, the teacher should "set out the subject-matter of a short but expressive (*argutum*) letter in the vernacular which has to be construed in Latin or Greek or both" (*CWE* 24: 678; ASD I-2, 130), while the vocabulary and style (*verba ac figura*) of a letter of Pliny or Cicero are suitable for practice in imitation (*CWE* 24: 679; ASD I-2, 132). To complement the students' efforts in letter writing, this compact, little handbook also advises Renaissance schoolmasters to focus their lectures on epistolary form, "set[ting] out the argument of the persuasive, dissuasive, exhortatory, dehortatory, narrative, congratulatory, expostulatory, commendatory, and consolatory letter ... point[ing] out the nature of each type, some features and set-phrases they have in common, and, once the argument has been set out, their peculiarities as well" (*CWE* 24: 680; ASD I-2, 133).

Routinely printed with *De ratione studii*, *De copia* also features the letter, both by demonstrating the richness of varied expression with 146 variations on a phrase presumably designed for epistolary writing—"Your letter pleased me mightily" (*CWE* 24: 348–54)—and by recommending letter-writing exercises in the service of refining that fundamental rhetorical skill of "characterization" or *prosopopoeia* (*CWE* 24: 585–86), long allied, as mentioned

---

3. On Erasmus's correspondence see Léon-E. Halkin, *Erasmus ex Erasmo: Erasme éditeur de sa correspondence* (Aubel, Belgium, 1983); Binns, "Letters of Erasmus," 55–79, and Jacques Chomarat, *Grammaire et rhétorique chez Érasme*, 2 vols. (Paris, 1981), 2: 1039–52.

above (p. 43), with epistolary composition.[4] Equally fundamental to good writing is good handwriting, a skill Erasmus exalts on the grounds of its prominent role in letter writing. So in *De recta pronuntiatione,* Erasmus has his fanciful interlocutor Lion defend this elementary but irreplaceable skill of penmanship against Bear's dismissive remarks. "Why, even when we get letters in their own hand from friends and fellow scholars," Lion argues,

> how we welcome them and seem to be listening to their voices and to be looking at them face to face.... A letter written by a third party hardly deserves to be called a letter at all. Secretaries often make their own changes. Even if you dictate rigidly, intimacy (*secretum*) will still be missing. Some things you will express differently, some you will not express at all, because you do not want to say them in front of the third person. So it is no longer a free discussion with a friend. And that leaves out the question of authenticity. Appending a signature is easy, to forge a whole letter very difficult indeed. Just as individual voices differ, so does every handwriting have something unique (*quiddam suum ac peculiare*) about it. (*CWE* 26: 391; ASD I-4, 34)

A letter written by someone else forfeits not only its uniqueness or what is *suum*—what belongs to it alone—but also its intimacy or *secretum* and therefore hardly deserves to be called a letter.[5] Invoking some of the most

---

4. The other phrase singled out for copious treatment—"Always, as long as I live, I shall remember you" (*CWE* 24: 354–64)—arguably also belongs to epistolary writing. On *De copia,* including these phrases, see Cave, *Cornucopian Text,* 3–34, and Chomarat, *Grammaire et rhétorique chez Erasme,* 2: 712–61. On the exercise of *prosopopoeia* as part of the writing curriculum since antiquity, see James J. Murphy, "The Key Role of Habit in Roman Writing Instruction," *Short History of Writing Instruction,* 62–69. And see Lisa Jardine, "Reading and the Technology of Textual Affect," in *Reading Shakespeare Historically,* ed. Jardine (London, 1996), 84, who suggests that "there are a number of indications in the *De Copia* that Erasmus has in mind familiar letter writing as the generalized model for textual production." For *familiaritas* as a topic in *De copia,* see *CWE* 24: 483. For possible medieval influences on *De copia,* including its treatment of *prosopopeia,* see George John Engelhardt, "Medieval Vestiges in the Rhetoric of Erasmus," *PMLA* 63 (1948): 739–44.

5. Elsewhere Bear reinforces the complementarity of reading and writing and identifies *secretum* as the goal of both activities: "The intimacy (*secretum*) which is the essence of intellectual communication, whether your aim is to put your own thoughts into writing or to get to know what great men have thought on a subject, vanishes equally in both cases" (*CWE* 26: 399; ASD I-4, 41). On *secretum* see Sen-

frequently repeated commonplaces about epistolary rhetoric, Lion's argument rehearses some of Erasmus's own pronouncements in his manual of letter writing, *De conscribendis epistolis.*

Singularly successful from its first publication at supplanting the many other manuals competing for the letter-writing market, Erasmus's *De conscribendis epistolis* does here and there add to the chorus of epistolary theorists describing the letter in terms of the style that defines a conversation between friends (e.g., *CWE* 25: 20, 50 and 79).[6] Writing such as this avoids artificiality, roughness, and tedium while seeking out "simplicity, frankness, humor and wit" (*CWE* 25: 20 and 50). But if letter writing calls for a simple or humble style, a *stilus humilior,* Erasmus concedes, it must be a *docta humilitas*—a "learned simplicity" (*CWE* 25: 21; ASD I-2, 225). Upholding Cicero's letters to Atticus as the standard for this genre, Erasmus demands from it a "careful and felicitous composition" (*CWE* 25: 14; ASD I-2, 214). For "letters which seem at times to have no order at all," Erasmus cautions, "are in fact carefully constructed" (*CWE* 25: 65; ASD I-2, 301). In keeping

---

eca, ep. 56.4–5, and Quintilian, 1.1.28–29, 10.3.22–23, and 10.3.30. On the intimacy of handwriting in an early print culture see Cathy Shrank, "'These fewe scribbled rules': Representing Scribal Intimacy in Early Modern Print," *Huntington Library Quarterly,* 67 (2004), 295–313.

6. For Erasmus on the deficiency of the manuals that his supplants, see ep. 117, *CWE* 1: 233–34. On the popularity of this influential treatise see *CWE* 25: lii and A. Gerlo, "The *Opus de Conscribendis Epistolis* of Erasmus and the Tradition of the *Ars Epistolica,*" in *Classical Influences on European Culture A.D. 500–1500,* ed. R. R. Bolgar (Cambridge, Eng., 1971), 107 and 112–13; on its complicated genesis, see Harry Vredeveld, "Towards a Critical Edition of Erasmus's *De conscribendis epistolis,*" *Humanistica Lovaniensia* 48 (1999): 8–13, and the following articles by Judith Rice Henderson: "Despauterius' Syntaxis (1509): The Earliest Publication of Erasmus' *De concribendis epistolis,*" *Humanistica Lovaniensia* 37 (1988): 175–210; "The Composition of Erasmus' *Opus de conscribendis epistolis*: Evidence for the Growth of a Mind," *Acta Conventus Neo-Latini Torontonensis* 37 (1988): 147–54; "Erasmus on the Art of Letter-Writing," in *Renaissance Eloquence,* ed. James J. Murphy (Berkeley, 1983), 331–55; "The Enigma of Erasmus' *Conficiendarum epistolarum formula,*" *Renaissance and Reformation,* n.s., 13 (1989): 313–30. And see Chomarat, *Grammaire et rhétorique chez Erasme,* 2: 1007–38; R. R. Bolgar, "The Teaching of Letter-Writing in the Sixteenth Century," *History of Education* 12 (1983): 245–53; Judith Rice Henderson, "Erasmian Ciceronians: Reformation Teachers of Letter-Writing," *Rhetorica* 10 (1992): 273–302; Rummel, "Erasmus' Manual of Letter-Writing"; and Baños, *El arte epistolar en el Renacimiento europeo,* 328–59.

with this expectation of careful construction, he advises his protégé in the art of letter writing to follow Cicero's lead in charting a middle course between "an untidy jumble" and "painstaking and finicky care" (*CWE* 25: 15; ASD I-2, 215). "[W]rite on the spur of the moment if you wish," he allows, "write whatever comes into your head, as long as it is the way Cicero wrote to Atticus" (*CWE* 25: 15; ASD I-2, 215).[7]

Somewhat unexpectedly, however, *De conscribendis* does not build its epistolary theory around the familiar letter. On the contrary, it first reduces the *genus familiare* to one of four main letter types and then features the other three, which as a group follow the Aristotelian—and Ciceronian— tripartite division of oratory into the deliberative, forensic, and epideictic (here encomiastic or demonstrative) kinds (*CWE* 25: 71; ASD I-2, 310–11). In keeping with this division, Erasmus's manual foregrounds the letter's persuasive over its expressive possibilities, its subject matter over its style, and its reliance on *decorum* (Aristotle's *to prepon*) over intimacy (Aristotle's *to oikeion*).[8]

Despite his preference, stated above, for discourse that is intimate rather than antagonistic, in other words, Erasmus follows the rhetoricians, and

---

7. For the Ciceronian epistolary formula *quidquid in buccam venerit* (whatever comes into your head), see *Ad Att.* 1.12.4, 12.1.2, 14.7.2; Seneca, ep. 118.1; Petrarch, *Fam.* 1.5, 12.10; and Erasmus, ep. 15, Allen 1: 89, *CWE* 1: 21 and cf. *Adagia* I.v.72 and 73. And see below, n. 31.

8. On the continued distinction between *decorum* and *proprietas*, see *CWE* 25: 26–27; ASD I-2, 236: "Thus it will be the function of the teacher, before setting out the form of the letter to be written, to explain the story to the pupils, going back as far as is necessary and with as much detail as is deemed suitable, specifying also the main turning-points of the story, the distinct characteristics of the personages involved (*personarum proprietatem*), and the other circumstances, so that they do not stray from propriety (*a decoro*) in their writing and say what is inappropriate." On the role of *decorum* in *De conscribendis*, see Jean Lecointe, *L'idéal et la différence: La perception de la personnalité littéraire à la Renaissance* (Geneva, 1993), 405, 433. In his inquiry into "la présence de la personne dans le style" (436), Lecointe briefly treats the influence of epistolary style (429–34).

That Erasmus is aware of the range of meanings of terms related to the *oikos* and even considers at least some of them colloquial is clear from Nosoponus's remark in the *Ciceronianus* that he knows Conradus Goclenius καὶ οἴκοθεν (*CWE* 28: 426; ASD I-2, 684) and Uranius's in the *Convivium religiosum*, regarding the meaning of 2 Cor 5:1–2, that *domus* is the proper Latin translation for Paul's *oikia* (*CWE* 39: 194, ll. 9–10; ASD I-3, 254).

especially Quintilian, in taking the persuasive oration as his point of departure for epistolary writing in *De conscribendis epistolis*. Like Quintilian, Erasmus not only locates the sources of persuasion in the traditional triad of *logos, pathos,* and *ēthos* but concentrates on the first two—the letter's argument and audience—to the near exclusion of the third, the writer's character, even though epistolary theory and practice as far back as Cicero, Demetrius, and Seneca, as we have seen, identify letter writing precisely with the writer's aim to reveal himself.[9] "One must but take into account the subject (*de re*) and recipient (*cui scribas*) of the letter," Erasmus reminds the schoolmaster (*CWE* 25: 18; ASD I-2, 281). Then citing Quintilian as his authority, Erasmus repeats that the style or *stilus* must be suited to the topic as well as the character of the listeners since one cannot write alike on all topics to all audiences (*CWE* 25: 19; ASD I-2, 222–23). Only as an afterthought does he include the variable of the writer as part of the equation (*CWE* 25: 19; ASD I-2, 223): "At the same time the style will also keep in mind the writer and not merely the recipient or the purpose for which it was sent" (*Sed interim et illud spectabit, unde veniat, non solum ad quem veniat, aut quibus de rebus legata*).[10]

In keeping with his subordination of *ēthos* to *logos,* moreover, Erasmus demurs on the very question of epistolary style, variously referred to as *stilus, character,* and *genus dicendi*: "[H]ow, I ask you, can a single style (*character*) be devised for such an infinitely varied content?" (*CWE* 25: 12; ASD I-2, 210). Although style shows the man, as Erasmus well knows, he is writing for the instruction of young boys, as he stresses repeatedly;[11] and so he focuses on a more accessible feature of epistolary composition. "Certainly a division based on general characteristics of style (*ex characteris conditione*) rather than on variety of subjects (*ex argumenti varietate*)," he admits, "seems to me quite unsuitable for teaching" (*CWE* 25: 70; ASD I-2, 309).

On these same grounds, Erasmus rejects the competing taxonomy of the

---

9. On the centrality of *ēthos* in Renaissance stylistics, see Lecointe, *L'idéal et la différence*, 418–68.

10. On the priority of *logos,* followed by *pathos* and finally *ēthos*, see also *CWE* 25: 74 and the introductory essay, where Fantazzi explains that "[b]efore the infinite variety of the epistolary genre Erasmus does not attempt to confine the writer within narrow limits, but counsels good judgment and adaptation of style to subject matter and person addressed" (8).

11. On Erasmus's invocation of the Socratic apophthegm, see *CWE* 23: xxvii; *Adagia* II.vi.54; Cave, *Cornucopian Text*, 48 n. 16; and above, p. 6. On the terminology and hierarchy of style, see Lecointe, *L'idéal et la différence*, 136–46.

late antique Greek epistolary theorists who designate the friendly or familiar letter as one kind among many. "For what they call 'friendly' (*philikon*)," he insists, " is not derived from the subject (*ab argumento*), but from the person (*a persona*). Besides, we also give advice, reproof, and encouragement to our close friends (*quos familiariter amamus*), and we joke or dispute with them" (*CWE* 25: 72; ASD I-2, 313–14). Because writing *familiariter* bears on the relation between the correspondents rather than on the subject matter about which they correspond, in other words, Erasmus addresses it only reluctantly. Part and parcel of both the ethical and the stylistic aspects of letter writing, *familiaritas* or intimacy gives way to other, more preliminary pedagogical concerns in *De conscribendis epistolis*.

Sidelining the *genus familiare* despite its currency in the field of humanist epistolary theory and practice, Erasmus again follows at least some of the ancient rhetoricians in relegating *familiaritas* itself to a single part of the letter, the exordium, which no less an authority than the young Cicero set aside for capturing good will (*De inventione* 1.16.22; cf. *CWE* 25: 108). For it is in the letter's opening, Erasmus reminds the schoolmaster, who should in turn instruct his pupils, that the letter writer must highlight the intimate bond between himself and his correspondent (*CWE* 25: 76–77)—a reminder Erasmus reinforces both in his summaries of *exordia* (e.g., *CWE* 25: 76) and in his sample letters, including the so-called *Encomium matrimonii* (*CWE* 25: 129).[12] As we have seen in chapter 1, however, the more mature Cicero eventually rejects this early isolation of *benevolentia* to the oration's opening remarks and concentrates instead on a thoroughgoing *conciliatio* or *commendatio,* roughly corresponding to Aristotelian *ēthos,* that permeates the entire speech, accounting in large measure for its persuasiveness (see above, pp. 21–25).

In Erasmus's *De conscribendis epistolis,* in contrast, conciliatory and commendatory impulses are either confined to the letter's opening or identified more narrowly with two kinds of letter, both of which fall under the persuasive category while preserving their close association with intimacy. "There is a class of letters, not unlike the commendatory class (*commendatorio*)," Erasmus explains, "which I thought should be called conciliatory (*conciliatorium*). For just as in recommendations (*commendatione*) we win favor (*conciliamus aliis favorem*) and good will for others with our friends, so when we are anxious to win over (*conciliare*) to ourselves men with whom we have had no previous acquaintance or friendship, we might be said to

---

12. See, on this work, *CWE* 26: 528–29.

be recommending ourselves (*nosmet ipsos commendamus*)" (*CWE* 25: 246; ASD I-2, 568). The aim of the conciliatory, like the commendatory, letter, then, is either to initiate or to strengthen *familiaritas*.

The kind of letter Cicero called *familiare et iocosum* in his widely quoted letter to Curio (*Ad fam.* 2.4.1; see above, p. 30), on the other hand, Erasmus invokes in passing in his treatment of abrupt openings, citing some examples from Cicero's two letter collections (*CWE* 25: 78; ASD I-2, 323). Cicero's equally famous definition of a letter as a communication designed to provide information (see above, p. 30) is offered to explain the *genera extraordinaria*—that is, those letters that fall outside the *ordo* imposed by the division into deliberative, judicial, and demonstrative—as replacement for what is labeled the *genus familiare* earlier in the manual:[13]

> We have so far dealt with what seemed to fall within one of the three classes of the persuasive, the demonstrative, and the judicial. We shall come now to the remaining kinds of letters, which, though they do not so much stand in need of rhetorical technique, yet occur more often than the kinds already described. Thus we will mention in particular the kind of letter in which we tell a friend of any news that he ought to know or will bring him pleasure, whether it be of a public or a private nature. (*CWE* 25: 225; ASD I-2, 541)

To supplement his surprisingly brief explanation of this class of letters that occurs most frequently even if it defies theorizing, Erasmus turns once again to illustrations from Cicero's *Ad familiares* and *Ad Atticum*.

If Erasmus thwarts our expectations in his *De conscribendis epistolis* by refusing to put not only an intimate style but any kind of style at the center of epistolary practice, his *Ciceronianus,* in contrast, zeroes in on the question of style, a move made all the more inescapable by the subtitle: *A Dialogue on the Ideal Latin Style* (*De optimo dicendi genere*).[14] In making this move, moreover, the *Ciceronianus* foregrounds epistolary style. For, in spite of their differences, all three interlocutors in this satirical dialogue approach the problem of writing from the perspective of writing letters. So when Bulephorus challenges Nosoponus to take a stand on the traditionally vexed relation in the rhetorical manuals between *res* and *verba*, Nosoponus takes

---

13. Neither Margolin (ASD) nor Fantazzi (*CWE*) flags either of these descriptions as variations on the Ciceronian kinds or *genera* in his letter to Curio.

14. On the controversy behind the dialogue, its publication history, its arguments, and its style, see Pierre Mesnard's introduction (ASD I-2, 583–96).

up the challenge in terms of epistolary composition, revealing by his answer to Bulephorus that he has as little understanding of the bond of *familiaritas* as of the epistolary *genus familiare*.[15]

Undertaking to write to his so-called friend regarding the loan of some books, a topic not uncommon in humanist letter writing, Nosoponus threatens in this correspondence to withdraw his affection entirely if the books are not returned immediately. To put this threatening subject matter into words, moreover, Nosoponus anticipates spending not just hours but days first rereading Cicero's letters and then pouring over his Ciceronian indices to insure the letter's purity of style (*CWE* 28: 353–55). Acknowledging a devotion to his Roman model that constitutes idolatry, Nosoponus admits to considering it "a finer thing to write three letters in a Ciceronian idiom than a hundred volumes in a style as polished as you like, but quite different from Cicero's" (*Equidem pulchrius esse duco tres epistolas scribere phrasi Ciceroniana, quam centum volumina stilo quamlibet expolito, modo a Ciceroniano discrepante*) (*CWE* 28: 362; ASD I-2, 621). And when Bulephorus, later in the conversation, counters Nosoponus's argument for a labored, literal-minded imitation of Cicero, he does so by highlighting the absurdities of writing letters in this fashion.

On the one hand, Bulephorus argues, few correspondents can appreciate a letter so fastidiously constructed; and, on the other, such fastidiousness is not practicable when, as sometimes happens, one must write more than twenty letters a day (*CWE* 28: 406–7).[16] Equally absurd is the restriction on contemporary letter writers to use none but the Ciceronian forms of salutation and valediction (*CWE* 28: 371–73) when Christian epistolary practice provides conventions of address and farewell that are more fitting.[17] Finally, at the end of the dialogue, when Bulephorus urges Nosoponus to identify from among ancient or modern writers from Pompey to Christophe de Longueil a single one who deserves to be labeled Ciceronian, his urging repeatedly elicits comments on their reputation as letter writers. For any Ciceronian seeking validation from the "four silly young Italians" fueling the literary craze that has snared Nosoponus must perform on this very "stage" (*CWE* 28: 406). Even Bulephorus upholds the Ciceronian letter

---

15. For Bulephorus on *res* over *verba*, see *CWE* 28: 402.

16. Consider Erasmus's letter to Henry Botteus (ep. 1985, mentioned above, n. 2), written in the same year as the *Ciceronianus*.

17. See Alexander Dalzell, "Greetings and Salutations in Erasmus," *Renaissance and Reformation*, n.s., 13 (1989): 251–61. On the *decorum peculiare* of the *Ciceronianus*, see Lecointe, *L'idéal et la différence*, 436–41.

as the standard of measure, although his criterion is intimacy rather than stylistic purity. "What have Seneca's *Letters* in common with letters," Bulephorus asks,

> except for the title? But in Cicero's *Letters* nothing is far-fetched and extraneous. Either he writes down the comments on serious and important matters which he would make in person if circumstances allowed, or he chats about personal affairs (*de familiaribus rebus*) and intellectual interests with his absent friends just as people do when they are together. What's more, Cicero did not publish his own *Letters,* and seems to have written some of them without his usual care for style. . . . we do not find in most of Longueil's *Letters* either the simplicity and charm of natural speech, or a feeling of reality. (*CWE* 28: 430; ASD I-2, 693)

Like Nosoponus in deriving his assumptions about writing from a rhetoric of letter writing, Bulephorus nevertheless rejects Nosoponus's obsession with stylistic purity in favor of the stylistic difference associated with intimacy.

For the inevitable and even desirable differences in writing styles reflect the deeper psychological differences among writers—differences that Petrarch, following Cicero and Quintilian, as we have seen, applauds.[18] Attributing the rebirth of eloquence to Petrarch's mind as well as his style, Bulephorus echoes this approval in his plan for Nosoponus's return to psychic health through the cultivation of what is his own (*suum*) rather than Cicero's.[19] "Every one of us (*singula mortalium ingenia*)," Bulephorus explains with an emphasis on the singularity of each and every *ingenium,*

---

18. For a discussion of "the key problem of identity and difference" (39) in the *Ciceronianus,* see Cave, *Cornucopian Text,* 35–49, where Cave reminds his reader that Erasmus places "personal" discourse, traditionally restricted to informal genres like the letter, "at the centre of the problem of rhetoric, thus renewing the ancient debate on the relationship between rhetoric and truth in terms of a new and potent grammar of identity and an intensified textual self-consciousness" (43). See also Fumaroli, *L'âge de L'éloquence,* 101–6, who stresses the writer's social and religious alienation that results from failing to nurture a "'je' personnel" (103), and Chomarat, *Grammaire et rhétorique chez Erasme,* 2: 815–40, who credits Erasmus with "en toute clarté la notion de personnalité" (833). See also Laurel Carrington, "The Boundaries between Text and Reader: Erasmus' Approach to Reading Scripture," *Archiv für Reformationsgeschichte* 88 (1997): 5–22.

19. With Nosoponus's consent, Bulephorus praises Petrarch as follows : "The leader in the rebirth of eloquence was, it seems, Francesco Petrarch, a great and celebrated figure in his own time, but now hardly read at all. He had an ardent mind

has his own personal inborn characteristics (*suum quiddam ac genuinum*), and these have such force that it is useless for a person fitted by nature for one style of speaking (*dicendi genus*) to strive to achieve a different one. (*CWE* 28: 396–97; ASD I-2, 647)[20]

Nosoponus responds—and Bulephorus reinforces his response—by acknowledging Quintilian as the authority for this attitude (*CWE* 28: 397, 407; cf. Quintilian, *Institutio oratoria* 2.8.1, 10.2.19, and above, p. 47); still Nosoponus is not ready to acquiesce in Bulephorus's approbation of the fundamentally epistolary aim of self-expression, despite Bulephorus's warning that if you express Cicero (*exprimere Ciceronem*), you cannot express yourself (*teipsum exprimere*), "and if you do not express yourself, your speech will be a lying mirror" (*CWE* 28: 399; ASD I-2, 649). Whereas Cicero's Antonius in *De oratore*, as we have seen, makes the case for the orator's need to express character (*mores exprimere*), Bulephorus particularizes the case to the challenge rooted in epistolary writing of expressing oneself.

If Bulephorus's assumptions about the best style of writing derive from writing letters, his assumptions about the best reading practices derive in turn from the paradigm of reading letters. Invoking now and again the traditional figure of the reader as consumer who digests what he reads (*CWE* 28: 402 and 442), Erasmus, through Bulephorus, endorses a model of read-

---

(*ingenium ardens*), a vast knowledge, and a not inconsiderable power of expression (*nec mediocris eloquendi vis*)" (*CWE* 28: 414; ASD I-2, 661). On Petrarch's reputation as the "restorer of the 'litterae'" that lay "altogether oppressed" (386), according to the northern humanist most influential on Erasmus, see Mommsen, "Rudolf Agricola's Life of Petrarch," 367–86.

In a letter to Alfonso Fonseca (ep. 2157; Allen 8: 155, ll. 379–83), Erasmus similarly credits Augustine with a style all *his* own (*suum quoddam dicendi genus*), one that demands a *lector familiaris*—an intimate reader—in order to be understood and appreciated. Erasmus's annotation on Romans 8:32 (*qui enim proprio filio suo*) may clarify his view on the formula used by Petrarch in regard to style (*proprium et suum*): "*Suo* is redundant in the Latin text; for ἴδιου, either *suo* or *proprio* is enough" (*CWE* 56: 229). For the legality of the term *idios*, see above, p. 36. For Petrarch's reputation as a prose writer among the quattrocento humanists, see M. L. McLaughlin, "Histories of Literature in the Quattrocento," in *The Languages of Literature in Renaissance Italy*, ed. Peter Hainsworth, Valerio Lucchesi, Christina Roaf, David Robey, and J. R. Woodhouse (Oxford, 1988), 63–80.

20. On the crucial role of *ingenium* in the *Ciceronianus* and its relation to genius, see Lecointe, *L'idéal et la différence*, 217–25, and Chomarat, *Grammaire et rhétorique chez Erasme*, 2: 833–37, 841–43.

ing grounded in the intimacy—here *consuetudo*—between the reader and the writer.[21] This intimacy assumes on the reader's part an attraction to the writer that resonates with Cicero's philosophical and rhetorical understanding of *conciliatio,* the Latin equivalent, as we have seen, of *oikeiōsis.* For Erasmus imagines that the best reading practice, impossible between *ingenia* that are inherently *aliena,* conciliates (*conciliat*) rather than repels the reader, fostering between him and the writer a meeting of the minds (*CWE* 28: 440; ASD I-2, 703), an *affinitas* characteristic of *familiaritas.*[22]

Erasmus expects from his reading, in other words, nothing less than an understanding of the writer's thoughts and feelings, an understanding modeled on the long years of living together characteristic of the most intimate friends. "Minds differ far more than voices and physical features do," Bulephorus affirms, recalling, once again, not only Cicero, Quintilian, and Petrarch, but Lion on handwriting,

> and the mirror will lie unless it reflects the true born image of the mind. The very thing which the reader enjoys is getting to know the writer's feelings, character, disposition, and type of mind (*affectus, indolem, sensum, ingeniumque*) from the way he writes, just as he would by living on familiar terms with him for several years (*quam si complures annos cum illo consuetudinem egeris*). (*CWE* 28: 440; ASD I-2, 703)[23]

---

21. On the near synonymy between *familiaritas* and *consuetudo,* see Hellegouarc'h, *Le vocabulaire latin des relations et des partis politiques sous la République,* 77: "consuetudo y prend un sens extrêmement voisin de celui de *familiaritas;* Cicéron emploie l'association *familiaris consuetudo.* Mais surtout, nous pouvons constater la fréquence des groupes où se trouvent associés *consuetudo* et *familiaritas.* Aussi *consuetudo* finit-il, comme *familiaritas,* par désigner une forme particulièrement forte de l'*amicitia* basée sur la fréquence et la constance des relations entre les individus qu'elle associe; comme la *familiaritas* par conséquent, elle ne peut exister qu'entre un nombre limité d'individus." Hellegouarc'h cites Cicero's *Pro rege Deiotaro,* 30: "Familiaritatem consuetudo attulit."

22. In his 1531 colloquy *Amicitia,* Erasmus's interlocutors discuss the affinities or *amicitiae* between humans and various animals and end with a reflection on *familiaritas,* which, unlike Christian *caritas* and these natural *amicitiae,* is felt by each person for very few others (*CWE* 40: 1033–55; ASD I-3, 700–709). On the *familiaritas* of this colloquy in contrast to *caritas,* see Chomarat, *Grammaire et rhétorique chez Erasme,* 2: 922, and Seth Lobis, "Erasmus and the Natural History of Friendship," *ERSY* 30 (2010): 23–39.

23. For Politian's influence on Erasmus's advocacy of a unique, personal style, including his choice of such terms as *indoles,* see Lecointe, *L'idéal et la différence,*

For Erasmus as for Petrarch, then, the flip side of a *rhetoric* of intimacy is a *hermeneutics* of intimacy, a deep understanding of what one reads based on the model of understanding a *familiaris*. With its attention to understanding the individuality and uniqueness of the writer's style and therefore his mind, this hermeneutics underwrites all of Erasmus's extensive editorial work, including his edition of Jerome.

If Erasmus recollects an early talent for writing familiar letters (see above, p. 74), he also admits to an early taste for reading them, especially Jerome's (*CWE* 61: 80; *Hieronymi opera* [*HO*], vol. 2 [Basel, 1516], part 1, preface, 4B).[24] So enduring was this youthful affinity for Jerome and so arduous the editorial project it engendered that Erasmus only half jokingly lays a proprietary claim to Jerome's letters, suggesting to Johann von Botzheim that they should figure as the last volume of his own *opera omnia* (ep. 396; *CWE* 61: 13).[25] Erasmus bases this claim, moreover, on his deep intimacy with the subject of his editorial efforts—an intimacy that is, like the traditional *familiaritas* of the letter, modeled on the affectionate conversation between friends. To accomplish his editorial aim, Erasmus explains in a 1516 preface to the Froben edition of Jerome, he has had to "rely on the intimacy (*familiaritate*) which repeated readings of Jerome's works gained for me just as face-to-face association with him might have done" (*CWE* 61: 80; *HO* II, part 1, 4B).

In his dedicatory letter to William Warham introducing the same edition (ep. 396), however, Erasmus, like Cicero and Petrarch before him, questions whether reading might not allow for even greater intimacy than conversation: whether written might not surpass oral discourse in effecting the Gadamerian miracle of understanding (see above, p. 6). "For such is my opinion," Erasmus offers, "if a man had lived in familiar converse (*domesticam consuetudinem*) with Cicero (to take him as an example) for several years, he will know less of Cicero than they do who by constant reading

---

325–26, 409, 450, who suggests that Politian's insistence on *indolem proferre* as the standard of style may rely on Demetrius's discussion of epistolary style (429); and compare ep. 2615, Allen 9: 447, ll. 51–52, quoted in Chomarat, *Grammaire et rhétorique chez Erasme*, 842 n. 563: "Pectus hominis nulla ex re magis deprehenditur quam ex stilo. In hoc certe speculo te utcumque vidisse mihi videor."

24. See John C. Olin, "Erasmus and Saint Jerome: The Close Bond and Its Significance," *ERSY* 7 (1987): 33–53, and Rice, *Saint Jerome in the Renaissance*, 116–36.

25. On the implications of this claim see Lisa Jardine, *Erasmus, Man of Letters: The Construction of Charisma in Print* (Princeton, 1993), 164–69, and my *Friends Hold All Things in Common*, 170–73.

of what he wrote converse with his spirit every day" (*CWE* 3: 256; Allen, 2: 212).²⁶ And this endorsement of the power of reading to effect intimacy caps off a description of the multiple ways that books communicate—ways that, recalling Erasmus's recommendation to the schoolmaster in *De ratione studii,* rehearse the traditional functions of the letter. Concerning the great literary figures of the past, Erasmus asserts:

> they live on for the world at large even after death, and live on in such fashion that they speak to more people, and more effectively dead than alive. They converse with us, instruct us, tell us what to do, give us advice and encouragement and consolation as loyally and as readily as anyone can. In fact, they then most truly come alive for us when they themselves have ceased to live. (*CWE* 3: 256; Allen, 2: 212)

Like the letter in Erasmus's lessons for the young, in other words, literature in general not only offers us the written counterpart to conversation or *sermo* but also fulfills, more specifically, epistolary writing's "persuasive, dissuasive, exhortatory, dehortatory, narrative, congratulatory, expostulatory, commendatory, and consolatory" aims (see above, p. 75).

If reading, on the model of reading letters, aspires to the intimacy that fosters understanding, it is the Erasmian editor, above all, who realizes this aspiration. For the editor—that is, the successful editor—is the most understanding reader. Erasmus himself, as we have already seen, boasts of precisely this intimacy or *familiaritas* with Jerome—an intimacy that he has come to enjoy, in the words of the *Ciceronianus,* through coming to understand "the writer's feelings, character, disposition, and type of mind" (*CWE* 28: 440; ASD I-2, 703); and this understanding is accessible in turn through what Erasmus defines in the most capacious terms in his edition of Jerome as *style.*

26. For *domestica* as a synonym of *familiaris* in the language of the humanists, see Gordon Griffiths, James Hankins, and David Thompson, eds., *The Humanism of Leonardo Bruni* (Binghamton, 1987), 310–11: "But 'household' (*domus*) here means the same thing as 'family' (*familia*) from which the expression 'household management' (*res familiaris*) is derived. The Latins were accustomed to indicate the various arts by attaching the appropriate qualifying adjective to this word *res*. For example: *res militaris, res publica, res familiaris, res rustica, res domestica,* which means the same as *res familiaris,* since household and family are the same thing." On greater intimacy afforded through reading than through daily conversation, see Christine Bénévent, "Erasme en sa correspondance: Conquête(s) et défaite(s) du langage," in Van Houdt et al., *Self-Presentation and Social Identification,* 57–85, esp. 70–72.

"The term style" (*vocabulum stili*), Erasmus explains in the same 1516 preface to this edition,

> comprehends all at once a multiplicity of things—manner in language and diction, texture, so to speak, and, further, thought and judgment, line of argumentation, inventive power, control of material, emotion, what the Greeks call ἦθος,—and within each one of these notions a profusion of shadings, no fewer, to be sure, than the differences in talent (*ingeniorum*), which are as numerous as men themselves. (*CWE* 61: 78; HO II, part 1, 3D-4A)

Anticipating Bulephorus's broader view in the *Ciceronianus* of what it means to write like Cicero (as well as Montaigne's reflections on individuality in the *Essais*), Erasmus insists that difference rules in the kingdom of style. "[I]n no other sphere," he claims, invoking the difference between one egg and another, "is there greater diversity" (*CWE* 61: 77; HO, II, part 1, 3D).[27] Constituting nothing less than the very character and quality (*character et habitus*) of speech, in other words, style (*stilus*) is every bit as individual as appearance, voice, character, and disposition (*mos et genius*). Indeed, it is even more individual; for "the quality of mind (*mentis habitus*)," Erasmus insists in terms he will later repeat in the *Ciceronianus,* "is manifest in speech even more than the likeness of the body is reflected in a mirror" (*CWE* 61: 76; HO, II, part 1, 3D). Understanding Jerome through his style, moreover, Erasmus claims to be following Jerome himself, who grounded his own editorial practices on the evidence of style (*CWE* 61: 76).

Eventually the mark of all good writing, stylistic individuality or uniqueness, as we have seen, finds its earliest foothold in the tradition of familiar letter writing, where readers expected writers to undertake first and foremost to express themselves—their thoughts, their feelings, their character. In keeping with this early alliance between individual style and epistolary writing, Erasmus reports, Cicero himself believed his letters to be inimitable, even by those determined to copy his style. For in these same letters, according to Erasmus, Cicero "says that he has given his writings [i.e., his letters] such distinctive features that it would not be difficult to distinguish them from the [epistolary] writing of others, for certain pieces in this genre by others' hands were being attributed to him" (*CWE* 61: 79; HO, II, part 1, 4A). Also in keeping with this alliance, Erasmus edits Jerome's letters by

---

27. In the conclusion (pp. 119–20), I take up in more detail both the question of difference as figured by two eggs and Montaigne's use of this figure.

calling into play an intimate understanding—a *familiaritas*—with "such distinctive features" of Jerome's style as can expose not just minor scribal errors but whole forgeries.[28] In his biography of Jerome, Erasmus refers to the end-product of such readerly intimacy in Gadamerian terms as "the [editorial] miracle of Jerome expressing himself (*sese exprimentem*)" (*CWE* 61: 24; HO, I, n. pg.).

Issuing his most famous call to reading in another 1516 preface—this one to his edition of the New Testament—Erasmus establishes the hermeneutics of *familiaritas* as the standard not just for editors but for all Christian readers. Most often appreciated for its advocacy of biblical translation into the vernacular, the *Paraclesis* exhorts Christians to read Scripture with the same expectation of intense feeling and intimate communication that they would bring to the letter of an absent and sorely missed friend. Whereas these same readers, Erasmus chides, "preserve the letters (*litteras*) written by a dear friend ... kiss them fondly ... carry them about ... read them again and again" (Olin 102; LB V, 142EF), they have not read the *litterae Christi* even once (LB V, 141D).[29] And yet these *divinae litterae* are composed with the same rhetoric of *familiaritas* that characterizes the familiar letter. Not only do they persuade, dissuade, narrate, console, and so on, but they use the power of language to compensate for distance, to bring the reader face to face with the writer, to render the absent present. Like the familiar letter, Erasmus insists, the *Euangelicae litterae* "bring you the living image of His holy mind ... and thus render Him so fully present that you would see less if you gazed upon Him with your very eyes" (Olin 106; LB V, 144D).[30]

28. For Petrarch's similar confidence in judging authenticity through style, in this case Cicero's, see McLaughlin, *Literary Imitation in the Italian Renaissance*, 33–34.

29. For quotations from the *Paraclesis* in English see John C. Olin, ed., *Christian Humanism and the Reformation: Selected Writings* (New York, 1965), with page numbers within parentheses in the text. In his introduction to the *Enchiridion*, John W. O'Malley describes the *Paraclesis* as the "most revealing document in Erasmus' entire corpus concerning what the Bible teaches and how it is to be regarded" (*CWE* 66: xxvi).

30. In the *Enchiridion*, a work that similarly emphasizes the affective dimension of reading, Erasmus makes a similar argument: "You give homage to an image of Christ's countenance represented in stone or wood or depicted in colour. With how much more religious feeling should you render homage to the image of his mind, which has been reproduced in the Gospels through the artistry of the Holy Spirit. No Apelles has ever portrayed with his brush the shape and features of the body in the way that

In the *Paraclesis*, then, Erasmus recites the same argument that served his turn when editing Jerome. There it was the readers of Cicero, and especially the readers of Cicero's letters, who could expect greater intimacy with the ancient Roman than those who had lived with him. Here, in his brief preface to the New Testament, Erasmus invokes this argument not once but twice, assuring his own readers that Christ "stands forth especially in this literature (*his litteris*), in which He lives for us even at this time, breathes and speaks, I should say almost more effectively than when He dwelt among men. The Jews saw and heard less than you see and hear in the books of the Gospels (*in Evangelicis litteris*)" (Olin 102; LB V, 142E).[31] And whereas Cicero admits, as we have seen in chapter 1, to being moved to kiss the letter of an absent friend,

---

speech reveals each person's mind and thought. This is especially so with Christ, for as he was the essence of simplicity and truth, there could be no dissimilarity between the archetype of the divine mind and the form of speech that issued from it" (*CWE* 66: 72). In the prefatory letter to the 1518 edition of the *Enchiridion*, addressed to Paul Volz (ep. 858), Erasmus similarly identifies the "letters" in the conventional debate between arms and letters with *litterae* in the narrower sense of *epistolae*: "In my opinion it will be found a good plan, long before we make the attempt by force of arms, to seek to win them by letters and pamphlets (*epistolis ac libellis*). What sort of letter (*qualibus epistolis*), you ask? No threats, no bluster; they must breathe the true fatherly affection and recall the spirit of Peter and Paul, they must not merely have the word 'apostolic' in the superscription, they must revive the activity of the apostles" (*CWE* 66: 11; Allen 3: 365). In the *Enchiridion* itself, Erasmus also features the reader as enemy after the model of the Israelites despoiling the Egyptians (*CWE* 66: 33; LB V, 7D), although he softens the Petrarchan appropriation of the Senecan figure of the reader as a spy in enemy territory by reconfiguring him as a *peregrinator* rather than an *explorator*: "In brief, it would be profitable to have a taste of all pagan literature, if, as I said, it is done at the appropriate time and with moderation, with caution and discrimination, as well as in a cursory manner, more in the manner of a foreign visitor than a resident (*deinde cursim, & peregrinantis non habitantis more*), and lastly and most important, if it all be related to Christ" (*CWE* 66: 33; LB V, 7E–8A).

31. Here again, Erasmus makes a similar point in the *Enchiridion* (*CWE* 66: 71; LB V, 32C). Although on occasion in the *Paraclesis* Erasmus will refer to the *Evangelici & Apostolici libri* (e.g., LB V, 142F), his preferred term by far for the works of the New Testament is *litterae*, the same term he uses for the familiar letters carried about. It is also worth noting that Erasmus slips into this work about the *litterae Christi* the frequently quoted formula from Cicero's epistolary writing, *quidquid in buccam venerit* (LB V, 141E). For the use of this formula, see above, n. 7.

Erasmus encourages the readers of Scripture to "covet [these *litterae*] ... embrace [them] ... fondly kiss [them]" (Olin 105; LB V, 144BC).[32]

If not all reading, then at least the most important reading, namely, reading Scripture, conforms to expectations established by the paradigm of reading letters. In the *Paraclesis,* a protreptic introduction to his New Testament, Erasmus understandably restricts his focus to the Gospels and apostolic letters, although he features the former, which he refers to, as we have seen, as the *litterae Christi* and the *Evangelicae litterae*. These writings distinguish themselves by their accessibility, accommodating all readers regardless of age, gender, fortune, or station in life, from the weakest and most vulnerable to the great and powerful (Olin 96). With the *Paraphrase on Romans,* in contrast, Erasmus openly offers an aid to reading in recognition of how difficult it is to understand Paul in what is arguably the letter with the greatest impact on the sixteenth century.[33]

32. On the power of presence in the *Paraclesis*, a fundamentally belletristic power summed up for Erasmus in *philosophia Christi*, see Dresden, "Erasme et les belles-lettres," 15–16. That Erasmus has an epistolary model in mind when imagining the reader's response to Scripture gains support from his distinction between the *Platonis libri* and the *Christi litterae* as well as by his reformulation of these *litterae* as *sermones mei* (John 14:15, 23): "He is not a Platonist who has not read the works of Plato; and is he a theologian, let alone a Christian, who has not read the literature of Christ (*Christi litteras*)? Who loves me, Christ says, keeps my word (*sermones meos servat*), a distinguishing mark which He himself prescribed" (Olin 99; LB V, 141D). In keeping with the importance of *sermo*, traditionally allied with *epistola* or *littera* as its corresponding written form, Erasmus insists that "our daily conversations reveal what we are" (Olin 97). On prayer as a conversation with God, see *Enchiridion*, *CWE* 66: 31.

On the relation between the terms *litera* and *epistola* among the humanists, see Silvia Rizzo, "Il latino del Petrarca nelle *Familiari*," in *Uses of Greek and Latin*, ed. A. C. Dionisotti, Anthony Grafton, and Jill Kraye (London, 1988), 48.

33. For the centrality of Paul's Letter to the Romans to the Reformation, see, for instance, John B. Payne, "Erasmus: Interpreter of Romans," *Sixteenth Century Essays and Studies* 2 (1971): 3–4. And see Payne, "Erasmus and Lefèvre d'Etaples as Interpreters of Paul," *Archiv für Reformationsgeschichte* 65 (1974): 54–83, and Robert D. Sider, "Historical Imagination and the Representation of Paul in Erasmus' Paraphrases on the Pauline Epistles," in *Holy Scripture Speaks: The Production and Reception Of Erasmus' "Paraphrases on the New Testament,"* ed. Hilmar M. Pabel and Mark Vessey (Toronto, 2002), 85–109, and "*Concedo Nulli*: Erasmus' Motto and the Figure of Paul in the Paraphrases," *Erasmus in English* 14 (1985–86): 7–10.

Written at roughly the same time as the *Paraclesis* and inaugurating the widely influential series of paraphrases on all the books of the New Testament except the Book of Revelation, the *Paraphrase on Romans* presents even a master paraphraser like Erasmus with special challenges.[34] This is so not because the task demands the integration of epistolary and *ethopoetic* or *prosopographic* writing, which had anyway been a standard feature of the schoolroom exercises for centuries and a fundamental part of Erasmus's own curriculum (see above, p. 43).[35] Rather, it is because Erasmus feels obliged to offer his readers, as he indicates both in the dedicatory letter to Cardinal Grimani (ep. 710) and in the summary argument to the paraphrase itself (*CWE* 42: 14), the very voice of Paul, even though Paul assumes a number of *personae* (Gr. *prosōpa*) or *ēthē* in the course of this one letter. More than the lexical and grammatical obscurities associated with Paul's *verba*, then, and even more than the conceptual obscurities associated with the complex *res* of this letter, the obscurities caused by Paul's "frequent and sudden change of masks (*personarum*)" (*CWE* 42: 13; LB VII, 777–78) confound the reader.[36]

Paul effects these sudden changes of "personality," Erasmus explains, in response to a shifting audience:

> he considers now the Jews, now the Gentiles, now both; sometimes he addresses believers, sometimes doubters; at one point he assumes the role

---

34. For an introduction to the publication history of the *Paraphrases*, see *CWE* 42: xx–xxix, 43: xv and 480, 44: xiii–xiv, and John J. Bateman, "The Textual Travail of the *Tomus secundus* of the *Paraphrases*," in Pabel and Vessey, *Holy Scripture Speaks*, 213–63; and see Chomarat, *Grammaire et rhétorique chez Erasme*, 1: 587–617, who demonstrates that the strategies deployed in the Pauline paraphrases are those recommended in *De copia*.

35. On the prosopographic agenda of the *Paraphrases*, see John J. Bateman, "From Soul to Soul: Persuasion in Erasmus' Paraphrases on the New Testament," *Erasmus in English* 15 (1987–88): 7–16 and Jane E. Phillips, "*Sub evangelistae persona*: The Speaking Voice in Erasmus' *Paraphrase on Luke*," in Pabel and Vessey, *Holy Scripture Speaks*, 127–50. In *CWE* 44: xv, Bateman reminds readers of Erasmus's Pauline paraphrases that "[i]n elaborating a document in this way, Erasmus is adapting to the task of paraphrasing a common practice of sixteenth-century letter-writing as may be illustrated from his own correspondence and from his treatise on letter-writing."

36. On the difficulties of both *res* and *verba* in this letter, see Payne, "Erasmus: Interpreter of Romans," 7.

of a weak man, at another of a strong; sometimes that of a godly man, sometimes of an ungodly man. The result of all this is that the reader, wandering about as though in some kind of confusing labyrinth or winding maze, does not see very well whence he has entered or how he may leave. (*CWE* 42: 13)

And just in case Erasmus's readers have forgotten this introductory explanation for their difficulties, Erasmus's Paul repeats it in chapter 7, encouraging these same readers to "imagine that I am two men in one (inasmuch as now, to make my point, I have put on the mask (*personam*) of a man still subject to vices and passions), one a carnal and gross man, and another more pure and less gross" (*CWE* 42: 44; LB VII, 800A).

Whatever his identity at the moment, however, Erasmus's Paul claims to write intimately and openly to the members of the Roman congregation. As we have seen in chapter 1, Cicero labeled this practice *writing familiariter*. Erasmus's Paul describes it to the Romans as writing *familiarius ac liberius*, intimately and freely (*CWE* 42: 85; LB VII, 828A), while in a letter of his own Erasmus advertises his Paul as writing *dilucide familiariterque*—clearly and intimately—and considers this style key to the success of his Pauline paraphrases (ep. 916; *CWE* 6: 238; Allen 3: 482).[37]

Without abandoning the philosophical pedigree of Paul's Letter to the Romans, including its responsiveness to the doctrinal and ethical questions facing the young Christian community at Rome, Erasmus adjusts the letter to conform to his readers' expectations of an *epistola familiaris*.[38] If this adjustment is evident in Erasmus's characterization of the letter's style as *familiare*, it is even more striking in his reconfiguration of the personal rela-

---

37. On a comparable intimacy between Jesus and his followers according to Erasmus's paraphrase of 1 John, see LB VII, 1141AB; and see Bateman, "From Soul to Soul," 9–10.

38. On the complex genre of the Pauline letter, see, for instance, George A. Kennedy, *New Testament Interpretation through Rhetorical Criticism* (Chapel Hill, 1984), 152–56; Jeffrey T. Reed, "Using Ancient Rhetorical Categories to Interpret Paul's Letters: A Question of Genre," in *Rhetoric and the New Testament: Essays from the 1992 Heidelberg Conference*, ed. Stanley E. Porter and Thomas H. Olbricht (Sheffield, 1993), 292–324; S. K. Stowers, *Letter Writing in Greco-Roman Antiquity* (Philadelphia, 1986) and *The Diatribe and Paul's Letter to the Romans* (Chico, Cal., 1981); John L. White, "Saint Paul and the Apostolic Letter Tradition," *Catholic Bible Quarterly* 45 (1983): 433–44.

tions that shape the letter. Not only does Erasmus's Paul assume a *familiaritas* with his correspondents at Rome, whom he has never met, but, in an effort to drive home Paul's insistence on God's limitless love for humankind, demonstrated by His sacrifice of an only Son, Erasmus models divine affection on an *amicitia* different from its human counterpart in degree only but not in kind.

Whereas Paul himself writes somewhat cryptically, in making the comparison between human and divine love, that someone who refuses to die for a righteous person (*dikaios*) might indeed die for a good person (*agathos*) (Romans 5:7), Erasmus clarifies the original Pauline passage by having his Paul imagine these two people more specifically as friends:

> And yet among men you would scarcely find anyone so much a friend (*amicum*) that he would rescue an honest and deserving friend (*amici*) from danger by his own death. But let us grant that someone might be found who would not refuse perhaps to undertake death for a good friend (*amico*); still, God has surpassed all examples of human love (*caritatis*), because he handed over his Son to death for the impious and the unworthy. (*CWE* 42: 33; LB VII, 792DE)

Also willing to hand over an only son, Abraham, who plays a singularly important role in the Pauline doctrine of faith, becomes a friend or *amicus* of God as a consequence of his faith (*CWE* 42: 30 and 32; LB VII, 790D, 792A). The *amicitia* between God and Abraham, moreover, serves as model for the relation between God and Erasmus's Christian reader, who "may have the peace of a conscience now free from anxiety and a steadfast friendship (*amicitiam*) with God" (*CWE* 42: 16; LB VII, 779D).[39] As paraphrased by Erasmus, then, Paul's Letter to the Romans qualifies the relationship transformed by faith and grace as an intimate relationship on the model of friendship. This relationship not only routinely found written

---

39. For Origen on the friendship between Abraham and God, see *Patrologia Graeca* 14, 970D, quoted in *CWE* 42: 145. For Origen's influence on Erasmus's understanding of Paul, see Payne, "Erasmus: Interpreter of Romans." It is also possible that Erasmus's hermeneutics of *familiaritas* is influenced more broadly by his knowledge of patristic hermeneutics. See, for instance, Jerome, *Tractatus lix in psalmos* 66, 1. 158: "antequam temptaretur, deus ei numquam locutus fuerat: postquam autem temptatus est, venit ad eum deus, et familiariter loquitur, quasi amicus cum amico suo." See also Margaret M. Mitchell, *The Heavenly Trumpet: John Chrysostom and the Art of Pauline Interpretation* (Louisville, 2002), for Chrysostom's "author-centered hermeneutics" (43), which is a "hermeneutics of love" (39–40).

expression in the familiar letter but also defined its style and thus the genre itself in terms of intimacy.[40]

Whether he is advising his own readers about how to read Scripture or rewriting it for them in the interest of deepening their understanding of its Author (or authors), Erasmus reinforces the expectation of intimacy characteristic of reading and writing letters. As we have seen, this epistolary genre resists classification according to subject matter. Instead, it is defined by its style; and this style reflects the close bond between the reader and a writer whose individuality or uniqueness as expressed in his writing makes this closeness possible. The rhetoric of intimacy, then, is a rhetoric rooted in style, the very style through which the reader comes to understand the writer. Fully appreciating the correspondence between this rhetoric and its hermeneutics, Montaigne, as we will see in the next chapter, claims to read and write intimately in search of such understanding.

---

40. In the 1508 prolegomena to the *Adages*, Erasmus stresses the *amicitia* not only between God and man but between God and Christ, citing Paul as his authority: "In fact that united in friendship (*amicitia*) with Christ, glued to Him by the same binding force that holds Him fast to the Father, imitating so far as we may that complete communion by which He and the Father are one, we should also be one with Him, and, as Paul says, should become one spirit and one flesh with God, so that by the laws of friendship (*amicitiae iure*) all that is His is shared with us and all that is ours is shared with him; and then that, linked one to another in the same bonds of friendship (*amicitiae vinculis*), as members of one Head and like one and the same body we may be filled with the same spirit, and weep and rejoice at the same things together" (*CWE* 31: 15; ASD II-1, 61–62).

CHAPTER 4 **Reading and Writing Intimately in Montaigne's *Essais***

*E*rasmian reform, whether educational or religious, as we have seen, takes epistolary writing and reading as its point of departure. The young student begins his rhetorical training by composing, translating, and paraphrasing letters, while the accomplished writer furthers his career by parading more advanced versions of these same skills. Meanwhile, the Erasmian Christian approaches Scripture as a letter reader would the long-awaited communication of a sorely missed friend. Only by reading the *litterae Christi* and the letters of Saint Paul, aided perhaps by Erasmus's own paraphrases, can the Christian experience an intimacy with the Divine Author and His apostle. Epistolary reading and writing, then, sets a standard that applies to more than just reading and writing letters; and this standard is defined by the stylistic quality of intimacy. As far back as Aristotle's *Rhetoric,* as we have seen in the first chapter, this quality of intimacy combines legal and affective dimensions—a combination that sets the conditions for early modern discussions of style and the individuality they promote. As we have seen in the second chapter, these dimensions shape the Petrarchan project of the *Familiares*. As we will now see, they also shape the *Essais* of Montaigne.

Recent scholarship on Montaigne has addressed in some detail both the Petrarchan and the Erasmian aspects of the essay, including its dependence on epistolary form.[1] Montaigne himself, on the other hand, is noticeably

---

1. On the Petrarchan and Erasmian pedigrees of Montaigne's literary agenda see Morris W. Croll, *Attic and Baroque Prose Style: The Anti-Ciceronian Movement*, ed. J. Max Patrick and Robert O. Evans with John W. Wallace (Princeton, 1966), 180; Dresden, "Erasme et les belles-lettres," 3; Gérard Defaux, "From Erasmus to Montaigne (and Beyond): Writing as Presence," *ERSY* 8 (1988): 35–69; M. Mann Phillips, "From the *Ciceronianus* to Montaigne," in *Classical Influences on European Culture A.D. 1500–1700*, ed. R. R. Bolgar (Cambridge, Eng., 1974), 191–97; Hugo Friedrich, *Montaigne*, trans. Dawn Eng (Berkeley, 1991), 25–26, 57, 66, 220–21, 355–60. On the epistolary pedigree of the *Essais*, see Fumaroli, "Genèse de l'épistolographie classique," who claims that "La rhétorique des *Essais* est toute erasmienne" (893 n. 25); Barry Weller, "The Rhetoric of Friendship in Montaigne's *Essais*," *New Literary History* 93

silent on the debt of his *Essais* to his humanist predecessors, even if he does boldly advertise its epistolary pedigree. As we might expect, this advertisement is heard most audibly in the essay entitled "A consideration upon Cicero" (I.40).[2]

(1978): 519; Jules Brody, "La première réception des *Essais* de Montaigne: Fortunes d'une forme," in *Automne de la Renaissance, 1580–1630*, ed. Jean Lafond and André Stegmann (Paris, 1981), 23–24, who makes the case that Montaigne's first readers considered his controversial literary production "un modèle de style epistolaire" (23) and a "version vernaculaire de la lettre humaniste" (24). Following Pierre Villey (*Les sources et l'évolution des "Essais" de Montaigne*, 2 vols. [Paris, 1908], 1: 189–90), on the other hand, Friedrich concludes that although the *Essais* represent "a final release of Petrarchan striving," Montaigne "probably only knew Petrarch's Italian works" (25). But Montaigne, on his own account, owned a hundred different volumes of letters printed in Italy (I.40), and so there is some likelihood that Petrarch's, first printed in Venice in 1492, was among them.

As a writer of essays Francis Bacon confirms the origin of this literary form in the letter (*Selected Writings of Francis Bacon* [New York, 1955], 6): "To write just treatises requireth leisure in the writer, and leisure in the reader ... which is the cause that hath made me choose to write certain brief notes, set down rather significantly than curiously, which I have called *Essays*. The word is late, but the thing is ancient. For Seneca's epistles to Lucilius, if one mark them well, are but *Essays*, that is dispersed meditations, though conveyed in the form of epistles."

2. According to Villey, *Les sources et l'évolution des "Essais" de Montaigne* (1: 125–26), although it is impossible to identify with certainty Montaigne's borrowings from Erasmus, and especially from the *Adages, Praise of Folly*, and *Colloquies*, since these works were so widely diffused, "il est probable que Montaigne avait presque toutes les oeuvres morales d'Erasme" (126). Montaigne actually mentions Erasmus only once in the *Essais* (III.2), where he admits that "it would have been hard for me not to take for adages and apophthegms everything he said to his valet and his hostess" (*The Complete Essays of Montaigne*, trans. Donald M. Frame [Stanford, Cal., 1965], 615). All translations of the *Essais* are from this edition and will be referred to in the text by page number in parenthesis. For the French edition I have used *Les Essais de Michel de Montaigne*, ed. Pierre Villey and V.-L. Saulnier, 2 vols. (Paris, 1978), also referred to parenthetically by page number in the text. According to Villey, *Les sources et l'évolution des Essais de Montaigne* (1: 189–90), there are in the *Essais* five quotations from Petrarch's Italian works, and in the essay "Of books" (II.10) Montaigne contrasts the restraint of the ancient poets to "Petrarchan flights" (Frame 299). It is also possible that on two occasions (II.10, Villey 1: 411; II.31, Villey 1: 716) Montaigne's reference to Cicero as "le pere de l'eloquence romaine"—the father of

Turning the reader's attention in this essay to the same two epistolary writers that Erasmus in *De conscribendis epistolis* considered the best antiquity had to offer, Montaigne, without mentioning the Dutchman or his singularly popular manual, overturns the Erasmian verdict. Cicero and Pliny deserve scorn rather than commendation for aspiring to "derive some great glory from mere babble and talk, to the point of publishing their private letters written to their friends" (Frame 183). Such writing, Montaigne concludes, is motivated by vanity—a motivation under constant scrutiny in the *Essais*. On the other hand, Montaigne admires the letters of Epicurus and Seneca, written, in contrast, to remedy the vanity of others. Their letters are not "empty and fleshless" but "stuffed full of fine arguments of wisdom, by which a man becomes not more eloquent but wiser" (Frame 185).

In the same essay, Montaigne assesses his own letter writing, informing his reader of not only his natural aptitude for epistolary composition but also his preference for writing familiar rather than dictaminal letters, which, in turn, he prefers to write in his own hand and to begin rather than finish (Frame 186–87). Montaigne's method for composing letters, moreover, resembles his method for composing essays in that as a letter writer he is "prone to begin without a plan (*sans project*); the first remark brings on the second" (Frame 186; Villey 1: 253).³ In keeping with this resemblance,

---

Roman eloquence—and "pere d'eloquence" echoes the Erasmian description in the introduction to his *De copia*, itself a possible echo of Petrarch's second letter to Cicero (*Fam.* 24.4). See chap. 3, n. 8.

It is an assumption of the argument that follows that Montaigne would have known both these writings and others of Petrarch and Erasmus even though he nowhere mentions them explicitly. In fact, Montaigne goes out of his way to keep silent on his more recent literary models, emphasizing instead the uniqueness of his literary undertaking. In "Of practice" (II.6) Montaigne acknowledges only ancient predecessors, whose works, if not their names, have been lost, while "[n]o one since has followed their lead" (Frame 273); and in the opening of "Of the affection of fathers for their children" (II.8), Montaigne characterizes his *Essais* as "the only book in the world of its kind" (Frame 278). "On some verses of Virgil" (III.5), on the other hand, offers an explanation: "When I write, I prefer to do so without the company and remembrance of books, for fear they may interfere with my style. Also because, in truth, the good authors humble and dishearten me too much" (Frame 666).

3. For Montaigne on this aleatory feature of his composition, see, for instance, "Of repentance" (III.2), where he claims that "[m]usical fancies are guided by art, mine by chance" (Frame 611), or the conclusion of "Of prompt or slow speech" (I.10), where Montaigne adds in 1588 regarding the "chance encounters" that "control" his

Montaigne even admits that he would have written letters rather than essays if he had had, as in the past, a fitting correspondent, some intimate friend to write to (Frame 185–86). Here as elsewhere, Montaigne's allusion to Etienne de la Boétie reinforces the alliance between the essay and the familiar letter on the grounds of their shared investment in friendship.[4]

Throughout the *Essais,* Montaigne returns to the two related topics of friendship and La Boétie, but in the essay entitled "Of friendship" (I.28), Montaigne showcases this relation. Even while insisting on the singularity, the uniqueness, of the mutual attachment between himself and his special friend, Montaigne rehearses the ancient ideals of friendship expressed, as we have seen in the opening chapter, in the writing of Aristotle, Cicero, and Seneca. Like them, Montaigne imagines a friendship nourished by communication, equality, intimacy (here *privauté*), and honest rebuke (Frame 136; Villey 1: 185). On these grounds, he discounts the possibility of friendship between parents and their children. Rarely experienced, such friendship, he reminds his reader, binds one man to another man—although never to a woman, who "by the common agreement of the ancient schools is excluded from [such friendship]" (Frame 138).[5] Like Petrarch, then, Montaigne both

---

essays, "If I erased every passage where this happens to me, there would be nothing left of myself" (Frame 27). Similarly in "Of Democritus and Heraclitus" (I.50), Montaigne claims to "take the first subject that chance offers.... Scattering a word here, there another, samples separated from their context, dispersed, without a plan and without a promise" (Frame 219). Not incidental to the assumption underlying this study of the complementarity of rhetoric and hermeneutics, Montaigne claims not only to write without a plan but to read without one: "sans ordre et sans dessein, à pieces descousues" (III.3; Frame 629; Villey 2: 828). See also Terence Cave, "Le récit montaignien: un voyage sans repentir," in *Pré-histoires: Textes troublés au seuil de la modernité* (Geneva, 1999), 164–76.

4. On the essay as a substitute letter, see Struever, "Montaigne's Ciceronian Pessimism," 52. For the role of friendship in Montaigne's *Essais,* see Weller, "Rhetoric of Friendship in Montaigne's *Essais,*" and Richard Scholar, *Montaigne and the Art of Free-Thinking* (Oxford, 2010), 135–58. For Montaigne's friendship with La Boétie, see Donald M. Frame, *Montaigne: A Biography* (London, 1965), 63–84.

5. On the maleness of this tradition, see Aristotle's discussion of friendship between worthy men in the *Rhetoric* (1.5.16), which Kennedy in his edition notes as "one of the rare specifications of maleness" in this text (61 n. 108). On Montaigne's later rethinking of this position, see II.17, Frame 502, and Scholar, *Montaigne and the Art of Free-Thinking,* 152–53. On this essay and the role of friendship in the early modern understanding of selfhood, see Terence Cave, "Fragments of a Future

celebrates his friendships and casts his lot with the ancients rather than the moderns, who, in any case, as he claims in the later essay "Of presumption" (II.17), pay little or no attention to what true friendship requires—what Montaigne calls *la culture de l'âme* (Frame 500; Villey 1: 658), echoing the Senecan *cura animi*. Of course, Montaigne exempts La Boétie from this criticism, judging him a "soul of the old stamp" (Frame 500).

In this later essay (II.17), Montaigne also returns to a favorite point pressed in earlier essays, including "A consideration upon Cicero," regarding the competition between words and deeds. Eventually finding in favor of the words that underwrite his rhetoric of intimacy, Montaigne begins with a defense of action. If Epicurus and Seneca, as we have seen, surpass Cicero and Pliny in their manner of letter writing, then Xenophon and Caesar are to be admired even more than these for seeking recognition on the basis not of what they wrote but of what they did. "If the deeds of Xenophon and Caesar had not far surpassed their eloquence," Montaigne insists, "I do not believe they would have written them down. They sought to recommend not their sayings but their doings" (Frame 183).[6]

In "Of practice" (II.6), Montaigne reverses this judgment on "sayings" and "doings," invoking first Cicero and then himself as illustrations of this reversal. Just as Cicero, not unlike Socrates before him and the saints after him, focused attention on himself, so Montaigne, defying those critics who call for him to "testify about myself by works and deeds (*ouvrages et effects*) not by bare words" (Frame 274; Villey 1: 379), follows Cicero's—and Socrates'—lead. In response to such criticism, Montaigne further proclaims that his *cogitations* not only cannot be captured in action but are almost too elusive for words:

> What I chiefly portray is my cogitations, a shapeless subject (*subject informe*) that does not lend itself to expression in actions (*en production ouvragere*). It is all I can do to couch my thoughts in this airy medium of words. Some of the wisest and most devout men have lived avoiding all noticeable actions (*effects*). My actions would tell more about fortune than

---

Self: From Pascal to Montaigne," in *Retrospectives: Essays in Literature, Poetics, and Cultural History*, ed. Neil Kenny and Wes Williams (London, 2009), 130–45. And see François Rigolot, "Friendship and Voluntary Servitude: Plato, Ficino and Montaigne," *Texas Studies in Literature and Language* 47 (2005): 326–44.

6. Compare "Of anger" (II.31), where Montaigne insists that "[s]aying is one thing and doing is another" (Frame 541). For Seneca on this same theme, see epp. 20.2, 16.3, 108.38.

about me.... It is not my deeds (*mes gestes*) that I write down; it is myself, it is my essence (*c'est moy, c'est mon essence*). (Frame 274; Villey 1: 379)[7]

The essential (as opposed to the accidental or fortuitous) Montaigne is the "thinking" or "cogitating" Montaigne; and the readers who would get to know him, he reiterates in "Of presumption," must do so through what he has said—and said about himself in writing—rather than through what he has done:

> Those whom Fortune (whether we should call her good or bad) has caused to spend their lives in some eminent station, can testify to what they are by their public actions. But those whom she has employed only in a mass, and of whom no one will speak unless they do so themselves, may be excused if they have the temerity to speak of themselves to those who have an interest in knowing them. (Frame 479)

Later in the same essay, Montaigne announces yet again this claim regarding his writerly intention: "But whatever I make myself known to be, provided I make myself known such as I am, I am carrying out my plan (*mon effect*)" (Frame 495; Villey 1: 653). The plan of Montaigne's essays in frankly disclosing his thoughts and feelings is to make himself known to his readers.[8] As far back as Cicero, as we have seen, this same aim has motivated the familiar letter writer, whose writing Cicero himself has described as *writing intimately* or *familiariter.*

Intimate writing, including essay writing, then, is identified with letter writing. In the tradition traced in these chapters, as we have seen, intimacy finds its fullest treatment as a feature of epistolary style; and Montaigne's frequent discussions of his own style confirm this identification.[9] In "A consid-

---

7. In "Of vanity" (III.9), Montaigne makes two comparable claims: that he "cannot keep a record of my life by my actions; fortune places them too low. I keep it by my thoughts (*mes fantaisies*)" (Frame 721; Villey 2: 945–46); and that he produces *essais* because he cannot produce *effaicts* (Frame 759; Villey 2: 992). See also III.5, Frame 643, where Montaigne confesses that he is "hungry to make myself known."

8. On Montaigne's express aim to make himself known, consider his claim in "Of the art of discussion" (III.8) that he takes "such great pleasure in being judged and known" (Frame 705) and in "Of vanity" (III.9) that he "would willingly come back from the other world to give the lie to any man who portrayed me other than I was, even if it were to honor me" (Frame 751).

9. On the earliest reception of the *Essais* as a reaction to style, see Brody, "La première réception des *Essais* de Montaigne," esp. 19–25. For a fuller discussion of

eration upon Cicero," for instance, Montaigne aligns his style with Seneca's and Erasmus's epistolary styles by describing it as "too compact, disorderly, abrupt, individual" (*trop serré, desordonné, couppé, particulier*) (Frame 186; Villey 1: 252)—a description that echoes a comparable list of adjectives in an earlier essay (I.26), including "sinewy," "brief," "compressed," "vehement," "brusque," "irregular," "disconnected," "bold," and "soldierly" (Frame 127).[10] But when in the same essay (I.40) Montaigne describes his style as "humorous and familiar" (Frame 186)—*comique et privé* (Villey 1: 252)—he invokes his affiliation not with Seneca and Erasmus but with the epistolary Cicero, who in his frequently cited letter to Curio (*Ad fam.* 2.4.1), discussed in chapter 1, approves of the letter that is *familiare et iocosum*.[11] The other

---

Montaigne's style, see Margaret M. McGowan, *Montaigne's Deceits: The Art of Persuasion in the "Essais"* (Philadelphia, 1974), esp. chap. 2, "Consciousness of Style," and Friedrich, *Montaigne*, 365–76.

10. On the Erasmian pedigree of this list, see ep. 1885, Allen 7: 194; M. Mann Phillips, "From the *Ciceronianus* to Montaigne"; and Defaux, "From Erasmus to Montaigne (and Beyond)," 37–38. On the Senecanism of this pedigree see ep. 114.22 and Brody, "La première réception des *Essais* de Montaigne," 23–24. On the list of adjectives that includes *nerveux, court, serré, vehement, brusque desreglé, descousu, hardy*, and *soldatesque*, see Villey 1: 171–72. Compare I.20 (Frame 56), where Montaigne uses a very similar list to describe the pleasure identical with virtue of which he approves, and II.17 (Frame 484), where he applies a number of them to "a Gascon dialect" equally worthy of approval. On the enormous influence of Seneca, Friedrich writes that "Montaigne began reading the Roman ethicist at about the same time as he began writing out the first essay. Books I and II are filled with borrowings from him. His influence has receded somewhat in the third book only to increase again after 1588" (60). On Seneca's influence, and especially that of the Letters to Lucilius, see also Villey, *Les sources et l'évolution des Essais de Montaigne*, 1: 214–17.

11. In "Genèse de l'épistolographie classique" (893 n. 25), Fumaroli notes this pair of stylistic qualities but associates it with Erasmus rather than Cicero. For *comique*, Villey offers *familier* (*Les sources et l'évolution des Essais de Montaigne*, 1: 254), while Maurice Rat (*Essais*, 3 vols. [Paris, 1958]) glosses the pair as "naturel et familier" (1: 284). John Florio translates it as "comical and familiar" (*The Essays of Montaigne*, ed. George Saintsbury, 3 vols. [London, 1893], 1: 271). On *privauté* as an occasional substitute for *familiarité*, see, for instance, "Three kinds of association" (III.3; Frame 625; Villey 2: 824) and "Of the art of discussion": "May we not include under the title of discourse and communication the sharp, abrupt repartee which good spirits and familiarity (*privauté*) introduce among friends, bantering and joking wittily and keenly with one another?" (III.8; Frame 717; Villey 2: 938). And see I.28, Frame 136,

kind of epistolary style earning Cicero's approval, as we have seen in the letter to Curio, is *severum et grave,* the same two adjectives—*severe* and *grave*—that Montaigne uses to identify *his* style in "Of presumption," an essay pointedly if unpredictably about style.

Beginning with the assumption that *form* is at once distinguishable from *content* and allied with *style,* Montaigne admits in the 1595 edition of this essay that although he does not "love a solemn and gloomy wisdom" (Frame 483), he practices a style that "prefers grave and austere matters" (*qui les veut plustot graves et severes*), provided the term *stile* is applicable to "a formless... way of talking" (*un parler informe*) (Villey 1: 637).[12] To position himself with regard to the essay's eponymous vice, moreover, Montaigne states his preference for Plutarch's style over Seneca's, even though, on his own account, his style more closely resembles Seneca's. "And if my inclination leads me more to imitate Seneca's style (*du parler de Seneque*)," he admits, "I nonetheless esteem Plutarch's more" (Frame 484; Villey 1: 638). Far from

---

discussed above, p. 99. In "The Style of Montaigne: Word-Pairs and Word-Groups," *Literary Style: A Symposium,* ed. Seymour Chatman (London, 1971), 383–405, esp. 384, R. A. Sayce identifies the doubling of words as Montaigne's signature technique and *domestique et privée* in the preface as the first instance. On the near synonymy of *domesticum* and *familiare* see above, chap. 3, p. 87. On the philosophers as the source of Montaigne's comic style, see Alison Calhoun, "Montaigne and the Comic: Exposing Private Life" (forthcoming in *Literature and Philosophy*).

12. Although Montaigne routinely uses the term *stile,* like Petrarch's and Erasmus's *stilus,* he also on occasion refers to what Frame and even John Florio call "style" as his *forme* or *façon.* On *forme* and *façon* as terms closely related to *stile,* see, in addition to the introduction (pp. 7–8), Montaigne's preface "Au lecteur," where he refers to both his *façon simple* and his *forme naïve* when defending his style. The preface affirms the epistolary pedigree of the *Essais,* moreover, by stressing its address to Montaigne's *familiares,* a record of his *conditions et humeurs,* so that these *parents et amis* can preserve their *conaissance* of him (Frame 2; Villey 1: 3). Indeed, even the metaphor of the portrait, the analogue in the visual arts to the letter in the literary arts, confirms the epistolary dimension of the project. On the notion that "Qui fait une lettre, fait son portrait" (quoted from P. Hercule in *Lettres à Philandre* [1637–1638]), see B. Beugnot, "Style ou styles épistolaires," *Revue d'histoire littéraire de la France* 6 (1978): 946. On *forme* as style, see also I.40, Frame 186, Villey 1: 252, where Montaigne's style is characterized as *une forme mienne*. In *Montaigne Philosophe* (Paris, 1996), Ian Maclean credits Montaigne's use of *forme* with "une precision et une abstraction toutes scolastiques" (37). On *façon* as *façon de dire* and *façon d'escrire,* see I.10, Frame 299, 301, and Villey 1: 411, 413.

presumptuous, it turns out, Montaigne actually suffers from the unnamed opposing vice—that of undervaluing what is his. For Montaigne bases his higher estimation of Plutarch's style on no other criterion than its dissimilarity or difference from his own. Either way, however, style is granted a value that is predicated on ownership—on the condition that it belongs to some one individual and to no one else.

If here as elsewhere in the *Essais* Montaigne foregrounds the question of style, in other words, here in particular he does so in a way that sets in high relief the legal, and in this sense, proprietary dimension of style discussed in previous chapters. For Montaigne diagnoses the vicious but unnamed opposite of presumption in terms of property law, as the inclination to "lower the value of the things I possess, because I possess them, and raise the value of things when they are foreign, absent, and not mine" (*je diminue du juste prix les choses que je possede, de ce que je les possede; et hausse le prix aux choses, d'autant qu'elles sont estrangieres, absentes et non miennes*) (Frame 480; Villey 1: 633–34). And Montaigne acknowledges his own susceptibility to this vice as it impacts not only his style but his other possessions as well, including his most basic possessions.[13]

13. According to Frame (*Montaigne: A Biography*), although there is no record of Montaigne's activities between the ages of thirteen and twenty-one or twenty-two, "his likeliest occupation for at least part of this period is still the study of law" (42–43), probably, Frame speculates, at Toulouse (45). In light of Montaigne's long career as magistrate, on the other hand, Frame notes his sparing use of legal language: "To be sure, Montaigne sprinkles through his book such terms as 'mortgaging' his will, his work, or the freedom of his soul, 'gains ceasing and . . . damages ensuing,' and begins several paragraphs of one chapter with the legal term 'Item.' But considering his long exposure to such terms, they leave few traces in his style, which he sought to make 'not lawyer-like, but rather soldierly'" (58). In "The Style of Montaigne," Sayce identifies the stylistic feature of doubling with "the language of law and administration" and attributes it to Montaigne's "legal training, which otherwise has left few traces in his style" (384). It is in part the aim of this chapter, in spite of Frame's and Sayce's assessment, to demonstrate Montaigne's alertness to and exploitation of the deeper connections between the legal, affective, and stylistic dimensions of intimacy. Indeed, Montaigne himself puts us on the lookout for the transfer of terms from one context to another: "In our language I find plenty of stuff but a little lack of fashioning. For there is nothing that might not be done with our jargon of hunting and war, which is a generous soil to borrow from. And forms of speech, like plants, improve and grow stronger by being transplanted" (III.5; Frame 665). On Montaigne's use of the art of jurisprudence, see Maclean, *Montaigne Philosophe*, 38–48; and see

For Aristotle, following Hesiod, as we have seen in chapter 1 (p. 15), these basic possessions are my house, my wife, and my ox, which not only belong to me but constitute where I belong, identifying me affectively as well as legally. Attuned to this mode of identification throughout the *Essais,* Montaigne here preserves the primacy of his house, transforms the Hesiodic ox into a horse, and, for the time being, leaves his wife out of an accounting of his belongings:

> The housekeeping, the house, the horse of my neighbor, if equal in value, seem better than my own, because they are not mine. (Frame 480)

> (L'OEconomie, la maison, le cheval de mon voisin, en esgale valeur, vault mieux que le mien, de ce qu'il n'est pas mien.) (Villey 1: 634)

Taking ownership as its point of departure, this essay presents a Montaigne challenged to value appropriately what is his own, including—even featuring—his own style.

In *De officiis,* as we have seen, Cicero uses the language of ownership—what is *proprium* and what is *suum*—alongside the stylistic concept of *decorum* to encourage his son Marcus to develop himself as distinct from anyone else (1.31.111–13). Returning to this Ciceronian passage in the 1595 edition, even quoting it in bits and pieces on three occasions, Montaigne identifies the soul or self as one's most valuable possession—what is most one's own.[14] As we have seen in the first chapter, Seneca presses a similar point with Lucilius in similar language when he insists that each man's soul or *animus* is what is most his own or *proprius* (ep. 41.7–8). In "Of vanity" (III.9)—an essay to which I will return in more detail—Montaigne echoes this Senecan insistence, first personalizing and then qualifying it. In keeping with his inclination to self-undervaluation, Montaigne asserts that "I have nothing of my own but myself and even there my possession is partly

---

Sue W. Farquhar, "Montaigne and the Law: 'De l'experience,'" *Montaigne Studies* 14 (2002): 37–48.

14. Montaigne quotes the Ciceronian passage in "Of presumption" (II.17; Frame 499; Villey 1: 658), "Of the useful and the honourable" (III.1; Frame 604; Villey 2: 795), and "Of vanity" (III.9; Frame 756; Villey 2: 989). On Montaigne's renewed interest in Cicero more generally and in *De officiis* in particular, see Villey, *Les sources et l'évolution des Essais de Montaigne,* 1: 98–104, esp. 101. On the various editions of the *Essais,* see David Maskell, "The Evolution of the *Essais,*" in *Montaigne: Essays in Memory of Richard Sayce,* ed. I. D. McFarlane and Ian Maclean (Oxford, 1982), 13–34.

defective and borrowed" (*Je n'ay rien mien que moy et si en est la possession en partie manque et empruntée*) (Frame 740; Villey 2: 968). Turning his attention from a rhetoric of intimacy to its corresponding hermeneutics, as we will see, Montaigne revisits not only the key question of style but both the legal language of *proprium* and *suum* and the distinction between what is borrowed and what is one's own.

Whereas "A consideration upon Cicero," discussed earlier, situates the essay in an epistolary context, "Of the art of discussion" (III.8), in keeping with traditional expectations, turns from *epistola* to *sermo*. In *De officiis*, Cicero both aligned *sermo* with *familiaritas* and laid down some rules of engagement. So does Montaigne, even rehearsing some of the same rules. For Montaigne advocates speaking freely—even rudely—in the interest of having the words of the interlocutors track their thoughts (Frame 705). Quoting Cicero on the inevitability of disagreement in discussion (*De finibus* 1.8), Montaigne encourages his companions in conversation to be quarrelsome rather than polite; and echoing the adjectives used elsewhere to describe his written style, he opts for an intimacy in conversation that is "strong" and "manly" (Frame 705)—*une familiarité forte et virile* (Villey 2: 924).[15] Comparing such exchanges to the bites and scratches of a vigorous lovemaking, Montaigne relishes the affective dimension of rhetorical intimacy—without overlooking the legal.

Many conversationalists, Montaigne cautions in this same essay, merely borrow their very best points. They do not possess them. Their arguments are not their own (Frame 715). And if this lack of ownership complicates the interlocutor's task in conversing, it also compromises the reader's ability to understand and assess what he reads.[16] To drive home this hermeneutic complication, Montaigne recounts his experience reading Philippe de Commines, one of whose remarks regarding the benefits of servants to their masters earned Montaigne's admiration until he discovered it in Tacitus. In light of this discovery, Montaigne issues a *caveat lector* that stands as a warning to his own readers:

15. For these same two stylistic qualities approved by Seneca, see ep. 114.15, 22.

16. On reading rather than conversing as the focus of this essay, see Weller, "Rhetoric of Friendship in Montaigne's *Essais*," 511–12. On Montaigne on reading more generally, see Cathleen M. Bauschatz, "Montaigne's Conception of Reading in the Context of Renaissance Poetics and Modern Criticism," in *The Reader in the Text: Essays on Audience and Interpretation*, ed. Susan R. Suleiman and Inge Crosman (Princeton, 1980), 264–91, and Terence Cave, "Problems of Reading in the *Essais*," in McFarlane and Maclean, *Montaigne: Essays in Memory of Richard Sayce*, 133–66.

The subject, according to what it is, may give a man a reputation for learning and a good memory; but in order to judge the qualities that are most his own (*les parties plus siennes*) and most worthy, the strength and beauty of his mind (*la force et beauté de son ame*), we must know what is his and what is not (*ce qui est sien et ce qui ne l'est point*); and in what is not his (*ce qui n'est pas sien*), how much is due him in consideration of the choice, arrangement, embellishment, and style (*en consideration du chois, disposition, ornement et langage*) that he has supplied. What if he has borrowed the matter and made the form (*la forme*) worse, as often happens? We who have little contact with books are in this strait, that when we see some fine piece of inventiveness in a new poet, some strong argument in a preacher, we dare not praise them for it until we have found out from some learned man whether this element is their own or someone else's (*si cette piece leur est propre ou si elle est estrangere*). Until then I always stand on my guard. (Frame 718; Villey 2: 940)

Like Petrarch, who called in his *Familiares* for a style at once *proprium* and *suum*, Montaigne both fastens on the question of style—here referred to as *forme* and divided into the elements of *disposition, ornement*, and *langage*— and distinguishes between what is *propre* and *sien* and what is not, what is *estrangere* (Petrarch's *alienum*).[17] Where style is concerned, in other words, what matters most to the reader is judging what belongs to a writer and what does not.

Addressing the challenges of reading a favorite French historian in his essay about conversation, Montaigne shifts the focus of attention from rhetoric to hermeneutics.[18] On this occasion, he claims to read with no other

---

17. In *The Cornucopian Text* (306–7), Cave highlights both the opposition between "what belongs to an individual (is proper or natural to him) and what is alien" and the further distinction of what is borrowed, but he does not discuss the legal dimensions of these concepts.

18. On Montaigne as a reader, see Friedrich, *Montaigne*, 42–44, who suggests in passing both that Montaigne seeks in books "above all the author who wrote them" and that the model for this reading is Erasmus: "This turning of one's eye from the work to the individual radiating forth from the work can be found even in Erasmus. It is conceivable that this recurs to an intensified degree in Montaigne" (44). See, in addition, Terence Cave, "Representations of Reading in the Renaissance," in Kenny and Williams, *Retrospectives*, 10–19, and "Problems of Reading in the *Essais*," 133–66, who maintains not only that the *Essais* is "a reassessment of the whole activity of reading" but that "the coherence of an individual's reading materials lies ultimately in their application to his own character and circumstances, rather than to those of

agenda than understanding what belongs to the writer. In keeping with the contrariety and contradictoriness flaunted throughout the *Essais,* however, Montaigne does not always claim to follow this reading practice. On another occasion (II.17; Frame 494), for instance, he admits to merely leafing through books rather than studying them and to remembering only the bits and pieces of subject matter that attract his attention while forgetting altogether the other details, including the author.

On most occasions, however, Montaigne both claims for himself and advocates for others the models of deeper reading applauded by Seneca and discussed in previous chapters.[19] As part of his program of education for the young, Montaigne recommends that they learn to read like consumers who slowly and fully digest their food instead of gobbling it down only to regurgitate it later; for "[t]he stomach has not done its work if it has not changed the condition and form of what has been given it to cook" (I.26; Frame 111). Elsewhere Montaigne couples the hasty consumer with the foolish householder as figures of superficial reading. Whereas the one fails to realize any lasting benefit from his neighbor's fire because after warming himself by it he neglects to carry some of it back home, the other fails to make himself bigger and stronger by eating because his belly is full of undigested meat

---

the defunct author. No doubt he will attempt to judge other writers through and in their works ... but the appropriation and digestion of all these materials for his own benefit remains his primary aim" (163). On Montaigne on reading, including the role of digestion, see also Bauschatz, "Montaigne's Conception of Reading in the Context of Renaissance Poetics and Modern Criticism," and Carol E. Clark, "Seneca's Letters to Lucilius as a Source of Some of Montaigne's Imagery," *Bibliothèque d'humanisme et Renaissance* 30 (1968): 249–66. Both Clark (250) and Bauschatz (275) mention in passing the relationship between reader and writer as one of friendship. For a fuller discussion, see Scholar, *Montaigne and the Art of Free-Thinking,* 154–58.

On the different reading practices of two of the earliest readers of Montaigne, Marie de Gournay and Estienne Pasquier, see Frame, *Montaigne: A Biography,* 310–11. While Gournay as Montaigne's protégé reads to know the writer better, Pasquier finds excuses for Montaigne's tendency to talk about himself and appreciates the *Essais* instead as "a real seed-bed of fine and notable sayings" and "a sort of diversified prairie of many flowers, pell-mell and without art" (311, quoting Pasquier, *Lettres,* 18.1, in *Choix de lettres sur la littérature,* ed. Dorothy Thickett [Geneva, 1956], 46–47). On the range of early modern reading practices, see above, introduction, n. 7.

19. On the influence of Seneca's second letter to Lucilius on Montaigne's theory of reading, see Clark, "Seneca's Letters to Lucilius as a Source of Some of Montaigne's Imagery," 255–56.

(I.25; Frame 101). Far too many schoolmasters, Montaigne laments, expect their students to remember from their reading of Plutarch the date of the destruction of Carthage without worrying about whether or not they have begun to understand Hannibal's or Scipio's character (I.26; Frame 115), even though it is this understanding of character, identified with epistolary writing as far back as Cicero, Demetrius, and Seneca, that motivates the kind of reading that Montaigne holds in the highest regard.[20]

In pursuit of this particular kind of understanding, Montaigne considers style—here again *la forme*—every bit as important as content, *la substance*. For only a style that is really owned can reveal the soul as one's most valuable possession. So Montaigne, taking more interest in the advocate himself than in the case he pleads, insists in defense of his hermeneutics that "every day I amuse myself reading authors without any care for their learning, looking for their style (*leur façon*), not their subject (*leur subject*). Just as I seek the company of some famous mind, not to have him teach me, but to come to know him" (Frame 708; Villey 2: 928).[21] As we have seen in chapter 1, Seneca rejects the Ciceronian oratorical aim of pleasing an audience for the epistolary aim of communicating the sources of his own feelings of pleasure. In keeping with this rejection, Montaigne replaces the audience's expectation of being taught, the first of the three Ciceronian oratorical offices, with that associated with reading letters: getting to know the thoughts and feelings of the writer.

From the earliest to the latest essays, Montaigne champions this hermeneutics of intimacy, claiming to read his favorite authors, including Seneca and Plutarch, for the kind of understanding associated with the closest friendships. "Plutarch's writings, if we savor them aright," Montaigne explains in "Of anger" (II.31), "reveal him to us well enough, and I think I know him even into his soul" (Frame 541).[22] Montaigne then opens the

---

20. So Montaigne considers himself a deeper reader of Livy than some others but not as deep as Plutarch (I.26; Frame 115). On Montaigne's reading habits, see also Peter Mack, *Reading and Rhetoric in Montaigne and Shakespeare* (London, 2010), 21–41.

21. For Montaigne's preference for biography on similar grounds, see "Of books" (II.10): "they spend more time on plans than on events, more on what comes from within than on what happens without.... That is why in every way Plutarch is my man. I am very sorry that we do not have a dozen Laertiuses, or that he is not either more receptive or more perceptive. For I consider no less curiously the fortunes and the lives of these great teachers of the world than the diversity of their doctrines and fancies" (Frame 303). On *façon* as style, see above, p. 103.

22. If Seneca is the source for Montaigne's contention that the soul is our most valuable possession (see chap. 1), he may also be the source for the insight already

next essay, "Defense of Seneca and Plutarch" (II.32), by identifying this deep understanding as *familiarité* (Frame 545; Villey 1: 721). But these are not the only authors worthy of being read *familiariter* (to return to Cicero's term). Quick to dismiss Cicero's letters in an earlier essay as wordy and vain (I.40), as we have seen, Montaigne eventually revises this blanket dismissal and admits to taking pleasure in the *Letters to Atticus*

> not only because they contain a very ample education in the history and affairs of his time, but much more because in them I discover [Cicero's] personal humors (*ses humeurs privées*). For I have a singular curiosity, as I have said elsewhere, to know the soul and the natural judgments of my authors. (II.10; Frame 302; Villey 1: 414–15)

Whereas others may read these letters for the information they provide, Montaigne stresses that he reads them, according to his usual practice, to understand the author as intimately as possible.[23] And luckily Montaigne is not alone among his contemporaries in this reading practice.

For Montaigne attributes the success of Jacques Amyot's translation of Plutarch, a work that figures prominently in the *Essais,* to the translator's intimate understanding of his ancient author.[24] Reading Amyot's Plu-

---

proverbial by Seneca's time (ep. 114.1–2) that style reveals the soul (*talis hominibus fuit oratio qualis vita*)—an insight, according to Cicero (*Tusc.* 5.47), that goes back to Socrates and that gives point to Socrates' practice, mentioned in *Essais* I.26 (Frame 110), of encouraging his students to speak before he spoke to them. See above, p. 79. On Montaigne's reading of Plutarch, see Friedrich, *Montaigne,* 71–72; Isabelle Konstantinovic, *Montaigne et Plutarque, Travaux d'humanisme et Renaissance* CCXXXI (Geneva, 1989); and Alison Calhoun, "Montaigne's Two Plutarchs," *Montaigne Studies* 21 (2009): 103–14, who argues on the basis of the Ciceronian element of *conferre* in *conférer* that "for Montaigne there was little differentiation between comparing the philosophers and getting to know them as he might a friend" (113). For Montaigne on the nature of the soul, see Carol E. Clark, "Talking about Souls: Montaigne on Human Psychology" in McFarlane and Maclean, *Montaigne: Essays in memory of Richard Sayce,* 57–76.

23. On Cicero's other letter collection, see "Of the greatness of Rome" (II.24; Frame 519), where Montaigne disputes the appropriateness of the French title *Epîtres familières* while accepting on Suetonius's authority the designation *ad familiares.* On the origin of the Ciceronian title, see chap. 2, p. 71.

24. For Montaigne's use of Amyot's translation, see Villey, *Les sources et l'évolution des Essais de Montaigne,* 2: 106–33. Like style in general, Amyot's style is at its best

tarch, Montaigne finds himself appreciating "a sense so beautiful, coherent, and sustained, that either [Amyot] has clearly understood the real thought (*l'imagination*) of the author, or at least, having by long acquaintance (*conversation*) implanted vividly in his own soul (*son ame*) a general idea of Plutarch's soul, he has attributed to him nothing that belies or contradicts him" (II.4; Frame 262; Villey 1: 363). Whereas Cicero and Seneca, as we have seen, figure letter reading (along with letter writing) as a substitute *sermo* occasioned by physical distance, Montaigne imagines the experience of a contemporary translator reading an ancient author who wrote not letters but essays as having all the intimacy and intensity of just such a *conversation*.

Like Petrarch and Erasmus before him, in other words, Montaigne extends the epistolary model of reading to reading more generally—and not only to a more general reading of the ancients. For Montaigne, like Petrarch, makes it unambiguously clear that he himself expects to be read in this way, at least by those who really want to understand him. So in the essay entitled "Of vanity" (III.9), Montaigne echoes the Petrarchan insistence that the reader should either pay the closest attention to what he reads or put off his reading altogether. Also like Petrarch, Montaigne invokes Seneca as the authority on how to read. Unlike Petrarch, however, Montaigne, here as elsewhere in the *Essais*, offers himself as an example to be taken in reverse:[25]

> Who is there that would not rather not be read than be read sleepily or in passing? *Nothing is so useful that it can be of value when taken on the run* [Seneca]. If to take up books were to take them in, and if to see them were to consider them, and to run through them were to grasp them, I should be wrong to make myself out quite as ignorant as I say I am. (Frame 761)

Identifying himself here with a reading practice he clearly discredits, Montaigne holds out hope that some unknown reader willing to spend several days—not just minutes or even hours—with his record of himself may

---

when it is *plus chez soy* (II.4; Frame 262; Villey 1: 364). See Cave, "Problems of Reading in the *Essais*," 138–39.

25. For other instances of Montaigne's presenting himself as a negative example, see "Of the art of discussion" (III.8), where he asserts that "the good that worthy men do the public by making themselves imitable, I shall perhaps do by making myself evitable" (Frame 703); and see "Of experience" (III.13): "In fine, all this fricassee that I am scribbling here is nothing but a record of the essays of my life, which, for spiritual health, is exemplary enough if you take its instruction in reverse" (Frame 826).

become a friend by virtue of the intimacy or *familiarité* afforded through reading.²⁶ This same intimacy, he insists, would require from an actual acquaintance long years of living together:

> Besides this profit that I derive from writing about myself, I hope for this other advantage, that if my humors (*mes humeurs*) happen to please and suit some worthy man (*honneste homme*) before I die, he will try to meet me. I give him a big advantage in ground covered; for all that long acquaintance (*connoissance*) and familiarity (*familiarité*) could have gained for him in several years, he can see in three days in this record (*ce registre*), and more surely and exactly. (III.9; Frame 749–50; Villey 2: 981)

Like the Erasmian Jesus, who is known more intimately to the readers of Scripture than to the Jews living in his own time and place, the Montaigne of the *Essais* is known "more surely and exactly" through his writing.²⁷ Accordingly (not to mention somewhat contrarily), Montaigne sends his "most faithful friends" (*mes amis plus feaux*) to the bookseller's shop for a more efficiently and effectively acquired intimacy (Frame 750; Villey 2: 981).

Taking up the rhetorical and hermeneutic concerns aired in a number of other essays, "Of vanity" must figure prominently in an account of reading and writing intimately in the Renaissance for two further reasons: first because it revisits the topic of friendship in the context of not just spatial but temporal distance; and second because it offers the essayist's most sustained meditation on *belonging*. In both cases, as we will see, Montaigne, who claims

---

26. In the same essay (III.9), Montaigne attributes the increased length of his essays in the third book to an accommodation to the attention span of his readers: "Because such frequent breaks into chapters as I used at the beginning seemed to me to disrupt and dissolve attention before it was aroused, making it disdain to settle and collect for so little, I have begun making them longer, requiring fixed purpose and assigned leisure. In such an occupation, if you will not give a man a single hour, you will not give him anything" (Frame 762).

27. See, on this passage, Cave, "Problems of Reading in the *Essais*," 155–56 and 159–60. On the comparable power of poetry to represent a reality more vivid than reality itself ("Venus is not so beautiful all naked, alive, and panting, as she is here in Virgil"), see "On some verses of Vergil" (III.5; Frame 645). For more immediate Erasmian elements in "Of vanity," see two articles by Mary B. McKinley: "Vanity's Bull: Montaigne's Itineraries in III, ix," in *Le parcours des "Essais": Montaigne 1588–1988*, ed. Marcel Tetel and G. Mallary Masters (Paris, 1989), 195–208, and "La présence du *Ciceronianus* dans 'De la vanité,'" in *Montaigne et la rhétorique*, ed. John O'Brien, Malcom Quainton, and James J. Supple (Paris, 1995), 51–65.

to be made differently (*autrement faict*) (Frame 747; Villey 2: 978), will forward, as he often does, the contrarian's case for, on the one hand, preferring absence to presence, and, on the other, feeling more at home among someone else's belongings.[28]

If the earlier essay "Of presumption," as we have seen, rehearses the Hesiodic paradigm of belonging among one's belongings by featuring the house and substituting the horse for an ox while leaving the wife out of the account, the later essay "Of vanity" keeps silent on the ox while it showcases the house and its manager, the wife. Here, as in the tradition we have been tracing, the house or household is characterized by both its legal and its affective dimensions.[29] So Montaigne insists that his ancestors bestowed on his estate not only their *nom,* thereby establishing legal title, but also their *affection* (Frame 741; Villey 2: 970);[30] and Montaigne himself cannot help but communicate his own affection for *ma maison* as one that "has always been free, very accessible, and at anyone's service" (Frame 737)—one deserving the same praise showered on Lycurgus, the Athenian, who served as the guardian of his fellow citizens' possessions (Frame 738).

Ma maison is remarkable not for its grandeur, in other words, but for its trustworthiness, and so is *ma femme,* in whose hands Montaigne confidently leaves the management of his household when he travels abroad.[31] Indeed, Montaigne defines the entire role of a wife in relation to the house, from which she derives her chief virtue, *la vertu oeconomique,* and her sole course of study, *la science du mesnage* (Frame 745; Villey 2: 975). Despite this admiration and even affection for his belongings, however, Montaigne resists the conclusion that home is where he belongs.

---

28. On the benefits of absence to friendship in "Of vanity," see Weller, "Rhetoric of Friendship in Montaigne's *Essais,*" 519–20, and Scholar, *Montaigne and the Art of Free-Thinking,* 141.

29. For an early meditation on the benefits of isolation from one's household, including wife, children, possessions, and servants, see "Of solitude" (I.39; Frame 177; Villey 1: 241). On the classical tradition behind the discussion of the household in III.9, see Friedrich, *Montaigne,* who recalls that "the treatment of household and family life is a convention of moral philosophy" (33) and mentions in this context not only Xenophon and the preface to Amyot's translation of Plutarch's *Moralia* but La Boétie's translation of Xenophon under the title *De la mesnagerie.* See also John O'Brien, "Le récit familial," *Montaigne Studies* 13 (2001): 7–12.

30. On the "taking true possession of said manor and house" by Montaigne's great-grandfather, see Frame, *Montaigne: A Biography,* 8.

31. On Montaigne's wife, Françoise de la Chassaigne, see ibid., 85–102.

On the contrary, Montaigne admits to finding mostly irritation in household management and to feeling more at ease in somebody else's home, when he is *hors de ma maison et esloigné des miens* (Villey 2: 978)—away from his house and all that is his.[32] This distance from his belongings, he claims, increases his feelings of affection (Frame 745) and encourages him to fulfill what he calls *les devoirs de l'amitié maritale* (Villey 2: 975). But if "Of vanity" freely communicates Montaigne's thoughts and feelings after the epistolary fashion, it also, after a more precisely Petrarchan fashion, reflects philosophically on the question of distance and the absence it occasions. Even more to the point, Montaigne's formulation of this reflection sets in high relief, as did Petrarch's, the affective dimension of what is legally our own. For Montaigne proclaims his enjoyment or *jouyssance* of his children as well as the contents of his coffers with all the proprietary right of an owner rather than a mere usufructuary.[33] "If we enjoy (*jouyssons*) only what we touch," he warns,

---

32. "On repentance" (III.2), in contrast, represents a Montaigne who is most himself *chez moi* (Frame 615; Villey 2: 811), which is the case, as we see in this essay, for the soul in general. For Montaigne's use of what Jules Brody calls "a powerful domiciliary metaphor," see "'Du repentir' (III.2): A Philological Reading," *Yale French Studies* 64 (1983): 249 n. 12. For the development from possession to affection in such expressions as "les miens," see Benveniste, *Indo-European Language and Society*, 283. On the use of *suum* and writing *familiariter* in seventeenth-century epistolography, see Justus Lipsius, *Principles of Letter Writing*, trans. and ed. R. V. Young and M. Thomas Hester (Carbondale, 1996), 11: "The ancients did this occasionally, but the declining age bestowed this term everywhere and on everyone, even to the extent that Pliny would greet the Emperor himself so very familiarly (*familiariter*) as 'his own' (*suum*) in the preface of his great work."

33. On the same "enjoyment and possession" applied to ideas, see "On presumption" (II.17; Frame 499; Villey 1: 658). In "That to philosophize is to learn to die" (I.20), Montaigne distinguishes *jouyssance* from *plaisir*, *volupté*, and *goût*, associating it here as elsewhere with *possession*, even if only to call the association into question: "Those who go on teaching us that the quest of it [pleasure] is rugged and laborious, though the enjoyment of it is agreeable, what are they doing but telling us that it is always disagreeable? For what human means ever attained the enjoyment of virtue? The most perfect have been quite content to aspire to it and to approach it, without possessing it (*sans la posséder*). But those others are wrong; since in all the pleasures that we know, even the pursuit is pleasant. The attempt is made fragrant by the quality of the thing it aims at, for it is a good part of the effect and consubstantial" (I.20; Frame 56–57; Villey 1: 82). And in "Of vanity" (III.9), Montaigne claims for himself

farewell to our crowns when they are in our coffers, and our children if they are off hunting. We want them nearer. In our garden—is that far? Half a day away? What about ten leagues—is that far or near? If it is near, what about eleven, twelve, thirteen, and so on, step by step? (Frame 746; Villey 2: 976)

Defusing the power of distance by disarming "farness" as a relative measure, Montaigne argues for an absence that poses no threat to either the proprietary or the affective dimensions of what is ours. On the contrary, as mentioned above, spatial distance increases their worth (Frame 745).

Referring elsewhere (III.3) to this same proprietary right in regard to his books, Montaigne clarifies further the legality of "enjoyment" as a feature of "possession":[34]

> I enjoy (*jouys*) [my books] as misers enjoy treasures, because I know that I can enjoy (*jouyray*) them when I please; my soul takes its fill of contentment from this right of possession (*ce droict de possession*). (Frame 628; Villey 2: 827)

Like the miser who not only need not use his wealth to enjoy owning it but actually enjoys it all the more when he does not use it, so this *paterfamilias* claims to enjoy his household; and what is true of Montaigne's house-

---

a *usage de mes biens* that is *liquide* and *quitte* (Villey 2: 975), the legality of which Florio translates as an "absolute use" and a "liquid fruition" (3.222). On other occasions, Florio, following Montaigne more closely, will translate legal *fructus* as "jovissance" (3.214, 223, 225). For the legal meaning of such terms as *jouissance, usage, liquide*, and *quitte*, see *Vocabulaire juridique*, ed. Gérard Cornu (Paris, 1987); *Amos and Walton's Introduction to French Law*, ed. F. H. Lawson, A. E. Anton, and L. Neville Brown (Oxford, 1967); and *French-English Dictionary of Legal Words and Phrases*, ed. A. W. Dalrymple (London, 1948), s.vv. On the legal concept of usufruct, its relation to ownership (and possession), and its role in early modern French law, see Jean Brissaud, *A History of French Private Law*, trans. Rapelje Howell (London, 1912), 418; and on usufruct in Roman law see David Daube, "Fashions and Idiosyncrasies in the Exposition of the Roman Law of Property," in Parel and Flanagan *Theories of Property*, 35–50. For a different but complementary discussion of *jouissance* in Montaigne's *Essais*, see Maclean, *Montaigne Philosophe*, 92, 115–16.

34. On the miserliness of fathers, who keep their children from sharing in the enjoyment of their property, and on the *affection et amour des siens* as the best defense against the infirmities of old age, see "Of the affection of fathers for their children" (II.8; Frame 285; Villey 1: 393). Throughout this essay, Montaigne invokes the legal concepts of *possession, jouyssance*, and *usage*.

hold, including the books of his library, as his principal belonging, is equally true of his friendships, considered in terms of the same legal language of ownership:

> Enjoyment and possession (*La jouyssance et la possession*) are principally a matter of imagination (*l'imagination*). It embraces (*embrasse*) more warmly what it is in quest of than what we have at hand, and more continually. Count up your daily musings, and you will find that you are most absent from your friend when he is in your company; his presence relaxes your attention and gives your thoughts liberty to absent themselves at any time and for any reason. (Frame 745; Villey 2: 975)

Montaigne's attenuation of this proprietary right as an act of the imagination and his reversal of the Petrarchan (and Ciceronian) values of absence and presence extend even to his own most valued friendship with La Boétie, a friendship that thrived on separation rather than on the living together—*simul vivere*—so celebrated by Petrarch (see above, pp. 64–65). "We filled and extended our possession (*la possession*) of life better by separating," Montaigne explains, because "[s]eparation in space (*La séparation du lieu*) made the conjunction of our wills richer (*plus riche*). This insatiable hunger for bodily presence (*la présence corporelle*) betrays a certain weakness in the enjoyment (*la jouyssance*) of souls" (Frame 746–47; Villey 2: 977). Far from diminishing our *droict de possession,* spatial distance enforces it. Montaigne is seemingly unfazed by the Petrarchan preoccupation with loss over time as well as space.[35] Indeed, he equates them, and the equation mitigates, if it does not entirely eradicate, the dislocation and disquiet occasioned by temporal distance.

To drive home this mitigation, Montaigne the contrarian insists that the wife whose husband has departed to the next world sustains no greater loss than she whose husband has traveled to the ends of this one (Frame 746). So indistinguishable is temporal from spatial distance, according to Montaigne, that "[w]e embrace (*embrassons*) both those who have been and those who are not yet, not merely the absent" (Frame 746; Villey 2: 976). And so unreckonable is temporal, like spatial, distance regarding the near and the far that the heroes of the Roman Republic are no more absent than

---

35. On the difference between Petrarch and Montaigne in this regard, see Friedrich, *Montaigne,* 39–42, who maintains that "Montaigne neither has a historicizing consciousness of the historical conditions of antiquity, as Budé does, for example, nor even—or at best only in momentary impulses—a transfiguring longing for it, as do the Italian humanists" (39).

the last generation of the house of Montaigne. "They are dead," Montaigne proclaims of Lucullus, Metellus, and Scipio:

> So indeed is my father, as completely as they; and he has moved as far from me and from life in eighteen years as they have in sixteen hundred. Nevertheless I do not cease to embrace (*embrasser*) and cherish his memory, his friendship, and his society, in a union that is perfect and very much alive. (Frame 762; Villey 2: 996)

Despite his seemingly unPetrarchan impassivity, Montaigne not only actively engages the past, even cherishes it, but, as noted earlier, actually prefers it, "throw[ing] himself back upon" it, as he says, whether by advocating passionately for Brutus and Pompey or by recollecting an ancient Rome whose sights he claims to know longer and better than those of his own country.[36]

As Frame translates it (762), Montaigne's "familiarity" with ancient Rome and her heroes may mistakenly recall Petrarch's *familiaritas* with Cicero (and Erasmus's with Jerome)—mistakenly because Montaigne does not here characterize these relations as *familiarité*.[37] This characterization

---

36. Frame 762–63: "Indeed, by inclination I pay greater service to the dead.... Finding myself useless for this age, I throw myself back upon that other, and am so bewitched by it that the state of that ancient Rome, free, just and flourishing (for I love neither her birth nor her old age), interests me passionately." Although Friedrich finds "a world of difference" between such comments in Montaigne and Petrarch's "effusive confession that he would like to forget the bustle about him and the commonness of men in order to live in the contemplation of even the tiniest fragments of the classical works handed down" (*Montaigne*, 40), I would emphasize an important continuity in their claims. For Petrarch's (like Montaigne's) involvement in politics despite the aspiration for reclusiveness, see Mann, *Petrarch*, 28–45.

37. Instead Montaigne refers here to his *connaissance* and *accointance* (Villey 2: 996). As we have seen, *familiarité* is the kind of *connaissance* that conversation, epistolary writing, and the kind of writing modeled on the epistolary aim to foster. Elsewhere Montaigne couples *familiarité* with *accointance* (e.g., II.8, Frame 288, Villey 1: 396; II.17, Frame 501, Villey 1: 660); and on one occasion he distinguishes this pair as the basis of ordinary friendships in contrast to his own unique friendship with La Boétie: "For the rest, what we ordinarily call friends and friendships are nothing but acquaintanceships and familiarities (*accoinctances et familiaritez*) formed by some chance or convenience, by means of which our souls mingle and blend with each other so completely that they efface the seam that joined them, and cannot find it again" (I.28; Frame 139; Villey 1: 188).

he saves for how he understands Plutarch and Seneca and for the way he aspires to be understood by his own readers. For Montaigne has in mind, as the argument of this chapter has tried to show, an intimacy that is rhetorical and hermeneutic, a special relation between *familiares* that comes to define the no less special relation between writer and reader. Grounded in the expression of thoughts and feelings freely and openly exchanged in conversation between friends, as we have seen, this rhetorical and hermeneutic intimacy finds its earliest and most ardent Renaissance spokesmen among epistolary writers and readers whose practice as well as theory serves, in turn, as a model for writing and reading more generally. I have called these spokesmen *Renaissance* because their explicit aim was to revive a style of communication that they identified with reading those representatives of a lost world whom they admired most. But these same spokesmen might just as aptly be called *early modern*. For what they discovered as part of their revival arguably created the conditions for some of our own reading and writing practices and, as I can only suggest in concluding, maybe even something more.

CONCLUSION **Rediscovering Individuality**

As we have seen in chapter 3 (p. 88), Erasmus stakes his editorial career on his ability to distinguish Jerome's writing from that of not only bumbling imitators but consummate forgers. In the kingdom of style, Erasmus explains in his preface to Jerome's *opera omnia*, difference rules. No other sphere fosters such diversity. "Indeed, those who are highly observant," Erasmus insists, "may distinguish one egg from another egg, one fig from another fig, and, proverbial wisdom notwithstanding, it is simply not true that one style is indistinguishable from another" (*CWE* 61: 77). In his preface to Jerome, in other words, Erasmus invokes the common wisdom in order to dismiss it, a strategy he uses again in the *Adages* (I.v.10; *CWE* 31: 393; ASD II-1, 486). Only there, the proverbial likeness between two eggs is further upended by the authority of Cicero, who presents as evidence an anecdote about some Delians who could tell not only one egg from another but which of the many hens in the yard had laid it.

On this occasion, Erasmus takes his Ciceronian anecdote from the *Academica* (2.18.57–58), where the subject under discussion is human perception rather than literary style. Speaking in the voice of his interlocutor Lucullus, the author of the anecdote is nevertheless recognizable as the same Cicero who advises son Marcus in his own voice in *De officiis*, as we have seen, to own fully what belongs to him: to cultivate his individuality (see above, p. 27). Both philosophical works, then, reveal a Cicero preoccupied with difference. And so does *On the Laws* (*De legibus*), where Cicero takes the opportunity of intimate conversation (*sermo familiaris*) with brother Quintus to differentiate himself from Plato, whose dialogue on the same topic of the laws serves as literary model. Readily acknowledging the inimitability of his Greek predecessor's style (*genus oratoris*), Cicero assures Quintus that he would not imitate this style even if he could because his goal in writing is to be himself (2.17–18). Cicero stages this brotherly exchange, moreover, in terms of legal ownership, the language of *meum* and *tuum*. To Cicero's assertion that he prefers to be his own person (... *esse vellem meus*), Quintus, approving this self-possession, echoes the legal terminology: *te esse malo tuum* (2.17).[1]

As an experienced reader of Cicero as well as of Jerome, Erasmus would not be surprised—as other, more recent readers might be—to find Cicero

---

1. Cicero, *De legibus*, trans. Clinton Walker Keyes (Cambridge, Mass., 1988).

the authority on individuality. What Erasmus very likely would find surprising, however, is the scholarly tendency of the last century to celebrate Montaigne as individuality's founding father, especially since Montaigne's pronouncements on this topic look back not only to Erasmus himself but to Erasmus's acknowledged ancient source. In "Of experience" (III.13), his most sustained and best known meditation on difference as a defining condition of humanity, Montaigne rehearses without attribution the Ciceronian anecdote about eggs cited by Erasmus. "Both the Greeks and the Latins," Montaigne explains,

> and we ourselves use eggs for the most express example of similarity. However, there have been men, and notably one at Delphi, who recognized marks of difference between eggs, so that he never took one for another; and although there were many hens, he could tell which one the egg came from. (Frame 815)

Whether or not Montaigne has knowingly changed the locale in the Ciceronian passage from Delos to Delphi (and the number of expert hen watchers from some to one), he has surely succeeded over the centuries in making his own the theme of difference epitomized by the distinctiveness of each individual egg.

Indeed, Montaigne's ownership of the theme of individuality is taken for granted in many quarters. When philosopher Charles Taylor in *Sources of the Self* reflects on the three forms of individualism that constitute modern identity, for instance, Montaigne provides the paradigmatic case of at least one of them.[2] In an article entitled "Montaigne's Individualism," Nannerl O. Keohane similarly confirms the Frenchman's status as exemplary of the early modern individual.[3] Both Taylor and Keohane, moreover, assume some alliance between individuality and intimacy. For Taylor, this alliance involves being present to oneself. For Keohane, it includes privacy and freedom and

---

2. *Sources of the Self*, 178–85, esp. 181–82, where Taylor credits Montaigne with inaugurating "a new kind of reflection which is intensely individual" and founding a "kind of modern individualism" whose "aim is to identify the individual in his or her unrepeatable difference."

3. Nannerl O. Keohane, "Montaigne's Individualism," *Political Theory* 5 (1977): 363–90, esp. 366: "Montaigne succeeded better than any other writer in making such a self-centered life attractive, in teaching man to think of this individualism as a satisfactory and appealing moral norm. He provided for modernity an alternative ideal, to be set over against the ancient ideal of the engaged citizen and the medieval ideal of the self-sacrificing saint."

is part and parcel of what Keohane calls Montaigne's "liberal individualism" as distinct from the "possessive individualism" of the next century.⁴

Bookending this study with the lineage from Demetrius to Ben Jonson that introduced it (see above, p. 2) and the line of descent along the unlikeness of eggs from Cicero through Erasmus to Montaigne that concludes it, I intend not only to reprise the case for a rediscovered rhetoric and hermeneutics of intimacy but also to suggest in conclusion that this rediscovery is not unrelated to an aspect of early modern culture that scholars of the period have considered determinative. Beginning with Jacob Burckhardt's vision of an Italian Renaissance "swarm[ing] with individuality," right up to Geoff Baldwin's recent retrospective assessment that "[t]wentieth-century scholarship of the early modern, or Renaissance, period has been dominated by a notion of *individualism*," the time between Petrarch and Montaigne has been marked as *individualist*.⁵ So dominant is this marking, in fact, that dissenting voices have felt compelled to remind us that "[n]o period in the history of philosophy has discussed individuality and its problems more often or more subtly than did the medieval schoolmen."⁶ And such reminders are as useful for thinking about intimacy as individuality.

---

4. See Taylor, *Sources of the Self*, 136, 139–40, and Keohane, "Montaigne's Individualism," 384, 387. On the importance of both self-awareness and privacy to the appearance of individuality, see Lionel Trilling, *Sincerity and Authenticity* (Cambridge, Mass., 1971), who remarks in regard to the statement that "at a certain point in history men became individuals": "Taken in isolation the statement is absurd. How was a man different from an individual? A person born before a certain date, a man—had he not eyes? Had he not hands, organs, dimensions, senses, affections, passions? . . . But certain things he did not have or do until he became an individual. He did not have an awareness of . . . internal space. He did not . . . imagine himself in more than one role, standing outside or above his own personality; he did not suppose that he might be an object of interest to his fellow man not for the reason that he had achieved something notable or been witness to great events but simply because as an individual he was of consequence. It is when he becomes an individual that a man lives more and more in private rooms; whether the privacy makes the individuality or the individuality requires the privacy the historians do not say" (24).

5. See Jacob Burckhardt, *The Civilization of the Renaissance in Italy*, trans. S. G. C. Middlemore (Oxford, 1945), 81, and Geoff Baldwin, "Individual and Self in the Late Renaissance," *Historical Journal* 44 (2001): 341–62, esp. 341. On Burckhardt's assessment, see Nelson, "Individualism as a Criterion of the Renaissance."

6. See Lynn Thorndike, "Renaissance Prenaissance?" *Journal of the History of Ideas* 4 (1943): 71, who continues: "Vittorino da Feltre and other humanist educa-

For nobody should doubt that there was intimate communication, including written correspondence, between friends and family before Petrarch discovered Cicero's letters to Atticus. And there is ample evidence that this epistolary practice took its cues at least some of the time from epistolary theory. But when one popular twelfth-century letter-writing manual addresses the issue of intimacy, it does so, according to the dictaminal rules, as part of its treatment of the *exordium* or introduction.[7] Advising the letter writer, like the orator, to secure the reader's good will at the opening of his letter, the manual recommends *familiaritas* as one item on a list of useful affective relations that includes *propinquitas, dilectio, dominium, servitus, societas, paternitas,* and *filatio*.[8] And while this recommendation also looks back to Cicero, the Cicero it looks back to is the pseudo-Ciceronian *Ad Herennium* and the early *De inventione*, not the Ciceronian letters or the late rhetorical works or even *De officiis*.

Petrarch's discovery of a rhetoric and hermeneutics of intimacy as part of his epistolary project—a discovery passed on to northern Europe through Erasmus's educational and religious reform and refitted by Montaigne to

---

tors may have suited their teaching to the individual pupil; at the medieval university the individual scholar suited himself. The humanists were imitative in their writing, not original. Vitruvius was the Bible of Renaissance architects who came to follow authority far more than their creative Gothic predecessors. For the middle ages loved variety; the Renaissance uniformity." For the status of the individual in scholastic philosophy and psychology, see also De Vogel, "Concept of Personality in Greek and Christian Thought," 21–23, and Nelson, "Individualism as a Criterion of the Renaissance," 319–21. In *Nous Michel de Montaigne* (Paris, 1980), Antoine Compagnon traces Montaigne's treatment of individuality back to Porphyry and Boethius and their legacy of nominalism.

7. On the *ars dictaminis* and its relation to humanist letter writing, see the introduction above, n. 10. For the vestiges of these rules in Erasmus's epistolary manual, see above, p. 78.

8. *The Principles of Letter Writing* (1135 CE) in *Three Medieval Rhetorical Arts*, ed. James J. Murphy (Berkeley, 1971), 17: "Goodwill will be secured also from the effect of circumstances if something is added which would be appropriate to both persons involved, or which would be in the purpose of things, or would be suitably or reasonably connected to goodwill, such as 'intimacy,' 'affections,' 'fellowship,' 'familiarity,' 'lordship and service,' 'fatherly feeling and filial feeling,' and the like." For the Latin see Ludwig Rockinger, ed., *Rationes dictandi* in *Briefsteller und formelbücher des eilften bis vierzehnten jahrhunderts*, (Munich, 1863; rpt. New York, 1961), chap. 6, p. 18.

vernacular specifications—is made possible, as I have tried to show, by the recovery of key ancient texts read and reread by these three authors. How these singularly influential early moderns wrote, I have also tried to show, was the result of not just which ancient texts they read but *how* they read them. And if these early moderns claimed to read as well as write *intimately,* they hoped in turn to be read in this way.

Finally, I have tried to show that the rhetorical and hermeneutical intimacy embraced by these humanists was a matter of style—that their concept of style was capacious enough to include the various *forms* and *fashions* that reveal the mind of the writer in all its individuality. Ready to underwrite individual differences, this capacious concept of style, as we have seen, actually invited reflection on what distinguishes two stylists, like two eggs, from one another. Wherever else individuality was demanding a hearing during the Renaissance, in other words, its case was being advocated loudly and clearly in the court of stylistic theory. Among the most compelling witnesses for this case, moreover, were the voices from antiquity, including those speaking the language of Greek and Roman law, especially property law. For the essence of private ownership is difference: the difference between what is mine and what is not mine—*meum* and *tuum*.[9]

If Keohane is right that Montaigne's brand of individualism predates the kind famously identified as "possessive" by C. B. Macpherson,[10] it is nevertheless worth noting that Montaigne's concept of style has deep roots in the legal concept of property. These roots reach down not only to Cicero's discussions of what is legally and psychologically *proprium* and *suum,* as we have seen, but to Aristotle's identification of the most excellent style as *oikeia,* from the *oikos* as the locus of belonging. This locus, as we have also seen, both corresponds to the Roman *familia* and provides Greek and Roman Stoicism with a point of origin for what has been called *personal identity* or *selfhood*; and this *selfhood* finds expression above all in one par-

---

9. In *A Democracy of Distinction,* in a chapter entitled "The Use of Property," Frank clarifies the relation between private ownership and individuation: "Insofar as Aristotelian property is a matter of holding things as one's own, it individuates and distinguishes.... Promoting integrated human activity and also individual ethical habituation, Aristotelian property reflects a dual commitment to collective action and individuation.... Property is mine, that is, not yours. In being mine, it differentiates me from you. At the same time, in differentiating me from you and you from me and each one from every other, it treats us as distinctly equal" (78–79).

10. C. B. Macpherson, *The Political Theory of Possessive Individualism: Hobbes to Locke* (Oxford, 1964), 53–61.

ticular form of written communication: the so-called *familiar letter*. When Petrarch discovers Cicero's letters to Atticus, then, he does something more than rediscover a rhetoric of intimacy; he sets in motion a stylistic movement or *fashion* that will give momentum in turn to the gathering forces of individuality.

Bibliography of Secondary Sources

Albright, Evelyn May. "Notes on the Status of Literary Property, 1500–1545." *Modern Philology* 17 (1919): 65–95.
Allen, P. S. *Erasmus: Lectures and Wayfaring Sketches.* Oxford, 1934.
———. "Erasmus' Relations with His Printers." *Transactions of the Bibliographical Society* 13 (1913–15): 297–321.
———. "Erasmus' Services to Learning." In *Erasmus: Lectures and Wayfaring Sketches,* 30–59.
Altman, Joel B. *The Improbability of Othello: Rhetorical Anthropology and Shakespearean Selfhood.* Chicago, 2010.
Antognini, Roberta. "*Familiarium rerum liber:* tradizione materiale e autobiografia." In *Petrarch and the Textual Origins of Interpretation,* ed. Teodolinda Barolini and H. Wayne Storey. Leiden, 2007: 205–29.
———. *Il progetto autobiografico delle "Familiares" di Petrarca.* Milan, 2008.
Aylmer, G. E. "The Meaning and Definition of 'Property' in Seventeenth-Century England." *Past and Present* 86 (1980): 87–97.
Baldwin, Geoff. "Individual and Self in the Late Renaissance." *Historical Journal* 44 (2001): 341–64.
Baños, Pedro Martín. *El arte epistolar en el Renacimiento europeo, 1400–1600.* Bilbao, 2005.
Baron, Hans. *From Petrarch to Leonardo Bruni: Studies in Humanistic and Political Literature.* Chicago, 1968.
Barwick, G. F. "The Laws Regulating Printing and Publishing in Italy." *Transactions of the Bibliographical Society* 14 (1919): 311–23.
Basso, Jeannine. "La lettera 'familiare' nella retorica epistolare del XVI e del XVII secolo in Italia." *Quaderni di retorica e poetica* 1 (1985): 57–65.
Bateman, John J. "From Soul to Soul: Persuasion in Erasmus' Paraphrases on the New Testament." *Erasmus in English* 15 (1987–88): 7–16.
———. "The Textual Travail of the *Tomus secundus* of the *Paraphrases.*" In *Holy Scripture Speaks: The Production and Reception of Erasmus' Paraphrases on the New Testament,* ed. Hilmar M. Pabel and Mark Vessey. Toronto, 2002: 213–63.
Batinski, Emily. "Seneca's Response to Stoic Hermeneutics." *Mnemosyne* 46 (1993): 69–77.
Bauschatz, Cathleen M. "Montaigne's Conception of Reading in the Context of Renaissance Poetics and Modern Criticism." In *The Reader in the Text: Essays on Audience and Interpretation,* ed. Susan R. Suleiman and Inge Crosman. Princeton, 1980: 264–91.

Beard, Mary. "Ciceronian Correspondences: Making a Book out of Letters." In *Classics in Progress: Essays on Ancient Greece and Rome,* ed. T. P. Wiseman. Oxford, 2002: 103–44.

Béné, Charles. "Érasme et Cicéron." In *Colloquia erasmiana turonensia,* vol. 2, ed. Jean-Claude Margolin. Toronto, 1972: 571–79.

Bénévent, Christine. "Érasme en sa correspondance: conquête(s) et défaite(s) du langage." In *Self-Presentation and Social Identification: The Rhetoric and Pragmatics of Letter Writing in Early Modern Times,* ed. Toon Van Houdt, Jan Papy, Gilbert Tournoy, and Constant Matheeussen. Leuven, 2002: 57–85.

Bernardo, Aldo S. "Petrarch, Dante, and the Medieval Tradition." In *Renaissance Humanism: Foundations, Forms, and Legacy,* ed. Albert J. Rabil Jr. Vol. 1. Philadelphia, 1988: 115–37.

Beugnot, Bernard B. "Style ou styles épistolaires" *Revue d'histoire littéraire de la France* 6 (1978): 939–57.

Bietenholz, Peter. "Erasmus and the German Public, 1518–1520: The Authorized and Unauthorized Circulation and Correspondence." *Sixteenth Century Journal* 8 (1977): 61–78.

Billanovich, G. "Petrarch and the Textual Tradition of Livy." *Journal of the Warburg and Courtauld Institutes* 14 (1951): 137–208.

Binns, J. W. "The Letters of Erasmus." In *Erasmus,* ed. T. A. Dorey. Albuquerque, 1970: 55–79.

Birrell, Augustine. *Seven Lectures on the Law and History of Copyright in Books.* London, 1899.

Black, Robert. "Cicero in the Curriculum of Italian Renaissance Grammar Schools." *Ciceroniana,* n.s., 9 (1996): 105–20.

———. *Humanism and Education in Medieval and Renaissance Italy: Tradition and Innovation in Latin Schools from the Twelfth to the Fifteenth Century.* Cambridge, Eng., 2001.

Blanc, Pierre. "Pétrarque lecteur de Cicéron. Les scolies pétrarquiennes du *De oratore* et de *l'Orator.*" *Studi Petrarcheschi* 9 (1978): 109–66.

Bobbio, Aurelia. "Seneca e la formazione spirituale e culturale del Petrarca." *La Bibliofilia* 43 (1941): 224–91.

Bolgar, R. R. "The Teaching of Letter Writing in the Sixteenth Century." *History of Education* 12 (1983): 245–53.

Boutcher, Warren. "Literature, Thought or Fact? Past and Present Directions in the Study of the Early Modern Letter." In *Self-Presentation and Social Identification: The Rhetoric and Pragmatics of Letter Writing in Early Modern Times,* ed. Toon Van Houdt, Jan Papy, Gilbert Tournoy, and Constant Matheeussen. Leuven, 2002: 137–63.

Boyle, Marjorie O'Rourke. *Christening Pagan Mysteries: Erasmus in Pursuit of Wisdom.* Toronto, 1981.

Bradley, Keith R. *Discovering the Roman Family*. Oxford, 1991.

Branca, Vittore. "Ciceronianesimo e anticiceronianesimo nell'esperienza epistolografica umanistica a Venezia." *Ciceroniana*, n.s., 10 (1998): 119–31.

Brink, C. O. "Οἰκείωσις and οἰκειότης: Theophrastus and Zeno on Nature in Moral Theory." *Phronesis* 1 (1956): 123–44.

Brody, Jules. "'Du repentir' (III:2): A Philological Reading." *Yale French Studies* 64 (1983): 238–72.

———. "La première réception des *Essais* de Montaigne: Fortunes d'une forme." In *Automne de la Renaissance, 1580–1630*, ed. Jean Lafond and André Stegmann. Paris, 1981: 19–30.

Brunschwig, Jacques. "The Cradle Argument in Epicureanism and Stoicism." In *The Norms of Nature: Studies in Hellenistic Ethics*, ed. Malcolm Schofield and Gisela Striker. Cambridge, Eng., 1986: 113–44.

Brunt, P. A. "'*Amicitia*' in the Late Roman Republic." *Proceedings of the Cambridge Philological Society* 191, n.s., 11 (1965): 1–20.

Bullock, Walter L. "The Precept of Plagiarism in the Cinquecento." *Modern Philology* 25 (1928): 293–312.

Campion, Edmund J. *Montaigne, Rabelais, and Marot as Readers of Erasmus*. Lewiston, N.Y., 1995.

Carruthers, Mary. *The Book of Memory: A Study of Memory in Medieval Culture*. Cambridge, Eng., 1990.

Cassirer, Ernst. "Some Remarks on the Question of the Originality of the Renaissance." *Journal of the History of Ideas* 4 (1943): 49–56.

Cavallo, Guglielmo. "Between *Volumen* and Codex: Reading in the Roman World." In *A History of Reading in the West*, ed. Guglielmo Cavallo and Roger Chartier, trans. Lydia G. Cochrane. Amherst, 1999: 64–89.

Cave, Terence. *The Cornucopian Text: Problems of Writing in the French Renaissance*. Oxford, 1979.

———. "Fragments of a Future Self: From Pascal to Montaigne." In *Retrospectives: Essays in Literature, Poetics, and Cultural History*, ed. Neil Kenny and Wes Williams. London, 2009: 130–45.

———. *How to Read Montaigne*. London, 2007.

———. *Pré-histoires: Textes troublés au seuil de la modernité*. Geneva, 1999.

———. "Problems of Reading in the *Essais*." In *Montaigne: Essays in Memory of Richard Sayce*, ed. I. D. McFarlane and Ian Maclean. Oxford, 1982: 133–66.

———. "Representations of Reading in the Renaissance." In *Retrospectives: Essays in Literature, Poetics, and Cultural History*, ed. Neil Kenny and Wes Williams. London, 2009: 10–19.

Chamberlain, Charles. "From 'Haunts' to 'Character': The Meaning of Ethos and Its Relation to Ethics." *Helios* 11 (1984): 97–108.

Charlier, Yvonne. *Érasme et l'amitié d'après sa correspondance*. Paris, 1977.

Cherchi, Paolo. "Petrarca (*Familiares* I, 1) e Plinio il Giovane (*Epistolae*, I, 1)." *Rassegna europea di litteratura italiana* 24 (2004): 101–5.

Chiron, Pierre. *Un rhéteur méconnu: Démétrios.* Paris, 2001.

Chomarat, Jacques. *Grammaire et rhétorique chez Érasme.* 2 vols. Paris, 1981.

———. "Grammar and Rhetoric in the Paraphrases of the Gospels by Erasmus." *Erasmus of Rotterdam Society Yearbook* 1 (1981): 30–68.

Clark, Carol E. "Seneca's Letters to Lucilius as a Source of Some of Montaigne's Imagery." *Bibliothèque d'humanisme et Renaissance* 30 (1968): 249–66.

———. "Talking about Souls: Montaigne on Human Psychology." In *Montaigne: Essays in Memory of Richard Sayce,* ed. I. D. McFarlane and Ian Maclean. Oxford, 1982: 57–76.

Clough, Cecil H. "The Cult of Antiquity: Letters and Letter Collections." In *Cultural Aspects of the Italian Renaissance: Essays in Honor of Paul Oskar Kristeller,* ed. Clough. New York, 1976: 33–67.

Compagnon, Antoine. *Nous, Michel de Montaigne.* Paris, 1980.

Constable, Giles. *Letters and Letter-Collections.* Turnhout, 1976.

Coogan, Robert. "The Pharisee against the Hellenist: Edward Lee Versus Erasmus." *Renaissance Quarterly* 39 (1986): 476–506.

Cotton, Hannah M. "Greek and Latin Epistolary Formulae: Some Light on Cicero's Letter Writing." *American Journal of Philology* 105 (1984): 409–25.

Cox, Virginia. "Ciceronian Rhetoric in Italy, 1260–1350." *Rhetorica* 17 (1999): 239–88.

Croll, Morris W. *Attic and Baroque Prose Style: The Anti-Ciceronian Movement.* Ed. J. Max Patrick and Robert O. Evans. Princeton, 1966.

Cugusi, Paolo. "L'epistola ciceroniana: Strumento di comunicazione quotidiana e modello letterario." *Ciceroniana,* n.s., 10 (1998): 163–89.

———. *Evoluzione e forme dell'epistolografia latina.* Rome, 1983.

Dalzell, Alexander. "Greetings and Salutations in Erasmus." *Renaissance and Reformation,* n.s., 13 (1989): 251–61.

Defaux, Gérard. "From Erasmus to Montaigne (and Beyond): Writing as Presence." *Erasmus of Rotterdam Society Yearbook* 8 (1988): 35–69.

Deissmann, Adolf. *Light from the Ancient East.* Trans. Lionel R. M. Strachan. London, 1927.

de Vogel, C. J. "The Concept of Personality in Greek and Christian Thought." In *Studies in Philosophy and the History of Philosophy,* ed. John K. Ryan. Washington, D.C., 1963: 20–60.

Dotti, Ugo. *Petrarca e la scoperta della coscienza moderna.* Milan, 1978.

———. "I primi sei libri delle 'Familiari' del Petrarca." *Giornale storico della letteratura italiana* 150 (1973): 1–20.

Dresden, Sem. "Erasme et les belles-lettres." In *Colloque Erasmien de Liège.* Paris, 1987: 3–16.

Dunn, E. Catherine. "Lipsius and the Art of Letter Writing." *Studies in the Renaissance* 3 (1956): 145–56.
Durling, Robert M. "The Ascent of Mt. Ventoux and the Crisis of Allegory." In *Petrarch,* ed. Harold Bloom. New York, 1989: 29–42.
Dyck, Andrew R. *A Commentary on Cicero, "De Officiis."* Ann Arbor, 1996.
Eden, Kathy. *Friends Hold All Things in Common: Tradition, Intellectual Property and the "Adages" of Erasmus.* New Haven, 2001.
———. "From the Cradle: Erasmus on Intimacy in Renaissance Letters." *Erasmus of Rotterdam Society Yearbook* 21 (2001): 30–43.
———. *Hermeneutics and the Rhetorical Tradition: Chapters in the Ancient Legacy and Its Humanist Reception.* New Haven, 1997.
———. "Literary Property and the Question of Style: A Prehistory." In *Borrowed Feathers: Plagiarism and the Limits of Imitation in Early Modern Europe,* ed. Hall Bjørnstad. Oslo, 2008: 21–38.
———. *Poetic and Legal Fiction in the Aristotelian Tradition.* Princeton, 1986.
Edwards, Catharine. "Self-Scrutiny and Self-Transformation in Seneca's Letters." *Greece and Rome* 44 (1997): 23–38.
Enenkel, Karl. "Die Grundlegung humanistischer Selbstpräsentation im Brief-Corpus: Francesco Petrarcas *Familiarium rerum libri* XXIV." In *Self-Presentation and Social Identification: The Rhetoric and Pragmatics of Letter Writing in Early Modern Times,* ed. Toon Van Houdt, Jan Papy, Gilbert Tournoy, and Constant Matheeussen. Leuven, 2002: 367–84.
———. "Modelling the Humanist: Petrarch's *Letter to Posterity* and Boccaccio's Biography of the Poet Laureate." In *Modelling the Individual: Biography and Portrait in the Renaissance,* ed. Karl Enenkel, Betsy de Jong-Crane, and Peter Liebregts. Amsterdam, 1998: 11–49.
Engberg-Pederson, Troels. "Discovering the Good: *Oikeiosis* and *Kathekonta* in Stoic Ethics." In *The Norms of Nature: Studies in Hellenistic Ethics,* ed. Malcolm Schofield and Gisela Striker. Cambridge, Eng., 1986: 145–83.
———. *The Stoic Theory of Oikeiosis.* Aarhus, Denmark, 1990.
Engelhardt, George John. "Medieval Vestiges in the Rhetoric of Erasmus." *PMLA* 63 (1948): 739–44.
Enos, Richard Leo. "Ancient Greek Writing Instruction." In *A Short History of Writing Instruction: From Ancient Greece to Modern America,* ed. James J. Murphy. Davis, Cal., 2001: 9–34.
Estes, James E. "The Achievement of P. S. Allen and the Role of *CWE.*" *Renaissance and Reformation,* n.s., 13 (1989): 289–98.
Fantazzi, Charles. "The *Epistolae ad Exercitationem Accommodatae* of Gasparino Barzizza." *Acta Conventus Neo-Latini Torontonensis* (Binghamton, 1991): 141–46.
———. "The Evolution of Erasmus' Epistolary Style." *Renaissance and Reformation,* n.s., 13 (1989): 263–88.

———. "Vives versus Erasmus on the Art of Letter-Writing." In *Self-Presentation and Social Identification: The Rhetoric and Pragmatics of Letter Writing in Early Modern Times*, ed. Toon Van Houdt, Jan Papy, Gilbert Tournoy, and Constant Matheeussen. Leuven, 2002: 39–56.

Fantham, Elaine. "Ciceronian *Conciliare* and Aristotelian Ethos." *Phoenix* 27 (1973): 262–75.

———. *The Roman World of Cicero's "De oratore."* Oxford, 2003.

Farquhar, Sue W. "Montaigne and the Law: 'De l'experience.'" *Montaigne Studies* 14 (2002): 37–48.

Fitzgerald, William. "The Letter's the Thing (in Pliny, Book 7)." In *Ancient Letters*, ed. Ruth Morello and A. D. Morrison. Oxford, 2007: 191–210.

Force, Pierre. "Innovation as Spiritual Exercise: Montaigne and Pascal." *Journal of the History of Ideas* (2005): 17–35.

Frame, Donald M. *Montaigne: A Biography*. London, 1965.

Frank, Jill. *A Democracy of Distinction: Aristotle and the Work of Politics*. Chicago, 2005.

Freedman, Joseph S. "Cicero in Sixteenth- and Seventeenth-Century Rhetoric Instruction." *Rhetorica* 4 (1986): 227–53.

Friedrich, Hugo. *Montaigne*. Trans. Dawn Eng. Berkeley, 1991.

Fubini, Ricardo. "La coscienza del Latino negli umanisti." *Studi medievale* 2 (1961): 505–50.

Fumaroli, Marc. *L'âge de l'éloquence: Rhétorique et 'res literaria' de la Renaissance au seuil de l'époque classique* (Paris, 1980).

———. "De l'âge de l'éloquence à l'âge de la conversation: la conversion de la rhétorique humaniste dans la France du XVIIe siècle." In *Art de la lettre, Art de la conversation à l'époque classique en France*, ed. Bernard Bray and Christoph Strosetzki. Klincksieck, 1995: 25–45.

———."Genèse de l'épistolographie classique: rhétorique humaniste de la lettre, de Pétrarque à Juste Lipse." *Revue d'histoire littéraire de la France* 78 (1978): 886–905.

Gambet, Daniel G. "Cicero in the Works of Seneca Philosophus." *TAPA* 101 (1970): 171–83.

Gardini, Nicola. *Rinascimento*. Milan, 2010.

Garin, Eugenio. *Italian Humanism: Philosophy and Civic Life in the Renaissance*. Trans. Peter Munz. New York, 1965.

Garrod, H. W. *The Study of Good Letters*. Oxford, 1963.

Garver, Eugene. *Aristotle's Rhetoric: An Art of Character*. Chicago, 1994.

Gentili, Bruno. *Poetry and Its Public in Ancient Greece: From Homer to the Fifth Century*. Trans. A. Thomas Cole. Baltimore, 1988.

George, Edward V. "Conceal or Disclose? The Limits of Self-Representation in the Letters of Juan Luis Vives." In *Self-Presentation and Social Identification: The*

Rhetoric and Pragmatics of Letter Writing in Early Modern Times, ed. Toon Van Houdt, Jan Papy, Gilbert Tournoy, and Constant Matheeussen. Leuven, 2002: 405–26.

Gérard, Mireille. "Art épistolaire et art de la conversation: les vertus de la familiarité." *Revue d'histoire littéraire de la France* 6 (1978): 958–76.

Geri, Lorenzo. *'Ferrea voluntas.' Il tema della scrittura nell'opera di Francesco Petrarca.* Rome, 2007.

Gerlo, A. "The *Opus de conscribendis epistolis* of Erasmus and the Tradition of the Ars Epistolica." In *Classical Influences on European Culture A.D. 500–1500,* ed. R. R. Bolgar. Cambridge, Eng., 1971: 103–14.

Gibson, Roy K., and A. D. Morrison. "What Is a Letter?" In *Ancient Letters: Classical and Late Antique Epistolography,* ed. Ruth Morello and A. D. Morrison. Oxford, 2007: 1–16.

Gill, Christopher. "Is There a Concept of Person in Greek Philosophy?" In *Companions to Ancient Thought: Psychology,* ed. Stephen Everson. Cambridge, Eng., 1991: 166–93.

———. "Personhood and Personality: The Four-*Personae* Theory in Cicero, *De Officiis I.*" *Oxford Studies in Ancient Philosophy* 6 (1988): 169–99.

———. "The Question of Character-Development: Plutarch and Tacitus." *Classical Quarterly* 33 (1983): 469–87.

———. *The Structured Self in Hellenistic and Roman Thought.* Oxford, 2006.

Gilman, Donald. "Energizing Rhetoric: Montaigne's 'De l'experience' and the Art of Imaging." In *Le visage changeant de Montaigne / The Changing Face of Montaigne,* ed. Keith Cameron and Laura Willett. Paris, 2003: 103–19.

Ginzburg, Carlo. *Wooden Eyes: Nine Reflections on Distance.* Trans. Martin Ryle and Kate Soper. New York, 2001.

Goldin Folena, Daniela. "*Familiarium rerum liber,* Petrarca e la problematica epistolare." In *Alla lettera: Teorie e pratiche epistolari dai Greci al novecento,* ed. Adriana Chernello. Milan, 1998: 51–82.

———. "Pluristilismo del *Familiarium rerum liber.*" In *Motivi e forme delle "Familiari" di Francesco Petrarca,* ed. Claudia Berra. Milan, 2003: 261–90.

Gombrich, E. H. "The Debate on Primitivism in Ancient Rhetoric." *Journal of the Warburg and Courtauld Institutes* 29 (1966): 24–38.

———. *Norm and Form: Studies in the Art of the Renaissance.* Vol. 1. Chicago, 1966.

———. "Style." In *International Encyclopedia of the Social Sciences,* ed. David L. Sills. vol. 15. New York, 1968: 352–61.

Grafton, Anthony. *Commerce with the Classics: Ancient Books and Renaissance Readers.* Ann Arbor, 1997.

———. "The Humanist as Reader." In *A History of Reading in the West,* ed. Guglielmo Cavallo and Roger Chartier, trans. Lydia G. Cochrane. Amherst, 1999: 179–212.

———. "Renaissance Readers and Ancient Texts: Comments on Some Commentaries." *Renaissance Quarterly* 38 (1985): 615–49.

Grendler, Paul F. *Schooling in Renaissance Italy: Literacy and Learning, 1300–1600.* Baltimore, 1989.

Grimaldi, William M. A., S. J. *Aristotle, Rhetoric I: A Commentary.* New York, 1980.

———. *Aristotle, Rhetoric II: A Commentary.* New York, 1988.

Guillén, Claudio. "Notes toward the Study of the Renaissance Letter." In *Renaissance Genres: Essays on Theory, History, and Interpretation,* ed. Barbara Kiefer Lewalski. Cambridge, Mass., 1986: 70–101.

Güntert, Georges. "Petrarca e il Ventoso: dalla '*Cupiditas vivendi*' al desiderio '*scribendi*.' L'epistola familiare IV, 1 come autoritratto lettarario-morale." In *Petrarca e i suoi lettori,* ed. Vittorio Caratozzolo and Georges Güntert. Ravenna, 2000: 143–56.

Hackel, Heidi Brayman. *Reading Material in Early Modern England: Print, Gender, and Literacy.* Cambridge, Eng., 2005.

Haebler, Konrad. *The Study of Incunabula.* Trans. Lucy Eugenia Osborne. New York, 1933.

Halkin, Léon-E. *Erasmus ex Erasmo: Érasme éditeur de sa correspondance.* Aubel, Belgium, 1983.

———. "Le traité d'art épistolaire d'Érasme." *Moreana* 21 (1984): 25–30.

Hall, Michael L. "Diverse Ways: Montaigne's *Ethos* and the Rhetoric of Indirection." *Montaigne Studies* 14 (2002): 65–80.

Halliwell, Stephen. "Traditional Greek Conceptions of Character." In *Characterization and Individuality in Greek Literature,* ed. Christopher Pelling. Oxford, 1990: 32–59.

Hands, A. R. "*Postremo Suo Tantum Ingenio Utebatur.*" *Classical Quarterly,* n.s., 24 (1974): 312–17.

Havelock, Eric A. *Preface to Plato.* Cambridge, Mass., 1963.

Hayum, Andrée. "Dürer's Portrait of Erasmus and the *Ars Typographorum.*" *Renaissance Quarterly* 38 (1985): 650–87.

Heidegger, Martin. "Letter on Humanism." In *Basic Writings,* ed. David Farrell Krell. New York, 1977: 189–242.

Hellegouarc'h, J. *Le vocabulaire latin des relations et des partis politiques sous la république.* Paris, 1963.

Henderson, Judith Rice. "The Composition of Erasmus' *Opus de conscribendis epistolis*: Evidence for the Growth of a Mind." *Acta Conventus Neo-Latini Torontonensis* 37 (1988): 147–54.

———. "Defining the Genre of the Letter: Juan Luis Vives' *De conscribendis epistolis.*" *Renaissance and Reformation / Renaissance et Réforme,* n.s., 7 (1983): 89–105.

———. "Despauterius' *Syntaxis* (1509): The Earliest Publication of Erasmus' *De Conscribendis Epistolis*." *Humanistica Lovaniensia* 37 (1988): 175–210.

———. "The Enigma of Erasmus' *Conficiendarum epistolarum formula*." *Renaissance and Reformation*, n.s., 13 (1989): 313–30.

———. "Erasmian Ciceronians: Reformation Teachers of Letter-Writing." *Rhetorica* 10 (1992): 273–302.

———. "Erasmus on the Art of Letter-Writing." In *Renaissance Eloquence*, ed. James J. Murphy. Berkeley, 1983: 331–55.

———. "Humanist Letter Writing: Private Conversation or Public Forum?" In *Self-Presentation and Social Identification: The Rhetoric and Pragmatics of Letter Writing in Early Modern Times*, ed. Toon Van Houdt, Jan Papy, Gilbert Tournoy, and Constant Matheeussen. Leuven, 2002: 17–38.

———. "On Reading the Rhetoric of the Renaissance Letter." In *Renaissance-Rhetorik / Renaissance Rhetoric*, ed. Heinrich F. Plett. Berlin, 1993: 143–62.

———. "Valla's *Elegantiae* and the Humanist Attack on the *Ars dictaminis*." *Rhetorica* 19 (2001): 249–68.

Henrion, Roger. "Les origines du mot *familia*." *L'antiquité classique* 10 (1941): 37–69 and 11 (1942): 253–87.

Hinds, Stephen. "Defamiliarizing Latin Literature, from Petrarch to Pulp Fiction." *TAPA* 135 (2005): 49–81.

———. "Petrarch, Cicero, Virgil: Virtual Community in *Familiares* 24, 4." In *Materiali e discussioni per l'analisi dei testi classici* 52 (2004): 157–75.

Hornbeak, Karen Gee. "The Complete Letter-Writer in English, 1568–1800." *Smith College Studies in Modern Languages* 15 (1934): 1–150.

Hughes, Frank W. "The Rhetoric of Letters." In *The Thessalonians Debate*, ed. Karl P. Donfried and Johannes Bentler. Grand Rapids, Mich., 2000: 194–240.

Hutchinson, G. O. *Cicero's Correspondence: A Literary Study*. Oxford, 1998.

Hutson, Lorna. "*Ethopoeia*, Source-Study and Legal History: A Post-Theoretical Approach to the Question of 'Character' in Shakespearean Drama." In *Post-Theory: New Directions in Criticism*, ed. Martin McQuillan, Graeme Macdonald, Robin Purves, and Stephen Thomson. Edinburgh, 1999: 139–60.

Hyde, Michael J., ed. *The "Ethos" of Rhetoric*. Columbia, S.C., 2004.

Inwood, Brad. "The Importance of Form in Seneca's Philosophical Letters." In *Ancient Letters: Classical and Late Latin Epistolography*, ed. Ruth Morello and A. D. Morrison. Oxford, 2007: 133–48.

———. *Reading Seneca: Stoic Philosophy at Rome*. Oxford, 2005.

Isnardi-Parente, Margherita. "Érasme, la République de Platon et la communauté des biens." In *Erasmus of Rotterdam: The Man and the Scholar*, ed. J. Sperna Weiland and W. Th. M. Frijhoff. Leiden, 1988: 40–45.

Jardine, Lisa. "Before Clarissa: Erasmus, 'Letters of Obscure Men,' and Epistolary Fictions." In *Self-Presentation and Social Identification: The Rhetoric and*

Pragmatics of Letter Writing in Early Modern Times, ed. Toon Van Houdt, Jan Papy, Gilbert Tournoy, and Constant Matheeussen. Leuven, 2002: 385–403.

———. *Erasmus, Man of Letters: The Construction of Charisma in Print.* Princeton, 1993.

———. "Reading and the Technology of Textual Affect." In *Reading Shakespeare Historically,* ed. Jardine. London, 1996: 78–97.

Johnson, R. "Isocrates' Methods of Teaching." *American Journal of Philology* 80 (1959): 25–36.

Jolidon, A. "L'évolution psychologique et littéraire d'Érasme d'après les variantes du '*De conscribendis epistolis.*'" *Acta Conventus Neo-Latini Amstelodamensis.* Munich, 1979: 566–87.

Juřen, Vladimír. "Les notes de Politien sur les lettres de Cicéron à Brutus, Quintus et Atticus." *Rinascimento,* n.s., 28 (1998): 235–56.

Kallendorf, Craig. "Marginalia and the Rise of Early Modern Subjectivity." In *On Renaissance Commentaries,* ed. Mariane Pade. Hildesheim, 2005: 111–28.

Kemp, Martin. "'Equal Excellences': Lomazzo and the Explanation of Individual Style in the Visual Arts." *Renaissance Studies* 1 (1987): 1–26.

Kennedy, George A. *Quintilian.* New York, 1969.

———. "The Rhetoric of Advocacy in Greece and Rome." *American Journal of Philology* 89 (1968): 385–436.

Kennedy, William J. *Rhetorical Norms in Renaissance Literature.* New Haven, 1978.

Keohane, Nannerl O. "Montaigne's Individualism." *Political Theory* 5 (1977): 363–90.

Kerferd, G. B. "The Search for Personal Identity in Stoic Thought." *Bulletin of the John Rylands University Library of Manchester* 55 (1972): 177–96.

Kircher, Timothy. *The Poet's Wisdom: The Humanists, the Church, and the Formation of Philosophy in the Early Renaissance.* Leiden, 2006.

Konstan, David. *Friendship in the Classical World.* Cambridge, Eng., 1997.

Konstantinovic, Isabelle. *Montaigne et Plutarque. Travaux d'humanisme et Renaissance CCXXXI.* Geneva, 1989.

Kraye, Jill. "Cicero, Stoicism, and Textual Criticism: Poliziano on ΚΑΤΟΡΘΩΜΑ." *Rinascimento,* n.s., 23 (1983): 79–110.

———. "Erasmus and the Canonization of Aristotle: The Letter to John More." In *England and the Continental Renaissance: Essays in Honor of J. B. Trapp,* ed. Edward Cheney and Peter Mack. Woodbridge, Eng., 1990: 37–52.

———. "Stoicism in the Renaissance from Petrarch to Lipsius." *Grotiana,* n.s., 22/23 (2001/2002): 21–45.

Kritzman, Lawrence D. *The Fabulous Imagination: On Montaigne's Essays.* New York, 2009.

Kushner, Eva. "Erasmus and the Paradox of Subjectivity." *Erasmus of Rotterdam Society Yearbook* 18 (1998): 1–20.

Kustas, George L. "The Literary Criticism of Photius." Ελληνικα 17 (1962): 132–69.
———. *Studies in Byzantine Rhetoric*. Thessaloniki, 1973.
Lamarque, Henri. "La lettre de Pétrarque à Sénèque (*Fam.*, XXIV, V)." *Revue des études italiennes* 50 (2004): 359–66.
Langer, Ullrich, ed. *The Cambridge Companion to Montaigne*. Cambridge, Eng., 2005.
———. *Perfect Friendship: Studies in Literature and Moral Philosophy from Boccaccio to Corneille*. Geneva, 1994.
Lanham, Carol Dana. "Freshman Composition in the Early Middle Ages: Epistolography and Rhetoric before the *Ars Dictaminis*." *Viator* 23 (1992): 115–34.
Lanzillotta, Maria Accame. "Le postille del Petrarca a Quintiliano (Cor. Parigino lat. 7720)." *Quaderni Petrarcheschi* 5 (1988): 1–201.
La Roncière, Charles de. "La vie privée des notables toscans au seuil de la Renaissance." In *De l'Europe féodale à la Renaissance*, ed. Georges Duby. Paris, 1985: 161–300.
Leach, Eleanor Winsor. "Absence and Desire in Cicero's *De amicitia*." *Classical World* 87 (1993): 3–20.
LeClercq, Jean. "L'amitié dans les lettres au moyen âge." *Revue du moyen âge latin* 1 (1945): 391–410.
———. "Le genre épistolaire au moyen âge." *Revue du moyen âge latin* 2 (1946): 63–70.
Lecointe, Jean. *L'idéal et la différence: La perception de la personalité littéraire à la Renaissance*. Geneva, 1993.
Leeman, A. D. *Orationis ratio: The Stylistic Theories and Practice of the Roman Orators, Historians, and Philosophers*. 2 vols. Amsterdam, 1986.
Lesses, Glenn. "Austere Friends: The Stoics and Friendship." *Apeiron* 26 (1993): 57–75.
Leushuis, Reinier. "The Mimesis of Marriage: Dialogue and Intimacy in Erasmus's Matrimonial Writings." *Renaissance Quarterly* 57 (2004): 1278–305.
Lévy, Carlos. "La conversation à Rome à la fin de la République: des pratiques sans théorie?" *Rhetorica* 11 (1993): 399–414.
Lewis, V. Bradley. "The Rhetoric of Philosophical Politics in Plato's Seventh Letter." *Philosophy and Rhetoric* 33 (2000): 23–38.
Lockwood, J. F. "Ηθικη Λεξις and Dinarchus." *Classical Quarterly* 23 (1929): 180–85.
Loewenstein, Joseph. "For a History of Literary Property: John Wolfe's Reformation." *English Literary Renaissance* 18 (1988): 389–412.
———. "The Script in the Marketplace." *Representations* 12 (1985): 101–14.
Lokaj, Rodney J. "Narrative Technique in Petrarch's *Familiares*." *Linguistica e letteratura* 24 (1999): 63–69.

Lorch, Maristella. "Petrarch, Cicero, and the Classical Pagan Tradition." In *Renaissance Humanism: Foundations, Forms, and Legacy,* ed. Albert J. Rabil Jr. Vol. 1. Philadelphia, 1988: 71–94.
MacDowell, Douglas M. *The Law in Classical Athens.* Ithaca, 1978.
———. "The ΟΙΚΟΣ in Athenian Law." *Classical Quarterly,* n.s., 39 (1989): 10–21.
Mack, Peter. *Reading and Rhetoric in Montaigne and Shakespeare.* London, 2010.
———. "Rhetoric and the Essay." *Rhetoric Society Quarterly* 23 (1993): 41–49.
———. "Rhetoric, Ethics and Reading in the Renaissance." *Renaissance Studies* 19 (2005): 1–21.
Maclean, Ian. *Montaigne Philosophe.* Paris, 1996.
———. "'Le païs au délà': Montaigne and Philosophical Speculation." In *Montaigne: Essays in Memory of Richard Sayce,* ed. I. D. McFarlane and Ian Maclean. Oxford, 1982: 101–32.
MacPhail, Eric. *The Voyage to Rome in French Renaissance Literature.* Stanford French and Italian Studies 68 (1990).
Malherbe, Abraham J. *Ancient Epistolary Theorists.* Atlanta, 1988.
Mallette, Karla. "Beyond Mimesis: Aristotle's *Poetics* in the Medieval Mediterranean." *PMLA* 124 (2009): 583–91.
Mann, Nicolas. *Petrarch.* Oxford, 1984.
Martellotti, Guido. "La questione dei due Seneca da Petrarca a Benvenuto." *Italia medioevale e umanistica* 15 (1972): 149–69.
Martin, Henri-Jean. *The History and Power of Writing.* Trans. Lydia G. Cochrane. Chicago, 1994.
Maskell, David. "The Evolution of the *Essais.*" In *Montaigne: Essays in Memory of Richard Sayce,* ed. I. D. McFarlane and Ian Maclean. Oxford, 1982: 13–34.
Massing, Jean Michel. *Erasmian Wit and Proverbial Wisdom: Illustrated Moral Compendium for François I.* London, 1997.
Mathie, W. "Property in the Political Science of Aristotle." In *Theories of Property: Aristotle to the Present,* ed. Anthony Parel and Thomas Flanagan. Waterloo, Ont., 1979: 13–32.
Mathieu-Castellani, Gisèle. "L'intertexte rhétorique: Tacite, Quintilien, et la poétique des *Essais.*" In *Montaigne et la rhétorique,* ed. John O'Brien, Malcom Quainton, and James J. Supple. Paris, 1995: 17–26.
May, James M. *Trials of Character: The Eloquence of Ciceronian Ethos.* Chapel Hill, 1988.
Mazzocco, Angelo. "Petrarch: Founder of Renaissance Humanism?" In *Interpretations of Renaissance Humanism,* ed. Mazzocco. Leiden, 2006: 215–42.
McCahill, Elizabeth May. "Finding a Job as a Humanist: The Epistolary Collection of Lapo da Castiglionchio the Younger." *Renaissance Quarterly* 57 (2004): 1308–45.
McKinley, Mary B. "La présence du *Ciceronianus* dans 'De la vanité.'" In *Montaigne*

et la rhétorique, ed. John O'Brien, Malcom Quainton, and James J. Supple. Paris, 1995: 51–65.

———. "Vanity's Bull: Montaigne's Itineraries in III, ix." In *Le parcours des "Essais": Montaigne 1588–1988,* ed. Marcel Tetel and G. Mallary Masters. Paris, 1989: 195–208.

McLaughlin, Martin L. "Histories of Literature in the Quattrocento." In *The Languages of Literature in Renaissance Italy,* ed. Peter Hainsworth, Valerio Lucchesi, Christina Roaf, David Robey, and J. R. Woodhouse. Oxford, 1988: 63–80.

———. *Literary Imitation in the Italian Renaissance: The Theory and Practice of Literary Imitation in Italy from Dante to Bembo.* Oxford, 1995.

Mellet, Sylvie. *L'imparfait de l'indicatif en latin classique: temps, aspect, modalité.* Louvain, 1998.

Merchant, Frank Ivan. "Seneca the Philosopher and His Theory of Style." *American Journal of Philology* 26 (1905): 44–59.

Mesnard, Pierre. "Le commerce épistolaire, comme expression sociale de l'individualisme humaniste." In *Individu et Société à la Renaissance: Travaux de l'Institut pour l'Etude de la Renaissance et de l'Humanisme.* Brussels, 1969: 17–31.

Mommsen, Theodor E. "Petrarch and the Story of the Choice of Hercules." *Journal of the Warburg and Courtauld Institutes* 16 (1953): 178–92.

———. "Petrarch's Conception of the 'Dark Ages.'" *Speculum* 17 (1942): 226–42.

———. "Rudolf Agricola's Life of Petrarch." *Traditio* 8 (1952): 367–86.

Monfasani, John. "Three Notes on Renaissance Rhetoric." *Rhetorica* 5 (1987): 107–18.

Monti, Carla Maria. "Seneca '*Preceptor morum incomparabilis*': la posizione di Petrarca (*Fam.* XXIV, 5)." In *Motivi e forme delle 'Familiari' di Francesco Petrarca,* ed. Claudia Berra. Milan, 2003: 189–228.

Moreau, Philippe. "Osculum, basium, sauium." *Revue de philologie, de littérature et d'histoire ancienne* 104 (1978): 87–97.

Morello, Ruth, and A. D. Morrison, eds. *Ancient Letters: Classical and Late Antique Epistolography.* Oxford, 2007.

Moss, Ann. *Printed Commonplace-Books and the Structuring of Renaissance Thought.* Oxford, 1996.

Mouchel, Christien. *Cicéron et Sénèque dans la rhétorique de la Renaissance.* Marburg, 1990.

Murphy, James J. *Rhetoric in the Middle Ages: A History of Rhetorical Theory from St. Augustine to the Renaissance.* Berkeley, 1974.

———. "Trends in Rhetorical Incunabula." *Rhetorica* 18 (2000): 389–97.

Murphy, James J., and Martin Davies. "Rhetorical Incunabula: A Short-Title Catalogue of Texts Printed to the Year 1500." *Rhetorica* 15 (1997): 355–470.

Najemy, John M. *Between Friends: Discourses of Power and Desire in the Machiavelli-Vettori Letters of 1513–1515.* Princeton, 1993.

Nelson, Norman. "Individualism as a Criterion of the Renaissance." *Journal of English and Germanic Philology* 32 (1933): 316–34.

Nicholson, John. "The Survival of Cicero's Letters." *Studies in Latin Literature and Roman History* 9 (1998): 63–105.

Nolhac, Pierre de. *Petrarch and the Ancient World.* Boston, 1907.

———. *Pétrarque et l'humanisme.* 2 vols. Paris, 1892; rpt. 1965.

O'Connell, Michael. "Authority and the Truth of Experience in Petrarch's 'Ascent of Mount Ventoux.'" *Philological Quarterly* 62 (1983): 507–19.

Olin, John C. "Erasmus and Saint Jerome: An Appraisal of the Bond." In *Erasmus of Rotterdam: The Man and the Scholar,* ed. J. Sperna Weiland and W. Th. M. Frijhoff. Leiden, 1988: 182–86.

———. "Erasmus and Saint Jerome: The Close Bond and Its Significance." *Erasmus of Rotterdam Society Yearbook* 7 (1987): 33–53.

Ong, Walter J. *Orality and Literacy: The Technologizing of the Word.* London, 1982.

O'Sullivan, Neil. *Alcidamas, Aristophanes and the Beginnings of Greek Stylistic Theory.* Stuttgart, 1992.

Panizza, Letizia A. "Gasparino Barzizza's Commentaries on Seneca's Letters." *Traditio* 33 (1977): 297–358.

———. "Textual Interpretation in Italy, 1350–1450: Seneca's Letter I to Lucilius." *Journal of the Warburg and Courtauld Institutes* 46 (1983): 40–62.

Papy, Jan. "Creating an 'Italian' Friendship: From Petrarch's Ideal Literary Critic 'Socrates' to the Historical Reader Ludovicus Sanctus of Beringen." In *Petrarch and His Readers in the Renaissance,* ed. Karl A. E. Enenkel and Jan Papy. Leiden, 2006: 13–30.

———. "Petrarch's 'Inner Eye' in the *Familiarium libri XXIV.*" In *Meditatio—Refashioning the Self: Theory and Practice in Late Medieval and Early Modern Intellectual Culture,* ed. Karl Enenkel and Walter Melion. Leiden, 2011: 45–68.

Patterson, Lyman Ray. *Copyright in Historical Perspective.* Nashville, 1968.

Payne, John B. "Erasmus and Lefèvre d'Étaples as Interpreters of Paul." *Archiv für Reformationsgeschichte* 65 (1974): 54–83.

———. "Erasmus: Interpreter of Romans." *Sixteenth Century Essays and Studies* 2 (1971): 1–35.

Pembroke, S. G. "Oikeiōsis." In *Problems in Stoicism,* ed. Anthony A. Long. London, 1971: 114–49.

Pennacini, Adriano. "Situazione e struttura dell'epistola familiare nella teoria classica." *Quaderni di retorica e poetica* 1 (1985): 11–15.

Petersen, Erik. "'Communication of the Dead.' Notes on the *Studia humanitatis* and the Nature of Humanist Philology." In *The Uses of Greek and Latin,* ed. A. C. Dionisotti, Anthony Grafton, and Jill Kraye. London, 1988: 57–69.

Petitmengin, P. "Comment étudier l'activité d'Érasme, éditeur de textes antiques?" *Colloquia erasmiana turonensia,* vol. 1. Toronto, 1972: 217–22.

Phillips, Jane E. "*Sub evangelista persona:* The Speaking Voice in Erasmus' Paraphrase on Luke." In *Holy Scripture Speaks: The Production and Reception of Erasmus' Paraphrases on the New Testament,* ed. Hilmar M. Pabel and Mark Vessey. Toronto, 2002: 127–50.

Phillips, Margaret Mann. "Érasme et Montaigne." *Colloquia erasmiana turonensia,* vol. 1. Toronto, 1972: 479–501.

———. "Erasmus and the Art of Writing." In *Scrinium Erasmianum,* ed. J. Coppens. Leiden, 1969: 335–50.

———. "Erasmus in France in the Later Sixteenth Century." *Journal of the Warburg and Courtauld Institutes* 34 (1971): 246–61.

———. "From the *Ciceronianus* to Montaigne." In *Classical Influences on European Culture A.D. 1500–1700,* ed. R. R. Bolgar. Cambridge, Eng., 1974: 191–97.

———. "The Mystery of the Metsys Portrait." *Erasmus in English* 7 (1975): 18–21.

Pigman, G. W., III. "Barzizza's Studies of Cicero." *Rinascimento* 21 (1981): 123–63.

———. "Versions of Imitation in the Renaissance." *Renaissance Quarterly* 33 (1980): 1–32.

Pocock, J. G. A. "The Mobility of Property and the Rise of Eighteenth-Century Sociology." In *Theories of Property: Aristotle to the Present,* ed. Anthony Parel and Thomas Flanagan. Waterloo, Ont., 1979: 141–66.

Pollard, Alfred W. "The Regulation of the Book Trade in the Sixteenth Century." *The Library* 7 (1916): 18–43.

Poster, Carol. "A Conversation Halved: Epistolary Theory in Greco-Roman Antiquity." In *Letter-Writing Manuals and Instruction from Antiquity to the Present,* ed. Carol Poster and Linda C. Mitchell. Columbia, S.C., 2007: 21–51.

———. "The Economy of Letter Writing in Graeco-Roman Antiquity." In *Rhetorical Argumentation in Biblical Texts,* ed. Anders Eriksson, Thomas H. Olbricht, and Walter Übelacker. Harrisburg, Penn., 2002: 112–24.

Poster, Carol and Linda C. Mitchell, eds. *Letter-Writing Manuals and Instruction from Antiquity to the Present.* Columbia, S.C., 2007.

Quacquarelli, Antonio. *Retorica e liturgia antenicena.* Rome, 1960.

Quillen, Carol Everhart. *Rereading the Renaissance: Petrarch, Augustine, and the Language of Humanism.* Ann Arbor, 1998.

Quint, David. *Montaigne and the Quality of Mercy: Ethical and Political Themes in the "Essais."* Princeton, 1998.

Rabil, Albert, Jr. "Cicero and Erasmus' Moral Philosophy." *Erasmus of Rotterdam Society Yearbook* 8 (1988): 70–90.

Rawson, Elizabeth. *Intellectual Life in the Late Roman Republic.* London, 1985.

Regosin, Richard L. *The Matter of My Book: Montaigne's* Essais *as the Book of the Self.* Berkeley, 1977.

———. "Montaigne and His Readers." In *A New History of French Literature,* ed. Denis Hollier. Cambridge, Mass., 1989: 248–53.

Reynolds, L. D. *The Medieval Tradition of Seneca's Letters.* Oxford, 1965.

Rice, Eugene F., Jr. *Saint Jerome in the Renaissance.* Baltimore, 1985.

Riggsby, Andrew M. "The Rhetoric of Character in the Roman Courts." In *Cicero the Advocate,* ed. Jonathan Powell and Jeremy Paterson. Oxford, 2004: 165–85.

Rigolot, François. "Friendship and Voluntary Servitude: Plato, Ficino and Montaigne." *Texas Studies in Literature and Language* 47 (2005): 326–44.

Rizzo, Silvia. "Il latino del Petrarca nelle *Familiari.*" In *The Uses of Greek and Latin,* ed. A. C. Dionisotti, Anthony Grafton, and Jill Kraye. London, 1988.

Robbins, Jill. "Petrarch Reading Augustine: 'The Ascent of Mont Ventoux.'" *Philological Quarterly* 64 (1985): 533–53.

Robertson, Jean. *The Art of Letter Writing: An Essay on the Handbooks Published in England during the Sixteenth and Seventeenth Centuries.* Folcraft, Penn., 1942; rpt. 1973.

Rosenmeyer, Patricia A. *Ancient Epistolary Fictions: The Letter in Greek Literature.* Cambridge, Eng., 2001.

Ross, David O., Jr. *Style and Tradition in Catullus.* Cambridge, Mass., 1969.

Roussel, Bernard. "Exegetical Fictions? Biblical Paraphrases of the Sixteenth and Seventeenth Centuries." In *Holy Scripture Speaks: The Production and Reception of Erasmus' Paraphrases on the New Testament,* ed. Hilmar M. Pabel and Mark Vessey. Toronto, 2002: 59–83.

Rummel, Erika. "Argumentis, non contumeliis: The Humanistic Model for Religious Debate and Erasmus' Apologetic Letters." In *Self-Presentation and Social Identification: The Rhetoric and Pragmatics of Letter Writing in Early Modern Times,* ed. Toon Van Houdt, Jan Papy, Gilbert Tournoy, and Constant Matheeussen. Leuven, 2002: 305–15.

———. *Erasmus as a Translator of the Classics.* Toronto, 1985.

———. "Erasmus' Manual of Letter-Writing: Tradition and Innovation." *Renaissance and Reformation,* n.s., 13 (1989): 299–312.

Sabbadini, Remigio. *Le scoperte dei codici latini e greci ne' secoli XIV e XV.* 2 vols. Florence, 1905, 1914.

———. *Storia del ciceronianismo e di altre questioni letterarie nell'età della Rinascenza.* Turin, 1885.

Saenger, Paul. "The Implications of Incunabula Description for the History of Reading Revisited." *Bibliographical Society of America* 91 (1997): 495–504.

Saller, Richard P. "'*Familia, Domus,*' and the Roman Conception of the Family." *Phoenix* 38 (1984): 336–55.

Sattler, William. "Conceptions of *Ethos* in Ancient Rhetoric." *Speech Monographs* 14 (1947): 55–65.

Sauerländer, Willibald. "From Stilus to Style: Reflections on the Fate of a Notion." *Art History* 6 (1983): 253–70.

Sayce, Richard A. *The Essays of Montaigne: A Critical Exploration.* London, 1972.

———. "The Style of Montaigne: Word-Pairs and Word-Groups." In *Literary Style: A Symposium*, ed. Seymour Chatman. London, 1971: 383–405.
Scaglione, Aldo. "Classical Heritage and Petrarchan Self-Consciousness in the Literary Emergence of the Interior 'I.'" In *Petrarch*, ed. Harold Bloom. New York, 1989: 125–37.
Schapiro, Meyer. "Style." In *Aesthetics Today*, ed. Morris Philipson and Paul J. Gudel. New York, 1980: 137–71.
Schenkeveld, Dirk M. "The Intended Public of Demetrius's *On Style*: The Place of the Treatise in the Hellenistic Educational System." *Rhetorica* 18 (2000): 29–48.
Schmidt, Peter L. "Die Rezeption des romischen Freundschaftsbriefes (Cicero-Plinius) im frühen Humanismus (Petrarca-Coluccio Salutati)." In *Der Brief im Zeitalter der Renaissance*, ed. Franz Josef Worstbrock. Weinheim, Ger., 1983.
Schmitz, Dietmar. "La théorie de l'art épistolaire et de la conversation dans la tradition latine et néolatine." In *Art de la lettre, art de la conversation à l'époque classique en France*, ed. Bernard Bray and Christoph Strosetzki. Klincksieck, 1995: 11–23.
Scholar, Richard. *Montaigne and the Art of Free-Thinking*. Oxford, 2010.
Scholderer, Victor. "Printing at Venice to the End of 1481." *The Library* 5 (1924): 129–52.
Screech, M. A. "Commonplaces of Law, Proverbial Wisdom and Philosophy: Their Importance in Renaissance Scholarship (Rabelais, Joachim du Bellay, Montaigne)." In *Classical Influences on European Culture A.D. 1500–1700*, ed. R. R. Bolgar. Cambridge, Eng., 1974: 127–34.
Seigel, Jerrold E. *Rhetoric and Philosophy in Renaissance Humanism: The Union of Eloquence and Wisdom, Petrarch to Valla*. Princeton, 1968.
Setaioli, Aldo. "On the Date of Publication of Cicero's Letters to Atticus." *Symbolae Osloenses* 51 (1976): 105–20.
Shrank, Cathy. "'These fewe scribbled rules': Representing Scribal Intimacy in Early Modern Print." *Huntington Library Quarterly* 67 (2004): 295–313.
Sider, Robert D. "*Concedo Nulli*: Erasmus' Motto and the Figure of Paul in the Paraphrases." *Erasmus in English* 14 (1985–6): 7–10.
———. "Historical Imagination and the Presentation of Paul in Erasmus' Paraphrases on the Pauline Epistles." In *Holy Scripture Speaks: The Production and Reception of Erasmus' "Paraphrases on the New Testament,"* ed. Hilmar M. Pabel and Mark Vessey. Toronto, 2002: 185–209.
———. "'In Terms Quite Plain and Clear': The Exposition of Grace in the New Testament Paraphrases of Erasmus." *Erasmus in English* 15 (1987–8): 16–25.
Smiley, Charles Newton. "*Latinitas* and Ἑλληνισμος." *Bulletin of the University of Wisconsin* 143 (1906): 205–72.
Smith, Craig R. "*Ethos* Dwells Pervasively." In *The "Ethos" of Rhetoric*, ed. Michael J. Hyde. Columbia, S.C., 2004: 1–19.

Southern, R. W. *Medieval Humanism and Other Studies.* Oxford, 1970.
Sowards, J. K. "Erasmus and the Apologetic Textbook: A Study of the *De Duplici Copia Verborum ac Rerum.*" *Studies in Philology* 55 (1958): 122–35.
Spitzer, Leo. *Linguistics and Literary History: Essays in Stylistics.* Princeton, 1948.
Stacey, Peter. *Roman Monarchy and the Renaissance Prince.* Cambridge, Eng., 2007.
Steiner, Deborah Tarn. *The Tyrant's Writ: Myths and Images of Writing in Ancient Greece.* Princeton, 1994.
Stirewalt, M. Luther, Jr. *Studies in Ancient Greek Epistolography.* Atlanta, 1993.
Stock, Brian. "Reading, Writing, and the Self: Petrarch and His Forerunners." *New Literary History* 26 (1995): 717–30.
Storey, H. Wayne. "Il *liber* nella formazione delle *Familiari.*" In *Motivi e forme delle "Familiari" di Francesco Petrarco,* ed. Claudia Berra. Milan, 2003: 495–506.
Stowers, Stanley K. *Letter Writing in Greco-Roman Antiquity.* Philadelphia, 1986.
Striker, Gisela. "The Role of *Oikeiosis* in Stoic Ethics." *Oxford Studies in Ancient Philosophy* 1 (1983): 145–67.
Struever, Nancy S. *The Language of History in the Renaissance: Rhetoric and Historical Consciousness in Florentine Humanism.* Princeton, 1970.
———. "Montaigne's Ciceronian Pessimism: Rhetoric, Politics, Ethics." *Montaigne Studies* 14 (2002): 49–64.
———. "The Rhetoric of Familiarity: A Pedagogy of Ethics." *Philosophy and Rhetoric* 31 (1998): 91–106.
———. *Theory as Practice: Ethical Inquiry in the Renaissance.* Chicago, 1992.
Sullivan, Robert G. "Classical Epistolary Theory and the Letters of Isocrates." In *Letter-Writing Manuals and Instruction from Antiquity to the Present,* ed. Carol Poster and Linda C. Mitchell. Columbia, S.C., 2007: 7–20.
Svenbro, Jesper. "Archaic and Classical Greece: The Invention of Silent Reading." In *A History of Reading in the West,* ed. Guglielmo Cavallo and Roger Chartier, trans. Lydia G. Cochrane. Amherst, 1999: 37–63.
Taylor, Charles. *Sources of the Self: The Making of the Modern Identity.* Cambridge, Mass., 1989.
Taylor, John. "Letters and Letter Collections in England, 1300–1420." *Nottingham Medieval Studies* 24 (1980): 57–70.
Tetel, Marcel. "De la subjectivité augustinienne dans le *Secretum* et *Les Essais.*" In *Augustinus in der Neuzeit,* ed. Dominique de Courcelles. Turnhout, 1998: 23–32.
Thompson, Elbert N. S. *Literary Bypaths of the Renaissance.* New Haven, 1924.
Thornton, Dora. *The Scholar in His Study: Ownership and Experience in Renaissance Italy.* New Haven, 1997.
Todd, William Mills, III. *The Familiar Letter as a Literary Genre in the Age of Pushkin.* Princeton, 1976.

Tracy, James D. "Erasmus among the Postmodernists: *Dissimulatio, Bonae Literae,* and *Docta Pietas* Revisited." In *Erasmus' Vision of the Church,* ed. Hilmar M. Pabel. Ann Arbor, 1995.

Trapp, J. B. *Erasmus, Colet and More: The Early Tudor Humanists and Their Books.* London, 1991.

Treggiari, Susan. "Sentiment and Property: Some Roman Attitudes." In *Theories of Property: Aristotle to the Present,* ed. Anthony Parel and Thomas Flanagan. Waterloo, Ont., 1979: 53–85.

———. "The Upper-Class House as a Symbol and Focus of Emotion in Cicero." *Journal of Roman Archaeology* 12 (1999): 33–56.

Trilling, Lionel. *Sincerity and Authenticity.* Cambridge, Mass., 1971.

Trimpi, Wesley. *Ben Jonson's Poems: A Study in the Plain Style.* Stanford, 1962.

Tripet, Arnaud. *Pétrarque ou la connaissance de soi.* Geneva, 1967.

Ullman, B. L. *Studies in the Italian Renaissance.* Rome, 1955.

Vaillancourt, Luc. *La lettre familière au XVIe siècle: Rhétorique humaniste de l'épistolaire.* Paris, 2003.

Vallese, Giulio. "Érasme et Cicéron: Les lettres-préfaces au *De Officiis* et aux *Tusculanes.*" In *Colloquia erasmiana turonensia,* vol. 1. Toronto, 1972: 241–46.

Vance, Jacob. "Duty, Conciliation, and Ontology in the *Essais.*" In *Montaigne after Theory, Theory after Montaigne,* ed. Fahi Zallona. Seattle, 2009: 75–99.

van Hook, Larue. *The Metaphorical Terminology of Greek Rhetoric and Literary Criticism.* Chicago, 1905.

van Poll-van de Lisdonk, Miekske L. "Humanists, Letters, and *Proverbia:* Some Aspects of Erasmus' First Collection of Proverbs." *Erasmus of Rotterdam Society Yearbook* 26 (2006): 1–15.

Vecchi, Giuseppe. "Il 'proverbio' nella pratica letteraria dei dettatori della scuola di Bologna." *Studi mediolatini e vulgari* 2 (1954): 283–302.

Vessey, Mark. "Erasmus' Lucubrations and the Renaissance Life of Texts." *Erasmus of Rotterdam Society Yearbook* 24 (2004): 23–51.

———. "The Tongue and the Book: Erasmus' *Paraphrases on the New Testament* and the Arts of Scripture." In *Holy Scripture Speaks: The Production and Reception of Erasmus' Paraphrases on the New Testament,* ed. Hilmar M. Pabel and Mark Vessey. Toronto, 2002: 29–58.

Villey, Pierre. *Les sources et l'évolution des Essais de Montaigne.* 2 vols. Paris, 1908; rpt. New York, 1968.

Ward, John O. "Rhetorical Theory and the Rise and Decline of *Dictamen* in the Middle Ages and Early Renaissance." *Rhetorica* 19 (2001): 175–223.

Waszink, J. H. "Classical Philology." In *Leiden University in the Seventeenth Century: An Exchange of Learning,* ed. Th. H. Lunsingh Scheurleer and G. H. M. Posthumus Meyjes. Leiden, 1975: 161–75.

Watson, Alan. *The Law of Property in the Later Roman Republic.* Oxford, 1968.

Weinberg, Bernard. "Translations and Commentaries of Demetrius, *On Style* to 1600: A Bibliography." *Philological Quarterly* 30 (1951): 353–80.
Weller, Barry. "The Rhetoric of Friendship in Montaigne's *Essais*." *New Literary History* 93 (1978): 503–23.
White, Peter. "*Amicitia* and the Profession of Poetry in Early Imperial Rome." *Journal of Roman Studies* 68 (1978): 74–92.
———. *Cicero in Letters: Epistolary Relations of the Late Republic*. Oxford, 2010.
Wilkins, Ernest Hatch. *Life of Petrarch*. Chicago, 1961.
———. *Petrarch's Correspondence*. Padua, 1960.
———. *Studies in the Life and Works of Petrarch*. Cambridge, Mass., 1955.
Wilson, Marcus. "Seneca's *Epistles* Reclassified." In *Texts, Ideas and the Classics: Scholarship, Theory, and Classical Literature*, ed. S. J. Harrison. Oxford, 2001: 164–87.
Wisse, Jacob. *Ethos and Pathos from Aristotle to Cicero*. Amsterdam, 1989.
Witt, Ronald. *'In the Footsteps of the Ancients': The Origins of Humanism from Lovato to Bruni*. Leiden, 2000.
———. "Medieval '*Ars Dictaminis*' and the Beginnings of Humanism: A New Construction of the Problem." *Renaissance Quarterly* 35 (1982): 1–35.
———. "Medieval Italian Culture and the Origins of Humanism as a Stylistic Ideal." In *Renaissance Humanism: Foundations, Forms, and Legacy*, ed. Albert Rabil Jr. Vol. 1. Philadelphia, 1988: 29–70.
Wohl, Victoria. "Plato avant la lettre: Authenticity in Plato's Epistles." *Ramus* 27 (1998): 60–93.
Wolff, Etienne. "Pétrarque et le genre épistolaire: réflexions sur *Familiares* I, 1." In *Epistulae Antiquae II: Actes du IIe Colloque International: Le genre épistolaire antique et ses prolongements européens*, ed. Léon Nadjo and Elisabeth Gavoille. Louvain, 2002: 379–85.

Index

akribeia, 13, 36
amicitia (*see also* friendship), 29, 66, 94
Amyot, Jacques: as translator of Plutarch, 110–11
Apollonius of Tyana: as letter writer, 72
Apuleius, 63
Aristotle: on character (see also *ēthos*; *mores*), 18–19, 21–22; on friendship, 17, 99; on genres of oratory, 11–15, 20, 78; on *kyrios*, 17–18, 35; on legal possession, 15–18, 33, 48, 105; letters of, 35, 72; on *lexis agōnistikē*, 12, 39; on *lexis graphikē*, 12, 35, 39, 56; *Nicomachean Ethics*, 24, 35; on *oikeion*, 8, 14–17, 19–20, 23, 25, 33, 35, 59, 96, 123; on *oikeiotēs*, 17, 59; on *oikos*, 8, 15–16, 19, 23, 33; *Poetics*, 19, 25; *Politics*, 15; *Rhetoric*, 11–17, 35, 39, 48, 59, 96; on style, 17–20, 34–36, 48, 64, 123; on *to prepon*, 15, 20; on writing, 11–14, 30, 64; on written vs. oral style, 12–14, 20, 64
ars dictaminis, 4, 122
Artemon, 35
Atticus: as addressee of Cicero, 2, 26, 28–34, 36, 49, 65–66, 69
Augustine, 51, 65; *Confessions*, 56

Baldwin, Geoff: on individualism, 121
Barzizza, Gasparo: *Liber epistolarum*, 70
Basil of Caesarea: as letter writer, 72
Boccaccio, Giovanni, 60, 63
Boétie, Etienne de la, 99–100
Bracciolini, Poggio, 69
Bruni, Leonardo, 69–70

Brutus: as addressee of Cicero, 65, 117
Burckhardt, Jacob: on the Italian Renaissance, 121

Caesar, Julius: as recorder of his deeds, 112; style of, 28
Cassiodorus, 51
Cato, 23–24, 66
character (see also *ēthos*; *mores*), 15, 18–22, 25, 27–29, 31, 34–37, 43–46, 75, 79, 84–85, 87–88, 109
Cicero: *Academica*, 23–24, 66, 119; on accommodating style to character, 43–44; on *aliena*, 26–27; on *alienatio*, 23–24, 34; and Aristotle's *Rhetoric*, 11; on *benevolentia*, 80; *Brutus*, 20; on character (*mores*), 15, 20–22, 25, 34, 43–44, 51; on *commendatio*, 22–24, 34, 80; on *conciliatio*, 21–25, 34, 37–38, 80; on *consuetudo*, 85; *De amicitia*, 66; *De finibus*, 23–24; *De inventione*, 80, 122; *De legibus*, 119; *De officiis*, 15, 25–27, 38, 59, 61, 66, 105–106, 122; *De oratore*, 20–21, 25, 28, 51, 84; on *decorum*, 15, 27–28; on defining a letter, 30–33, 64, 79, 81; on distance in friendship, 64, 90, 111, 116; on divisions of oratory, 14–15, 20, 28, 31–33, 57, 78, 109; on *dominus*, 26–27; on *domus*, 26–27, 38; on epistolary theory, 14, 20, 30–33, 52–54, 58, 64, 80–81; on *exordium*, 80; on friendship, 28–29, 99; imitation of, 75, 78, 82–90, 101, 121; letters of, 2, 4, 29–33, 36, 39,

145

Cicero (*continued*)
48–50, 55–56, 66, 69, 72, 77–78, 110, 119, 121, 124; *Letters to Friends* (*Epistolae ad familiares*), 30–33, 71–72; Montaigne on, 99–103, 105; moral philosophy of, 23, 25–27, 38, 51; *On Old Age*, 66; *Orator*, 15, 20, 22, 25, 32; Petrarch on, 48–60; on *proprium*, 26–28, 33–34, 59, 105, 123; on *sermo*, 29–33, 38–39, 64, 65, 106, 111, 119; and spontaneity, 31–32, 54–56, 58–59, 66–67; and Stoicism, 22–23, 25, 51; on *suum*, 26–27, 34, 59, 105, 123; *Tusculan Disputations*, 66

Colonna, Giovanni, 56, 64
commendatio, 23–24, 35, 80, 87, 98, 122
conciliatio, 23, 25, 29, 37, 80, 85
consuetudo, 11, 85

decorum (*to prepon*), 15, 20, 27–28, 34, 45, 78, 105
Demetrius: on *akribeia*, 36; on character, 34, 36, 109; on dialogue, 34; on epistolary theory, 1–2, 14, 34–36, 79; on *idios*, 35–36; on the legal concept of private property, 36; *On Style* (*Peri hermēneias*), 34–36; on persuasiveness (*to pithanon*), 36; rediscovery of, 2; on soul, 34; on *synētheia*, 35–36; on vividness (*enargeia*), 36
Democritus: as letter writer, 72
Demosthenes: as letter writer, 72
dialogue (see also *sermo*), 14, 34–35, 66, 81–82, 119
dictaminal theory. See *ars dictaminis*
domus (see also *familia* and *oikos*), 16, 26–27, 38

Ennius, 63, 66
Epicurus, 40, 62; letters of, 98, 100

epistolary novels, 2, 71
epistolary theory, 1–2, 11, 14, 20, 29–33, 38–39, 52–59, 74, 77–81, 93–94, 98–99, 101–103, 122
Erasmus: and Aristotle's *Rhetoric*, 11; *Ciceronianus*, 80–85; on Cicero's letters, 73–74, 77, 81; on *commendatio*, 80; on *conciliatio*, 80; *De conscribendis epistolis*, 77–81; *De copia*, 75; *De ratione studii*, 75–76, 87; *De recta pronuntiatione*, 76; on the *genus familiare*, 74, 78, 80–82, 93; on Jerome, 86–89; *Paraclesis*, 89–92; *Paraphrase on Romans*, 91–94, 96; on penmanship, 76; on *prosopopoiia*, 75, 92
ethologia (see also *prosopopoiia*), 43, 75, 92
ēthos (see also character; *mores*), 15, 18–22, 25, 34–35, 43, 45, 51, 79–80, 88, 92
Euripides: as letter writer, 72

familia (see also *domus*; *oikos*), 8, 16, 33, 59, 69, 73
familiaritas (see also *oikeiotēs*), 28, 39, 41, 48, 53, 59, 67, 73–75, 80–82, 85–87, 89, 94, 106, 117, 122
Ficino, Marsilio, 70
Filelfo, Francesco, 69–70
friendship (see also *amicitia*), 40–41, 52, 66–67, 69, 80, 94, 99–100, 109, 112, 116–117

Gadamer, Hans-Georg, 4–10, 86, 89; on the miracle of understanding, 86; on rhetoric and hermeneutics, 4–5, 7; on self-expression, 89; on style, 8–10; *Truth and Method*, 5, 7
Gerard, Cornelius: correspondence with Erasmus, 74

Goethe: on style, 9–10
Grimani, Domenico: addressee of Erasmus, 92

Heraclitus: as letter writer, 72
Herodotus, 36
Hesiod, 15, 105, 113
Hippocrates: as letter writer, 72
Homer: *Odyssey,* 18; Petrarch's letter to, 67–68
Horace, 67
Hoskyns, John: *Directions for Speech and Style* (c. 1599), 1–4, 8

imitation: 9, 42–44, 47, 61–62, 72, 75, 82
individualism: Cicero on, 27–28, 120; Montaigne on, 120–124; Petrarch on, 9–10, 119–124
ingenium: in *Ciceronianus,* 83, 85; in Petrarch, 62; in Quintilian, 47; in Seneca, 40–41

Jerome, St., 72, 86–90, 117, 119
Jonson, Ben: *Timber, or Discoveries* (1641), 1–2, 4, 8, 121
Julian the Apostate: as letter writer, 72

Keohane, Nannerl O.: on individualism in the Renaissance, 120–121, 123

Laelius: as interlocutor in Cicero, 65–66
legal possession, 8, 45; in Aristotle, 16, 105; in Cicero, 26–28, 105; in Demetrius, 36; in Hesiod, 15–16, 105, 113; in Montaigne, 104–106, 113–116, 123; in Petrarch, 59–61; in Seneca, 38, 41–42, 46; and style, 7, 9, 17–19, 27–28, 33, 45–46, 59–61, 105–107, 123

letter writing, 1–3, 5, 8, 11, 14, 20, 25, 28–39, 41–42, 47–48, 49–64, 66–72, 73–84, 86–95, 96, 98–103, 109–111, 122, 124
Libanius: as letter writer, 72
Lipsius, Justus: *Institutio epistolica* (1590), 1
Longueil, Christophe de: in *Ciceronianus,* 82–83
Lycurgus: Montaigne on, 113

Macpherson, C. B.: on individualism, 123
Macrobius, 61
Montaigne: as anti-Ciceronian, 55, 98; on Aristotle, 99, 105; on Cicero, 98–103, 105; on distance in friendship, 111–112, 114–116; and Italian letter collections, 70; on legal possession, 104–106, 113–116, 123; on Plutarch, 103–104, 109–110, 118; on Seneca, 98–100, 102–103, 105, 108–110, 118
mores (*see also* character; *ēthos*), 21–22, 25, 37, 45, 84

Nelli, Francesco, 57, 68

oikeion, 8, 14–17, 19–20, 23–27, 34, 36, 45, 59, 78
oikeiotēs (see also *familiaritas*), 17, 35, 59, 84
oikos (see also *domus; familia*), 8, 15, 19, 23, 33, 35, 59, 123
oratory: vs. epistolary writing, 2, 11, 14, 20, 32, 36–37, 39, 42, 49, 74–75, 84, 109, 122

pathos, 15, 45, 79
Paul, St., 56, 91–94
Petrarch: on *alienum,* 107; and Aristotle's *Rhetoric,* 11; in *Ciceronianus,*

INDEX | 147

Petrarch (*continued*)
83; Cicero's influence on, 48–61, 66–67, 69; on conversation (*conversatio*), 64–65; *De vita solitaria*, 67; on distance in friendship, 64, 67–68, 114, 116; on *familiaria*, 52–53; on *familiaritas*, 52–54, 55, 59, 67, 117; on *familiariter*, 54, 63; and friends, 64–67; on overcoming absence, 68; on *proprietas*, 59–61; on *proprium*, 9, 61, 107; Quintilian's influence on, 47–48, 62; Seneca's influence on, 51–52, 61–63, 69, 111; and spontaneity, 54–56, 58–59; on *suum*, 60–61, 107

Phalaris (sixth-century Greek tyrant), 71–72

Philostratus: as letter writer, 72

Piccolomini, Aeneas Silvius, 69–71; *A Tale of Two Lovers* (*De duobus amantibus historia*), 71

Pico della Mirandola, Giovanni, 70

Plato: *Gorgias*, 11; as letter writer, 72; *Phaedrus*, 11; *Republic*, 15; *Sophist*, 14; on types of discourse, 14

Plautus, 63

Pliny the Younger: imitation of 75; Letters of, 72; Montaigne on, 98, 100

Plutarch: on character, 109; Montaigne on, 103–104, 109–110, 118

Poliziano, Angelo, 70

Pompey: in *Ciceronianus*, 82; Montaigne on, 117

to prepon. See *decorum*

proprietas, 41, 45–47, 59

proprium (of property or style), 9, 26–27, 34, 38, 45, 59, 61, 79, 105–107, 123

prosopopoiia (see also *ethologia*), 43, 92

Quintilian: on the centrality of oratory, 42, 46; on character, 43–45; in *Ciceronianus*, 84–85; on conversation (*sermocinatrix*), 14, 42; on *ethologia*, 43; on *genera dicendi*, 46–47; influence on Erasmus, 75, 79; influence on Petrarch, 47, 83; on *ingenium*, 46–47, 62; on *pathos*, 45; on *proprietas*, 45–47; on self-expression, 44, 46–47; on style, 43–44, 46–47

Quintus: as addressee of Cicero, 32, 119

Rhetorica ad Herennium, 122

Salutati, Coluccio, 69–71

Seneca: on aims of writing, 36–38, 109; on character, 37; in *Ciceronianus*, 83; on *conciliatio*, 37; on digestion, 41, 63; on distance, 111; on *familiaritas*, 39, 41; on *familiariter*, 39–41, 48, 63; on *ingenium*, 41; on legal possession, 38–39, 41–42, 46; letters of, 26, 36–43, 51; Montaigne on, 98–100, 102–103, 105, 108–110, 118; as Platonizing philosopher, 46; on *proprietas*, 41–42, 46; reading Epicurus, 39–40, 61; on self-expression, 36–37; on the soul, 38–39, 105; and spontaneity, 38; on travel, 41

sermo (see also dialogue), 14, 29–33, 36, 38, 42–43, 87, 91, 106, 111, 119; Cicero on, 106, 111, 119; Montaigne on, 106; Seneca on, 38, 42, 111

spontaneity (in style), 31–32, 54–56, 58–59, 66–67

Stoicism, 49; and selfhood, 22–25, 34, 123

suum (of property or style), 18–19, 26–27, 34, 60–61, 76, 83–84, 105–107, 123

synētheia, 35–36

Taylor, Charles, 3; on individualism, 120
Terence, 66
Thucydides, 36
to prepon. See *decorum*

Varro, Marcus: as interlocutor of Cicero, 65–66
Virgil, 63, 67

Warham, William, Archbishop of Canterbury: as addressee of Erasmus, 86

Xenophon: *Economics,* 66; Montaigne on, 112

Zeno: Cicero on, 37

www.ingramcontent.com/pod-product-compliance
Lightning Source LLC
Chambersburg PA
CBHW051402290426
44108CB00015B/2122